Classroom-Based Language and Literacy Intervention

A Programs and Case Studies Approach

Francine C. Falk-Ross

Northern Illinois University

Allyn and Bacon

Boston ■ London ■ Toronto ■ Sydney ■ Tokyo ■ Singapore

Series Editor: Steve Dragin
Editorial Assistant: Barbara Strickland
Production Editor: Michelle Limoges
Production Manager: Susan Brown
Compositor: Peggy Cabot, Cabot Computer Services
Composition and Prepress Buyer: Linda Cox
Manufacturing Buyer: Chris Marson
Cover Administrator: Kristina Mose-Libon

Library of Congress Cataloging-in-Publication Data

Falk-Ross, Francine C.
   Classroom-based language and literacy intervention : a programs and case studies
approach / Francine C. Falk-Ross—1st ed.
      p.   cm.
   Includes bibliographical references and index.
   ISBN 0-205-31885-1 (alk. paper)
      1. Speech therapy for children.   2. Children—Language—Case studies.
   3. Language disorders in children.   I. Title.

LB3454. F37 2001
371.91'.42—dc21   2001022104

Printed in the United States of America

10   9   8   7   6   5   4   3   2   1   06   05   04   03   02   01

*To Carlyn, Jennifer, and David, who, by example, have taught
me that each child shines in his or her own individual way.*

CONTENTS

PREFACE

This book introduces school specialists and classroom educators to a deeper investigation of the process of language and literacy intervention for struggling students. Models of language development and remedial approaches abound, solidly supported by quantitative and qualitative research; however, the everyday process of developing compensatory strategies for classroom activities and language inclusion is not as clear. Integrating language support systems for children in inclusive classroom settings requires a delicate balance of modified instruction and professional collaboration.

The purpose of this book is twofold: to build educators' knowledge of the importance of language competence in literacy routines that characterize classroom activities; and to walk both teachers and specialists through the day-to-day process of supporting struggling students' language constructions in the context of the classroom. The book uses a case-study approach throughout to expand awareness of children's language competencies and the roles that classroom discourse plays within curricular activities, specifically literacy events. I will also initate a cycle of inquiry by identifying three struggling students early in the book. Next, through an explanation of theoretical perspectives, we develop information targeted at broadening educators' knowledge of language routines and disorders. We then survey intervention approaches and offer suggestions for classroom application, in general. Last, detailed narratives reveal the year-long intervention programs developed for each of the three students and highlight problems and progress encountered in intervention programs of this nature.

The cases described herein provide representative examples of expressive language difficulties, compensatory teaching approaches, and collaborative teacher teaming. These are not prescriptive of all language and literacy intervention approaches, many of which will require different measures and forms of individual attention and supportive services. Taken together, however, they provide a viable and inclusive alternative to the more traditional model of language and literacy support, which separates students from their classmates. This classroom-based approach is supported by a social-constructivist view of teaching and learning, and offers specialists and educators new ideas for accommodating student diversity in the classroom.

ACKNOWLEDGMENTS

The author wishes to thank the teachers and students whose cooperation and suggestions were so helpful in developing and designing the intervention programs provided in this text. Thanks are also extended to Christine Pappas and Mavis Donahue for sharing their insights into the value of fostering students' own language and literacy constructions and for their careful consideration of the social systems within schools. The support and encouragement offered by Stephen Dragin throughout the development of the book is greatly appreciated, as is feedback from reviewers during successive drafts of the manuscript. Steven Ross, Linda McElhiney, Sally Bintz, and Barbara Treccani receive gold stars for their suggestions, encouragement, and ongoing support from the conception to completion of this project. Corinne and Richard Falk receive "Teacher-of-the-Century" awards for their models of patience and compassion as they guided my learning.

SUMMARY

A commonly held perspective in language learning and use is that both of these capacities are socially motivated and culturally supported. Thus, this book provides suggestions and practical applications for development of a classroom-based language-intervention program as an alternative to the traditional, resource-based "pull-out" delivery system, characterized by taking a student out of his or her regular education classroom to an alternative setting; a system that still prevails in most schools. To illustrate the routine implementation of inclusive language-remediation programs, we introduce and describe the experiences of three elementary school–aged children who are experiencing expressive language difficulties in the classroom. We provide examples and explanations to trace the progressive changes in these students' language, the modifications in classroom-discourse routines to accommodate these students, and the perceptions of all classroom members as the remediation program is developed over a school-year period.

In the case studies, program descriptions are presented in two phases. In Phase One, which lasted for the first three months of the school year, the speech and language specialist developed compensatory language strategies from classroom observations of the teachers' existing linguistic routines during literacy and other curricular activities. She also observed the children's particular participation in these classroom interactions. In Phase Two, lasting for the remaining six months of the school year, she designed new language strategies and cues. The language specialist supported them in the classroom during everyday discourse, and, following a period of collaborative consultation, the classroom teacher did the same.

The three case studies document the development of communicative competence of the three children in the study. For example, the students responded to teachers' questions more appropriately and expressed their thoughts more effectively within the classroom language routines after the study's language program. This constituted the first year that these three children made these types of noticeable gains. The accounts of these children weave in descriptions of the ongoing process required to implement this new program into the regular classroom. Heightened awareness of issues in teacher readiness for classroom-based, language-remediation programs was also an important outcome of the study.

SECTION ONE

Perspectives

1 Introduction

Diversity and Disability in School Classrooms

Each school year, approximately 2.3 percent of the school population is identified as having a speech or language disability (U.S. Department of Education, 2000). This figure increases when we include the presence of second-language learners in the classroom who bring a diversity of language dialects from family and cultural practices. These learners may also have undiagnosed language disorders. Owing to their low intelligibility, delayed oral responses, and possible problems with language comprehension, the majority of such students struggle to participate in the important classroom discourse during literacy activities. In addition, they frequently have related problems associated with reading and writing—problems stemming from weaknesses in areas such as phonological awareness (e.g., Ball, 1997; Catts & Kamhi, 1999; Chall, 1996), word retrieval (e.g., McGregor & Windsor, 1996; Nippold, 1992; Wolf, 1991), language comprehension (Kamhi, 1997), metalinguistic awareness (Menyuk & Chesnick, 1997), and expressive language organization (e.g., Duchan, 1994). How can we limit the impact of these language and literacy difficulties on students' future educational achievement? What adaptations or modifications in teaching and learning activities and routines will elicit and benefit students' language constructions within everyday instructional activities? Who is responsible for creating and facilitating alternative strategies for these students' success? As educators, we need to collaborate to develop a working rationale and applicable methods for improving the quantity and quality of support for students with language disorders or difficulties in the classroom.

Recent transitions in curriculum theory and program development have directed our attention toward the importance of using balanced language approaches in developing language-support strategies within meaningful literacy activities (Ball, 1997; Catts & Kamhi, 1999). As a result, the field of education has witnessed renewed interest and insight into the oral-language connection with reading and the importance of compensatory instructional language activities to struggling students as they participate in literacy events in the classroom. Schools have opened their classrooms to diversity in language use through inclusive and heterogeneous classroom organizations. However, to facilitate change, teaching methods used within these classrooms need to be aligned with what we know about these learners. It has taken time for speech and language pathologists and classroom teachers to collaboratively develop appropriate approaches to fostering students' contributions in classroom-based communicative routines.

Transitions in Educational Policy

Over the last thirty years, educational programming has experienced a shift toward increased development of special educational services for language and literacy difficulties, and integration of these services into regular education classrooms (American Speech-Language-Hearing Association, 1993; Cirrin & Penner, 1995). Considerable discussion has percolated among educational specialists about the role and benefits of previously separate systems of instruction within the school (Wang, Haertel, & Walberg, 1998; Lipsky & Gartner, 1997; Moody, Vaughn, Hughes, & Fischer, 2000). Programs intended for children with language difficulties have been coupled with the legally mandated goal, stated by the Individuals with Disabilities Education Act (IDEA, 1997), of bringing these children from the fringes of classroom participation to the heart of learning activities in the least restrictive environments. The classroom is the first environment considered for placement, according to the policies set forth by IDEA. (The Act further provides for extra services, assistive devices, and specific individual educational plans to accommodate students' special needs for successful achievement.) As a result, and in accordance with the 1997 amendments to the IDEA, students identified as having special language and literacy needs receive assistance targeted toward supporting their involvement and progress in the general-education curriculum.

Texts and literature abound on special-education approaches to language-development problems (e.g., Duchan, Hewitt, & Sonnenmeier, 1994; Fey, Windsor, & Warren, 1995; Klein & Moses, 1999; Merritt & Culatta, 1996; Nelson, 1993; Owens, 1995), learning disabilities (e.g., Mercer & Mercer, 1998; Meyen, Vergason, & Whelan, 1996; Wallach & Butler, 1994), reading disabilities (e.g., Catts & Kamhi, 1999; Wolf, 1982), and at-risk status (e.g., Vaughn, Bos, & Schumm, 1997). However, evidence suggests mixed feelings on the part of special and general educators about how to implement these changes in their classrooms and how they feel about doing so (Minke, Bear, Deemer, & Griffen, 1996; Udvari-Solner, 1997; Vaughn, Bos, & Schumm, 1997).

There has also been a movement toward expanding the traditional roles of all educators to include more varied teaching methods with a more diverse student population. More information in the hands and minds of all educators can stimulate deeper and more practical discussions. Through consideration of detailed case studies describing students with special needs and the classroom programs developed for them, teachers, specialists, administrators, and parents can follow the processes of staff collaboration, student accommodations, curriculum adaptation, and program implementation throughout a school year.

Another new trend is the growing need for collaborative consultation opportunities between special-education specialists—including, but not limited to, learning specialists, speech and language pathologists, social workers, psychologists, occupational therapists, physical therapists, itinerant teachers, and paraprofessionals—and regular-education teachers for the purpose of developing the expertise of all educators (Blosser & Kratcowski, 1997; Friend & Bursuck, 2002; Secord, 1990). A collaborative consultation approach can close many of the gaps in knowledge of language accommodation for regular-education teachers and knowledge of curricular content for special-education teachers. This approach can benefit all children in the classroom. At a time when children with physical handicaps, cognitive impairments, and limited English proficiency are finally being included with their peers in regular classrooms, general educators' teaching styles must incorporate individual adaptations for children's special needs. As stated in the IDEA, once a child has qualified for special-education services, a group-determined set of language goals are specified for integration into the regular-education program according to the Individualized Education Program (I.E.P.). An I.E.P. is a written document that describes the student's levels of functioning, goals of the program, lists of services to be provided, criteria for monitoring progress, and dates documenting the duration of the program. Besides speech and language pathologists, regular-education classroom teachers and paraprofessionals or teacher aides are included as part-time implementers of these goals. Thus, classroom teachers have been asked to absorb and share more responsibilities for teaching children with special-education needs—children who would have been excluded in the past.

Learning through Case Studies

Most educators who work with students having special language needs in the general-education classroom have experienced challenging, personally meaningful episodes that reflect some of the dilemmas inherent in integrating the theory and practice of special-education services with general-education programs (e.g., Bland & Prelock, 1995; Farber & Klein, 1999). As an educator in the field of special education who has extensive experience teaching elementary-aged schoolchildren, I also have anecdotes to share that illuminate these kinds of problems. These special stories illustrate both the pitfalls and possibilities presented by those struggles, and the children's and teachers' determination to find a comfort level for all classroom members.

This book aims to explain, describe, and model teaching and learning strategies that can help students with language and literacy disabilities in the classroom. These strategies incorporate application of theory through the portrayal of the everyday struggles and strengths of three young boys and their learning experiences. Through these case examples, the lessons of organizational flexibility, curriculum modification, and classroom intervention can build a new perspective for teachers, parents, and administrators that is consistent with the broader view of education in most schools' missions today.

To tell the story of Mickey, a first grader; Vincent, a second grader; and Henry, a fourth grader, I first explain how their unique problems represent the majority of children with language and communication difficulties. I then show how their experiences informed working models of intervention in the school. Language specialists, including myself, in the boys' elementary schools often received referrals from classroom teachers for evaluation of children they felt were experiencing problems with participation in classroom discourse. These specialists were then charged with the task of investigating so as to determine whether a specific child would require language-intervention services. If so, the specialists would develop a remediation program that would help that child use language more appropriately in the classroom and thus learn more effectively.

A pilot case study conducted in a fifth-grade classroom revealed some of the problems caused by language difficulties in the classroom. The case study, which described a student named Robin, also shed light on the inconsistencies in formal and informal test results that may interfere with efforts to determine the appropriate form of support. For one thing, Robin's classroom talk and the effectiveness of the resulting traditional language-resource program—that is, individual therapy outside the classroom (Ross, 1992)—proved problematic. The descriptions of her language in the classroom and other school contexts were not consistent with her performance on standardized tests. Standardized test scores indicated age-appropriate language and word-retrieval skills; however, observations of this child's discourse in a variety of school contexts clearly showed her to have trouble finding words quickly enough to converse fluently in many classroom situations.

In addition, strategies targeting vocabulary development and memory skills that had been developed and practiced in the resource room had limited success, or carryover, into the classroom. However, by using information taken from classroom observation to build compensatory language strategies, the child and her teacher developed successful language routines within the classroom.

Thus, it became clear to me that the traditional forms of addressing children's language difficulties—that is, pull-out resource programs—raised issues of validity in this case for the identification of the problem, assessment of its severity in the classroom, and development of remediation strategies. Clearly, I faced some critical challenges: (1) to view the actual nature of schoolchildren's language difficulties in an authentic context, meaning the classroom; (2) to study the rich language routines typical there; and (3) to find ways to support this classroom language use in these routines. Three interrelated responsibilities became foci for developing compensatory programs for children referred for language support: (1) assessment approaches, or measurement of the problem's severity; (2) identification terms, or categorization of the problem; and (3) intervention strategies. Let's explore each of these areas briefly here; I discuss them in greater detail later in the book.

Dilemmas for Consideration

The Evaluation Process

Students with language disorders and difficulties are identified through a combination of evaluation procedures. Discrepancies often show up between the estimated language abilities of many children who have been formally tested in a resource room and teachers' reports of the students' language use in the classroom. One reason for these differences is that the test stimuli in formal language testing generally consist of picture identifications and labeling, phrase and sentence completions, and elicitations of picture descriptions following question probes. Because the language of the classroom—meaning the language exchanges that created participation problems for these children—were not primarily the same as those sampled in these tests, the validity of standardized tests bears careful consideration (McCauley & Swisher, 1984).

    This alternative view rests on the basic premise that the interpretation of assessment and remediation results need to include careful, rich descriptions of relevant, classroom-based language, to balance school- and state-driven dependence on formal testing instruments (Calkins, Montgomery, & Santman, 1998). Results of any one form of evaluation, especially standardized tests, may give the evaluator a limited view of a child's problems and potential. That is, to help these children, the speech and language specialist must gain the primary evaluative information describing any language difficulties in the classroom by observing routine social uses of dialogue between students and their teachers. I discuss the discrepancies in standardized test results and informal, classroom-based evaluation in later chapters.

Coming to Terms with Identification

Identifying a particular child's language problem is a challenging endeavor. One problem is that labels often obscure the nature of the difficulty because teachers, when referring students for help, frequently use different vocabulary labels to explain their observations. In the case of word-retrieval problems, which all three boys in this study were commonly described as having, teachers used the terms *word-finding mistakes, language-processing difficulties,* and *disorganized language use* to describe similar combinations of language behaviors. Moreover, when I have asked for examples of typical language difficulties expressed by children, teachers' descriptions of differently labeled problems overlap. Owing to the separated roles of regular classroom teachers and resource teachers in traditional education models, the lack of shared vocabulary has been all too common. For example, Prelock and Lupella (1989) found similarities and differences in the views of professionals from different disciplines concerning several issues, such as discrepancies in the use of descriptive terms to label behaviors. Another general example of this is the assignment of the terms *minimal brain dysfunction* (used by neurologists and physicians), *specific language impairment* (used by speech and language pathologists), and *learning disability* (used by special educators) to describe similar characteristics of language dysfunction. The differences in terminology both confuse and delay the diagnostic process.

Possibly, administrators and educators must modify the vocabulary that is used to explain the orientation of educational programs before they modify the programs. The term *special,* as it is used in the schools, has taken on an all-inclusive definition; that is, any student who is not absolutely "average" is special. "Special" has come to mean different, with a questionable, possibly negative, connotation. Yet changes in the characteristics and needs of the present population of schoolchildren have emerged quickly in the past few years and promise to challenge the teachers and administrators of the future even more. There are fewer and fewer "average" children in classes today. Rather than segregating children with special needs and backgrounds into special-education classes, teachers need to educate children with peers, so that the teachers can acknowledge and support their students' strengths and difficulties. What if we assumed that *all* students are special individuals with differences to share? Truly special teachers and students are those who address differences in language expression as part of the classroom culture, and who help and support children in their everyday conversational routines.

Classroom-Based Language and Literacy Intervention Programs

Problems of validity occur in intervention programs as well. Let's assume that the goal of an intervention program is to build on and improve children's classroom communicative competence; that is, their ability to use language appropriately to convey an understanding, an idea, or a question in a variety of meaningful social ways (Halliday, 1978; Simon, 1979). If we use this assumption, then how can effective strategies for the classroom be primarily taught in a context other than the classroom? Clearly, addressing children's language difficulties so as to help them achieve communicative competence in their classroom interactions is not easily accomplished through contrived activities in the resource room. Concerns focusing on the social and educational advantages provided by a more integrated, natural, and collaborative model of special-education services lead language interventionists to consider classroom-based over individual treatment procedures for children who are experiencing language difficulties. (Elksnin & Capilouto, 1994; McCormick, Loeb, & Schielfelbusch, 1997; Wilcox, Louri, & Caswell, 1991).

A main goal in using in-depth study of three case examples, then, was to reconstruct the difficulties of children with language problems in a different manner than in previous investigations. Specifically, I wanted to move the prime evaluation and intervention sites from a separated resource room to the everyday classroom. It is difficult to isolate any one problem from the complex of internal and external relationships that contribute to our language behavior (Damico & Damico, 1993;

Lerner, 1996). Using the reasoning inherent in systems theory, we can say that expressive language disorders are affected by other subsystems, such as biological and cognitive factors (Minuchin, 1985; Nelson, 1993) as well as by the reactions of other people (McGregor & Leonard, 1989). Change must occur within individuals and extend out to their environment. Each of the students discussed in these case studies, as all children, had unique histories that contributed to their language difficulties and their ways of coping with these problems.

The approach described in this book draws from a classroom-based program model, both for assessing metacommunicative awareness and for fostering more appropriate forms of it. *Metacommunicative awareness* is a student's explicit knowledge of language meaning and use at the discourse level. Students' metacommunicative awareness in the classroom differs from metalinguistic awareness in its focus on language. That is, it involves conscious reflection on communicative forms and meaning (Falk-Ross, 1997; Green, 1985; Wallach & Butler, 1994) as opposed to discrete elements of linguistic form. In many ways, this approach to language and literacy intervention is still considered alternative. It challenges the ways in which speech and language pathologists have traditionally approached language support and "delivered" it in schools; that is, through predominantly individual therapy outside the classroom.

A primarily in-classroom, curriculum-based approach introduces new ways for classroom teachers and speech and language pathologists to assist students, the majority of whom do not require separated therapeutic instructional attention, in the construction of verbal contributions in everyday instructional discourse. Students learn to anticipate and approach competent language routines already in use in the classroom in order to better understand and use discourse routines. Researchers have widely suggested this approach, but it is still new and often uncomfortable for special educators and classroom teachers (Elksnin & Capilouto, 1994; Ross & Wax, 1993). Still, efforts to become more familiar with and proficient at integrated, classroom-based programs are worthwhile endeavors. Students with communication disorders who received language intervention in the classroom (often referred to as LIC) evidenced more intelligible and complete oral language than those who received more traditional pull-out instruction (Bland & Prelock, 1995).

Teachers can also benefit from further education in the areas of classroom organization and management. Children working in groups, sharing and comparing new information, strengthens the learning of each member (Slavin, 1995). Students who actively share in their education, selecting and critiquing texts and topics, experience meaningful learning (Pappas, Keifer, & Levstick, 1999; Wells & Chang-Wells, 1992). The children in this study had less difficulty with language that they initiated and that interested them than they did with material selected for them or questions that struck them as contrived. In the classroom, these students more readily chose to share a personal anecdote or an idea with peers when they were participating in whole-class discussions and small-group learning circles than when they were in structured resource settings. This is true of all children's language and literacy skills; information that children can connect to their own experiences and needs is the most meaningful and valuable to them.

In summary, the major purpose of this book is to describe models of expressive language support from theory into practice through an in-depth recounting of one such program. I share details of an ethnographic inquiry intended to provide relevant, useful, and authentic language and literacy intervention for three elementary children with expressive language difficulties. The classroom and student descriptions capture the evolving stories of the expressive language difficulties that three elementary school–aged boys—Mickey, Vincent, and Henry (in grades one, two, and four, respectively)—experienced and grappled with at the time of the study. Through examination of their language difficulties as they occurred in school contexts using a functional approach, I first determined how these problems might affect these children's everyday classroom discourse. Thus, these case studies illustrate new ways to address language difficulties in the classroom. As such, they can extend our present knowledge of expressive language difficulties beyond that which has already been documented in studies and standardized tests using predetermined controlled stimuli to elicit language behaviors.

Many changes occurred during the school year that this book describes. Relationships among all classroom members—the children, teacher, aide, and myself—varied among the three classrooms and with time. For example, some of the children and their peers needed to become acclimated to the presence of another teacher in the room, as did a few of the teachers. The teachers and aides formed opinions concerning my role in the classroom and speculated as to how it differed from theirs. Clearly, all of these changes shaped the ongoing evaluation and remediation of discourse competencies for the focal children. Consequently, this book also addresses the process involved in creating a new system of special-education resource service delivery in a traditional school setting. Moreover, it sheds light on the changing attitudes the process creates for those involved with students having special language needs in the classroom.

Overview of the Book

As the case studies described in this book unfolded, the changing nature of language that each child used continually surfaced. The changing roles that each member of the study assumed—including the three focal students, their peers, their classroom teachers, and myself—also resufaced from week to week. Remember: The major aim in the classroom observations and interventions was to foster the competence of the children's language constructions in discourse. Thus the nature of support-strategies efforts continually changed as teachers and students adapted to constructive suggestions regarding their roles in classroom discourse. This shift required a higher-than-usual level of metalinguistic awareness on the part of each participant. Enabling each member to develop this awareness became a part of the new program as well.

Before the study began, dissatisfaction had grown over the lack of transfer, or generalization, of new skills and strategies taught in the special-education resource rooms into the everyday language routines in the regular classrooms. The process of new role negotiation introduced unprecedented forms of collaboration, because the responsibilities of the regular-education teachers and students had traditionally been separated from those involved in the special-education programs. Thus, the teacher-student relationship and language routines in these two general programs differed markedly. To bring remediation work into the classrooms would necessitate changes in the roles of the participants and the language strategies that each used.

Several themes crop up repeatedly throughout this book. The first of these themes stresses the importance of considering the different types of linguistic skills, language awareness, and literacy experiences that individual children bring to the classroom. Viewing each child in terms of strengths and potential instead of weaknesses and limitations empowers that child by recognizing his or her unique qualities. Variations exist in the learning styles—that is, the cognitive skills and cultural backgrounds—of each child in that classroom. These differences contribute to the anxiety, motivation, and success of each child individually, thereby influencing the specific language-support program developed for him or her.

A second theme emphasizes the advantages of basing language assessment on everyday samples taken from performance in the classroom and related settings. Assessment protocols outside the classroom are most often standardized using a specified population, as well as task-oriented language elicitations based on psycholinguistic models of performance. These tests provide results that reflect isolated skills in specific environments. However, the structure of the classroom routines and the nature of the exchanges therein change frequently and are not free from what more traditional testing systems would consider "confounding" variables. The susceptibility of children's expressive language difficulties to these everyday classroom variations will not show up in individual standardized testing in a resource room.

A third theme refers to the challenge of initiating an interactive language and literacy support program sensitive to the social needs of students and the unique instructional approaches of the teacher in the classroom. The United States' present educational system frequently encourages conformity, not diversity, of interests, knowledge, and styles of interaction. Children with special needs are particularly confined by too narrow definitions of acceptable behavior. However, educational reformers have recently pushed to reverse this system—to encourage teachers and children to work with differences within the classroom. The perspective on educational programs in this book reflects that push.

All the chapters in the book refer to the three above-mentioned themes in some portion. They are central to the theory and practice of assessing and instructing children with special language needs. Viewed separately, each theme mandates a change in the organization of the traditional classroom; taken together, these themes lay out a model of effective, inclusive instruction within general-education classes.

Chapter 2 develops the theoretical perspective that frames the classroom-based model of language and literacy instruction. It also introduces the three case studies and describes the assessment and remediation methods employed to support the children's classroom communication. Each of the three children experienced problems with word-processing and word-retrieval difficulties, which is common among students with language and learning disabilities (Donahue, 1994). Thus this chapter includes specific information relating to this aspect of language use and describes the assessment instruments used to qualify and measure them. The chapter also includes a brief description of the typical forms of language difficulties observed in children's classroom discourse. Discussion of testing methods and the ways in which these test results contribute to identification of the disorder follows.

Section 2 (Chapters 3–6) details the methodological approach used to (1) gather descriptive data to characterize students' language and literacy constructions in the classroom and (2) develop compensatory instructional strategies to foster competent participation in curricular events. The section encompasses the details of the two phases of focus in the book's series of case studies and discusses the key roles of collaborative networks and effective classroom management. In addition, it compares different testing methods in terms of the nature of the tasks and situational contexts of the language being examined.

Section 3 (Chapters 7–9) presents the classrooms and children from the time they were first observed (i.e., the first few months after the school year began) through the goal development of the program's second phase. Each chapter in the section traces the program's movement for each focal student. That is, it introduces the goal of the first phase, which was to gather information about language use in the classroom with and without remedial and compensatory support. That information would in turn help me make decisions concerning the specific details of the focused language and literacy assistance I would need to provide. These chapters also include specific information concerning the times and organization of language support.

Section 3 also describes the goals of the second phase, to help students competently participate in classroom discourse and to support their independent efforts. It explains the classroom-based assessment of the three children's language and addresses the classroom interventions used with them throughout the remainder of the school year. It also provides background information about each of the children selected for study. The second part of each chapter in Section 3 foreshadows each child's language strengths and the problems that determined the different approaches used to observe and evaluate them. Reactions of each of the focal students' peers are also noted, as is contextual information, such as classroom structure and teacher insights. All of this builds a clearer picture of each child's environment. These chapters specify the observations of Phase 1 and the interventions of Phase 2, providing examples of techniques that helped the boys to develop useful, authentic strategies to communicate effectively within the language routines of their classrooms.

Section 4 (Chapters 10–11) comprises a reconsideration of the three children's struggles with language difficulties and the usefulness of the language compensations and accommodations provided for them within their regular classroom. It also considers teachers' and students' responses to the new responsibilities imposed by an inclusionary model. This section considers implications of the study for future investigation. Moreover, it hints at the changes in perspective that regular- and special-education teachers can make regarding the importance of effective classroom discourse in classroom activities. Finally, the appendix provides a key to the transcription conventions used throughout the text.

2 Theoretical Frameworks for Working within Classroom Settings

Constructing Language

The language perspective that these three case studies reflect rests on a socioconstructivist model of language learning and language use. From this angle, we can view language as purposefully motivated, situationally embedded, and culturally influenced. It represents a social exchange of meanings constructed by the speaker in response to a need to impart a message; that is, it's a reaction to the language preceding it and a catalyst for the language that follows. This dialogic dimension of language empowers the speaker to explain, clarify, and question ideas and understandings of the environment, thus linking language and learning together.

Language is part of children's understanding of the surrounding world from the very start of their perception of sound. Vygotsky (1978) explains that as children become aware of their environment, the movements and sounds of language associated with specific actions become symbols of meaning. Children use these symbols as tools to code, organize, and internalize all sensory information as new knowledge. This semiotic mediation occurs first on a social, or interpersonal, plane and then on a psychological, or intrapersonal, plane (Wertsch, 1985). More specifically, as children learn how things work from verbal interaction, or external speech, they transform these learnings into organized thought, or inner speech, as they internalize cognitive understandings of the world. According to Mikhail Bakhtin (Holquist, 1990), language shapes a young child's experiences early on. Thus, language learning and learning through language, even in their earliest forms, have as basic components personal meaning and purposeful construction through social interaction (Halliday, 1993).

The model representing the social process through which learning occurs, including language learning, consists of a series of "assisted performances" (Vygotsky, 1978). That is, the learner, by using interactional exchanges in the form of verbal feedback from more knowledgeable adults or peers, comes to understand or accomplish a task within, and slightly above, his or her capability. Vygotsky refers to this range of skill levels as the "zone of proximal development." The range begins at a novice level of incompetence that requires assistance completing a task appropriately, and ends at an expert level of competence that does not require supervision.

As learners move through this zone, they slowly assume more and more responsibility for completing the task alone, while the expert provides less and less direction. Usually learners need a series of progressively difficult movements, or interactions, to complete the process, each move based on the success of the previous one. Bruner (1983) refers to the final shift in responsibility to the student alone as the "handover." Learning through "apprenticeship" (Rogoff, 1990), which is tailored to individual needs and abilities, the student gains new knowledge in some culturally familiar situation. Thus begins a new zone of proximal development as continual changes accompany new levels of knowledge and accomplishment. This socialization process mediates intellectual conversation and educational instruction through language, which plays the important role of providing feedback throughout the process and guiding new steps in learning. Students in classrooms must be active participants in the pedagogical discourse in order to receive the mentoring that brings them to new understandings.

Language has another significant characteristic as well: the shared contextual nature of discourse. Speakers share common experiences, mutual needs, and physical surroundings that define their conversational constructions (Bloome, 1982). All events—encompassed by language, participants, and social constructions—are further defined by how they are historically situated. That is, each event is related to, and affected by, those events that have occurred previously (Bakhtin, 1981; Bloome, 1982). Language through discourse provides for the development of meaning.

Meaning in the classroom is constructed and signaled through the specific communicative interactions between teachers and students, students and peers, and the teacher and the class (Bloome & Theodorou, 1988; Green, 1983). As these interactions become ritualized over time, a subtle predictability develops as to the discourse patterns that define communication in the classroom. The students develop a procedural knowledge that guides them through the everyday routines (Bloome, 1982; Green, Harker, & Wallet, 1988).

Participants do not necessarily explicitly verbalize these common understandings. Rather, they assume them. This shared knowledge, or everything the participants know and understand together, develops over time in continuous patterns. It enriches social connections and often lessens participants' need to verbally explicate details that they commonly acknowledge (Edwards & Mercer, 1987). Edwards and Mercer explain that both context and continuity contribute to the building and maintaining of competence in the classroom as learners plan and in complete tasks independently through educational discourse.

A Sociolinguistic Model of Language Study

As an underlying premise, a social-constructivist model of language assumes that the linguistic and functional, social, and cultural features of any language unit are symbiotic. That is, the particulars of language at once reflect and shape an individual's experiences. In addition to suprasegmental markers, such as vocal pitch, inflectional patterns, and phonemic characteristics, language form has signifi-cance in the listener's interpretation of the message. To better understand a speaker's intentions—that is, to engage in discourse analysis—listeners need to un-cover the history and significance of the speaker's experiences (Bakhtin, 1986) and clarify the situational meaning (Gee, 1999).

Language, in any form, occurs within some specific situational frame. Ana-lyzing only the words in a sample of language provides limited information. Halliday and Hasan (1985) distinguish between "text" (a unit of language that exists as a unified whole) and a collection of unrelated sentences. That is, text ". . . is a unit of language in use. . . . It does not consist of sentences; it is realized by, or encoded in sentences" (pp. 1–2). In these authors' view, unrelated sentences are merely grammatical specimens. Therefore, text, or functional language, is both a *process,* or an ongoing series of semantic choices, and a *product,* or the result of those choices that observers can identify and study (Halliday & Hasan, 1985).

The unique environment in which text is embedded influences the process in which a speaker makes semantic choices. Malinowski (1923) first referred to the prime elements of this environment as, "context of situation" and "context of cul-ture." This context shapes the meaning intended by the speaker and interpreted by the listener. Therefore, textual descriptions must clearly specify it. In an attempt to identify and organize its components, researchers with different perspectives have described "context of situation" in similar but different ways.

For example, Hymes (1985), taking an ethnographic perspective, views lan-guage use as specific to, and reflexive of, our cultural identities. Language is so em-bedded in the speaker's environmental evolution that it cannot be understood apart from these influences. Hymes names sixteen elements to describe context, building on a framework developed by Firth (1950). Of these concepts, he combines the seven more salient to spell the acronym SPEAKING: **s**etting, **p**articipants, **e**nds (outcomes, goals), **a**ct sequence, **k**ey (tone), **i**nstrumentalities (channels), **n**orms, and **g**enre. These situational features give language a real, purposive dimension that we don't find in structural analyses of language (e.g., Chomsky, 1975), which gen-erally assume ideal speaker-listener forms. Hymes's discussion of the unique rela-tionship between linguistic means and social meaning describes both the diversity of speech patterns among cultures and the commonalities within communities.

Halliday and Hasan (1976, 1985) view language from a social-semiotic per-spective. This view emphasizes the special relationship of the social environment and the functional organization of language. That is, language relates to social struc-ture. Thus, each semantic unit, or text, represents a message that social cues have influenced. Halliday and Hasan (1976) offer three descriptors of situational context to characterize the social environment of the text: (1) "field of discourse" refers to the nature of the social action in which language plays some essential role; (2) "tenor of discourse" refers to the nature of the participants, their status, roles, and formal relationships; and (3) "mode of discourse" describes the part the language is playing and the channel (oral and written) used by the participants.

These terms, "field," "tenor," and "mode," are not simply components of the speech setting; they provide a conceptual framework for interpreting social exchanges of meaning through language (Halliday, 1978). In other words, the field reflects the experiential meanings, the tenor reflects the interpersonal meanings, and the mode reflects the textual meanings. Specific combinations, or configurations, of these components reoccur in common situational environments. These "registers," as Halliday and Hasan (1985) call them, resemble the language "genres" described by Hymes (1974). The language that these similar situational configurations create is generally similar as well, offering predictability in routines. As the field, tenor, and mode change, so do the meanings of the text created. Thus, the particular features of these three constructs define the social situation of context that relates to language formulation. We can more fully appreciate the changes in children's language competencies in the classroom by applying these descriptors to transcriptions of language samples. To situate the examples of the three students' language constructions, field notes described the context of use of the focal children's language in all original transcriptions. The interpretive narratives discuss context as well.

Thus, a social perspective of language lends insight into interpretation of linguistic organization or structure. Language is not just what somebody says; it may also reflect something that a participant has *not* said but shares with another participant in the physical situation. Bakhtin (Holquist, 1990) provides an example of this extraverbal context while relating the story of two people who are sitting in a room in the month of May and notice that it has begun to snow outside. One of the two men comments to the other, "Well!" The clues to the meaning of this utterance lie mostly in the context of the situation and the history that each man has about seeing snow in the month of May. Bakhtin (1986) and Holquist (1990) discuss the dialogic quality of language as a reflection of all human interaction and as an attribute of language, or "utterance." This is comparable to Halliday's and Hasan's concept of "text." The words spoken during an exchange are deeply embedded in their own contextual and experiential histories.

The use of referential terms, such as pronouns and adjectival articles *(the, that),* also reflects shared understandings. These terms tie together parts of spoken or written texts into a unified whole and lend cohesion, or "texture," to the text (Halliday & Hasan, 1976). For example, the statement, "She gave it to him there," requires that the speaker has appropriately and adequately provided information to the listener for a joint understanding of the "she," "it," "him," and "there" in that comment. Cohesion, then, yields one description of a speaker's organization of meaning in any particular text (Liles, 1982) and provides for a clear message.

Language and Learning in the Classroom

Mediation through Assisted Language Performances

Talk in the classroom shares the many properties of general conversation, but is unique in several ways. The participants in the classroom and the physical characteristics of the school are among the more obvious of these distinctions. Within reading activities in classroom settings, pedagogic language routines take the forms of various language routines that accompany specific curricular activities (Bernstein, 1990; Cazden, 1988; Wells, 1998). These language routines, which the teacher sets up and peers use to question and respond to new information, shapes students' learning in the classroom (Cazden, 1988; Lemke, 1985; Tharp & Gallimore, 1988). Gutierrez (1995b) argues that these instructional language patterns provide a context that influences learning and literacy development. Specifically, language routines give students opportunities to clarify and repair misunderstandings (Pennington, 1998), and shape students' understandings and thinking processes (Wells, 1998). Thus, language is the medium of education (e.g., Lemke, 1985; Nystrand, Gamoran, Kachur, & Prendergast, 1997; Tharp & Gallimore, 1988). In order for students to participate competently in the oral communication within the classroom, they must thus learn to adapt their talk to language-interaction patterns specific to particular social-activity structures within the classroom (Christie, 1995; Pappas, 1999). The content, dialogue, and flow of classroom discourse are possibly less understood but equally defining.

A social context predominantly centered on educational tasks and discussions shapes and contrains the content of classroom discourse. The school becomes a major source of intellectual and literate stimulation in the child's early life, and language serves as the medium of the curriculum. Researchers have identified a strong relationship between language and literacy strategies (Blachman, 1994; Catts & Kamhi, 1999). They have shown that by building knowledge of the components of language, educators strengthen literacy skills and strategies. In general, social interactions with teacher and peers pave the way for children to personally engage in and internalize the lessons of the classroom (Wells & Chang-Wells, 1992). What and how well they learn often depends on the communication system set up in classrooms (Barnes, 1976). In fact, teachers often use a student's contribution to classroom discourse to assess his or her specific knowledge and comprehension in a lesson.

The dialogue of discourse reflects the special classroom context in the various combinations, or configurations, of interactional exchanges between students and teachers. In each classroom, common linguistic patterns within specific activity structures are identifiable. These language "registers" are referred to as "curriculum genres" (Christie, 1987; Pappas, 1995). Studies of classroom discourse reveal that students must master specific rules of language participation to succeed in the verbal interactional exchanges in the classroom (Cazden, 1988; Garcia, 1992; Gumperz, 1983; Pappas, 1991; Tharp & Gallimore, 1988). These rules become shared knowledge within the classroom, setting guidelines, or ground rules, of discourse that help learners make sense of classroom talk (Edwards & Mercer, 1987). The different curriculum genres reify a large part of the shared, or common, knowledge, owing to students' familiarity with the genre's and their understanding of the boundaries for their participation.

As recognizable, goal-oriented social processes, curriculum genres organize and frame learning and teaching episodes in the classroom (Martin, Christie, & Rothery, 1987). Familiar examples of curriculum genres include presentations ("show and tell"), students' reading their own writing aloud ("author's chair"), students taking turns at reading ("round-robin"), and recitations. Other researchers describe the situational context in terms of "activity settings" (Lemke, 1985), or "participation structures" (Erikson, 1977). Each refers to the routines characterizing a set of tasks and the turn-taking language interaction that accompanies it. Children learn at early ages to recognize and participate appropriately within these curriculum genres in order to acquire communicative competence in the classroom (Cazden, 1988; Tharp & Gallimore, 1988). Thus they become familiar with the distinctive language conventions that make up these routines. This familiarity provides a predictable form of language that children can use and a creative outlet as the language routine changes, or evolves, over time (Pappas, Keifer, & Levstik, 1999). The rules for participation in these curriculum genres vary among teachers and classrooms. For example, although researchers observed similarities in the general form of turn-taking routines in a longitudinal study of the same six different classrooms, Morine-Dershimer (1988), Ramirez (1988), Shuy (1988), and Tenenberg (1988) found six different systems of classroom talk.

The flow of discourse revolves around shared knowledge about the structure of turn allocation and contingent participatory moves in classroom routines. In general, the ability to participate in classroom tasks requires students to master the necessary linguistic routines in which the teacher presents the material. In many classrooms, these linguistic routines consist of discourse that the teacher initiates and controls in a familiar pattern: The teacher initiates a question or direction to the student(s), the nominated student responds with an answer or comment, and then the teacher provides evaluation, or feedback, for the student's response with an acknowledgment or judgmental comment, referred to as an IRE or IRF pattern (Cazden, 1988; Edwards & Mercer, 1987). A large percentage of these routines take the form of questions, and often the teacher determines their amount, content, and form (Edwards & Mercer, 1987; Flanders, 1970; Young, 1992). The complexities of the acts of reading and writing build on the domains of oral language but require variations on pragmatic strategies (Snow, 1994).

It has been argued that mainstream cultural norms influence the content, dialogue, and flow of traditional classroom discourse. That is, these norms limit the type and form of communication that takes place in the classroom and possibly the children's access to school knowledge (Eisenhart & Cutts-Dougherty, 1991). Some researchers have argued for more expansive forms of interaction that derive from students' inquiry and experience (Freire, 1970; Wells, 1999) and that reflect shared teacher authority in the classroom (Nystrand, Gamoran, Kachur, & Prendergast, 1997; Oyler, 1996). However, the predominant and persistant form of classroom discourse remains one of teacher initiation, student response, and teacher evaluation (Nystrand, Gamoran, Kacher, & Prendergast, 1997). Children with language differences or difficulties may also struggle with interactional routines in the class-room because of the ways they express themselves in classroom discourse. Under-standing these differences and accommodating for them in verbal exchanges can increase learning and success in school (Au & Jordan, 1981). Figure 2.1 compares traditional and inclusive school classrooms.

The study of classroom discourse is embedded in a communicative-compe-tence perspective, which in turn rests on a social-constructivist point of view (Hymes, 1974). This view assumes that social, cultural, and historical context cre-ates, shapes, constrains, and gives meaning to language (Wertsch, 1985). In a recip-rocal manner, language form and content also affect the speaker's social environment. That is, language and context share a dynamic, symbiotic relationship, and the social and linguistic characteristics of language are inseparable. Language, then, is never value-free (Green, 1983), never neutral (Bakhtin, 1986). The "text," or unit of functional language within a social situation, is both a product and a process (Halliday & Hasan, 1985). Students' contributions to classroom discourse, then, are language choices. Evaluating these choices in the social context can provide clues to which language remediation strategies teachers might use in the classroom. Strengthening the awareness of the routines that students and teachers use for ques-tioning, commenting, and clarifying information in the classroom can help students with language difficulties develop participation strategies (Falk-Ross, 1997; Menyuk & Chesnick, 1997).

Language Difficulties in Classroom Discourse and Literacy Activities

The term "language difficulties" encompasses a large number of specific problems. Part of the challenge of studying language difficulties lies in the assessment and identification stages—that is, in efforts to discriminate between similar problems to find differentiating factors responsible for specific problems with language behav-iors. Within the complex psychosocial system that shapes the way we organize in-formation into language forms, different contributing factors overlap. Attempts to isolate and label these factors can pose problems, owing to the individualistic nature of experiential knowledge and of contextual influences on language learning and language use. In this book, I do not stress differences in language use (such as varia-tions in dialect or linguistic style) that children learn in the context of another set of cultural norms. Neither do I emphasize difficulties that stem from a disordered lan-guage form, content, or use relative to a general norm of development. Instead, I focus on language difficulties—in theory and in example—that differ in form and use from the language of children's close family members and school peers. That is, the focal children's language difficulties appear social-developmental in nature and not culturally different from that of the school population in which the students are situated.

FIGURE 2.1   Comparison of Traditional and Inclusive Schools

Dimensions	Traditional Schools		Inclusive Schools
	Special Education	Language Intervention	Special Education and Language Intervention
Focus of Intervention	Developmental skills Functional/adaptive skills	Linguistic concepts/rules Linguistic forms and structures	Teacher-child interactions Peer interactions Curriculum adaptations
Methods and Procedures	Contrived instructional contexts Adult controlled Individual instruction Massed trials	Contrived therapy contexts Adult controlled Individual instruction Massed trials	Milieu language teaching Scaffolding Routines and script training Interactive modeling Situated pragmatics Direct instruction
Instructional Environment	Special education classroom Resource room Homogeneous groupings	Therapy room Special education classroom Homogeneous groupings	Regular classroom Other school settings (playground, cafeteria, etc.) Home/community environments Heterogeneous groupings
Professional Relationships and Responsibilities	Autonomous decision making Little opportunity for collegial interactions Periodic unidiscipline in-service training	Autonomous decision making Little opportunity for collegial interactions Periodic unidiscipline in-service training	Interdependent/shared decision making Many opportunities for collegial interactions Continuous transdisciplinary training
Scheduling	Individual instruction Small-group instruction	Individual or small-group therapy weekly or biweekly	Block scheduling (half or full day blocks per class) Consultation weekly or biweekly
Measurement and Evaluation	Formative and summative evaluation Quantitative data	Formative and summative evaluation Quantitative data	Formative and summative evaluation Authentic assessment Qualitative *and* quantitative data

From L. McCormick, D. F. Loeb, & R. L. Schiefelbusch, *Supporting Children with Communication Difficulties in Inclusive Settings: School-Based Language Intervention.* © 1997 by Allyn & Bacon. Reprinted/Adapted by permission.

What role do language difficulties play in the classroom, especially in the development of literacy skills? Children with language difficulties often produce texts—oral and written—that are less cohesive or meaningfully tied together than those of other children (Donahue, 1994; Feagans & Short, 1984, 1986; Liles, 1985; Wolman, 1991). Also, the rate and accuracy of naming behaviors strongly predict success in reading experiences in the areas of word identification, phonological awareness, and graphophonic representations (McGregor & Windsor, 1996; Troia, Roth, & Yeni Komshian, 1996). Speech and language pathologists often use reading as a communicative context for language instruction because investigating narratives helps children learn how to organize complex discourse structure and semantic complexity (Hoffman, 1990). The complexity of the act of reading builds on the domains of oral language but requires various pragmatic or problem-solving strategies for all students' language abilities (Snow, 1994).

Children's expressive communicative competence influences their educational achievement through the impressions, real or perceived, that it imposes. Because teachers often value speed of reply in the regular classroom (Allington, 1980), expressive language problems in the form of extended pauses or time fillers will give the impression that the child doesn't know the answer. Educators might judge expressive language difficulties in the form of word substitutions or circumlocutions as unacceptable. Thus, teachers and peers may underestimate and undervalue children's communicative competence in the classroom. As a result, such students may have fewer opportunities to participate in classroom lessons (Silliman & Wilkinson, 1991). Although many teachers may be as sensitive to children's classroom interactional difficulties as they are to children's academic problems (Ysseldyke, Algozzine, Shinn, & McGue, 1982), others are not. Therefore, children with language problems may also be at a disadvantage in attempting to convey their comprehension of content material.

Facilitative Strategies for Classroom Language Participation

Strategies for helping children with language difficulties are a matter for discussion among specialists. Recent research studies have uncovered flaws in the rationale supporting solely separate programming in the form of resource rooms and modified curriculum for children with language or learning disabilities (Moody, Vaughn, Hughes, & Fischer, 2000). In the long view, it has been suggested that resource programs to remediate language difficulties may not lead to improved and lasting growth in specific language skills (Madden & Slavin, 1983; Wang, Peverly, & Randolf, 1984; Will, 1986). More recent views of educational organization supported by social-constructivist theories of learning have turned these models around. Again, in Figure 2.1, Linda McCormick et al. (1997) show the changes in approaches to assessment and instruction taken by inclusive schools. The perspective supporting the newer models of cooperative teaching between general and special educators in the classroom argue that having children with disabilities remain in the classroom for as much time as possible with consultative help from special-education personnel offers social, emotional, and academic advantages (Bean, Zigmond, & Eichelberger, 1990; Dohan & Schultz, 1998; Friend & Cook, 1992; Hines, 1994; Phillips, Alfred, Brulle, & Shank, 1990; Stainback & Stainback, 1984; Wang, Reynolds, & Walberg, 1986). Figure 2.1 shows many of the beneficial program changes that develop from an inclusive approach to language intervention. Clearly, McCormick, Loeb, and Schiefelbusch provide more integrated and interactive methods of instruction and evaluation for teachers and students using classroom-based language and literacy support.

In summary, children's language problems can interfere with their participation in the important verbal exchanges that are an essential part of many classroom activities. To successfully communicate and learn in the classroom, they must be able to engage in language routines for participation set by the classroom teacher and peer group members. Language support and intervention provided by the speech and language pathologist and in collaboration with the teacher may be more effective than resource work alone (Chalfant, Pysh, & Moultrie, 1979).

Preparing for Classroom-Based Intervention

CHAPTER

3

Choosing an Ethnographic Study Approach

The use of discrete-skill evaluative methods to study and measure children's language behaviors and achievement progress has predominated in schools, judging from the large number and variety of these tests being administered in classrooms and special-education resource rooms. Speech and language pathologists quantify and analyze the results of such evaluations before defining children's abilities in school and determining their placements in the classroom. These language specialists often base their decisions on the belief that quantification provides accountability for administrators and predictability for teachers. That is, by measuring a few reactions in a large number of people, social behaviorists expect to achieve higher levels of validity, reliability, and replicability of their data from a detached viewpoint (Schubert, 1986). Although standardized testing allows comparisons among large numbers of students, they do not clearly present individual differences in strengths and weaknesses between students. Moreover, the characteristics of the normed population frequently do not often match those of students being tested. Relying solely on this approach to assessment prevents educators from capturing the complexities associated with classroom interaction. A closer focus on the nature of specific social interactions lets observers discern the essence of any experience (Eisner, 1985) and the true nature of a problem. Teachers and speech and language pathologists thus acquire a depth of knowledge about these complex phenomena (Hammersley, 1990).

Qualitative descriptions provide practical information based on experiential interaction (Schubert, 1986) and an emphasis on "thick" descriptions; that is, they gain an indepth perspective (Geertz, 1987). In particular, ethnography sheds light on sociocultural influences on interpersonal interactions, through participant observation, interviews, written documents, and other related sources (Wolcott, 1988). This immersion in the social environment of the researched group or case enriches observers' understanding of the total study experience. Hammersley (1990) refers to ethnography as "participatory research"; that is, research by and for the participants. Qualitative forms of inquiry also reflect a collective effort between the researcher or clinician and the researched; each brings his or her own values to the collaboration

(Roman & Apple, 1990). Through descriptive, critical, and often subjective language, the researcher interprets the meaning of everyday events and group relationships and proposes future work. This naturalistic approach provides its own validity and reliability in the depth of knowledge it uncovers and in its documentation of series of social events. More specifically, the case-study method helps break down empirical theories into detailed descriptions of direct experiences and social relationships that occur in real, ongoing events (Hamel, Dufour, & Fortin. 1993). As such, case studies extend people's understanding through naturalistic, psychological generalizations (Lincoln & Guba, 1985; Stake, 1999). The advantages of case studies for teaching and learning include application of theory to practice, activation of problem-solving skills, and immersion in authentic and relevant experiences (Elksnin, 1998).

Case-Study Methodology

I chose case-study focus within an ethnographic methodology to describe the three students' discourse patterns, their educators' contextualization (or facilitation) cues, and the collaborative intervention approaches characteristic of each child's classroom-based experience. The three boys described in these case studies were chosen for language and literacy intervention programs because they exhibited several expressive language difficulties observed frequently in students with classroom-discourse problems. Mickey, Vincent, and Henry had received language services only through a special-education resource program. Each child had learned to engage in small-group conversations in the resource classes, but each was still having difficulty transferring these strategies to the classroom.

The case studies related in this book follow the three boys' experiences and successes as the speech and language pathologists changed their expressive language support from traditional, predominantly skills-oriented exercises in an isolated setting to an integrated, discourse-based application in the classroom. We cannot know the impact of the prior individual therapy on the success of the classroom-based intervention. However, the difficulties the students experienced as they struggled in their classrooms indicated that the separated nature of the resource program had not helped them develop useful language strategies.

To best account for the ongoing observation and evaluation processes and to document the students' changing language behaviors, we must distinguish between two general phases: (1) initial observation, evaluation, and goal setting, and (2) subsequent interaction, instruction, and reevaluation. The first phase serves as the focus of discussion in this chapter. The main purpose of this phase was to gain information and set goals for focused instruction in the second phase. This initial phase lasted for three months—from mid-September through mid-December—owing to the early fall schedule of classroom organization, school-based reading and mathematical placement tests, and state testing administrations. Coding of classroom observations, teacher consultations, and parent interviews during the first three months of the school year (Phase One) shaped subsequent choices of three focused remediation goals. These, in turn, led to choices for implementing the language-intervention strategies (Phase Two) for the remainder of the year's program.

Phases of Study

Phase One.   Phase One began during the second week in September, when all placements were finalized. It consisted of classroom observations focused on the language used in the classroom and the three boys' participation within this environment. During this period of time, the focal students' use of language in various contexts in the classroom provided information about the specific verbal interactions and typical behavioral patterns in various curriculum genres, such as teacher-led reading instruction using basal materials and follow-up independent student work. Observation and, later, interaction with each child extended to at least ninety minutes each week during the school year in a variety of learning contexts. In addition, parents and teachers were interviewed for their impressions of the focal children and I audiotaped ongoing informal discussions with each classroom teacher about the boys' communicative competence, achievement levels, social skills, general progress, and any other concerns. Conversations with each child's parents concerning their knowledge of these same issues occurred during parent-teacher conference days and at other times, as appropriate. Language support was provided for each student in the classroom during this phase, mostly as the form of dynamic assessment for the purpose of developing appropriate goals for the boys' classroom-based language programs. Goals during this phase focused on discovering the boys' language needs and communicative competence in classroom discourse. The speech and language assessment protocol is illustrated in Figure 3.1.

The classroom observations, teachers' suggestions through consultations, and parent recommendations from interviews—all of which occurred during the first three months of the school year—helped me determine useful, collaboratively developed remediation goals for each child. Each piece of information shaped my choices of remediation goals. These goals, in turn, informed program-implementation decisions.

Phase Two.   Phase Two of the study began the second week in December, just before winter vacation. This phase entailed active implementation of interaction and language support in the classroom. In general, this support consisted of word-retrieval strategies for appropriate and focused classroom participation, and models for language constructions that would be acceptable within the classroom's language routines. As the speech and language specialist, I introduced, modeled, and modified these using coaching and conferencing strategies in the classroom, and using tutoring and collaboration strategies occasionally outside the classroom. The emphasis on language support was intended to help the boys communicate more competently than they had in the past, and, therefore, to learn more. Each boy and I

FIGURE 3.1   Speech and Language Assessment Protocol

Student's Name _____   Date _____

Student's Homeroom _____   Age/Grade_____

STUDENT INTERVIEW

e.g., Open question format, reading survey, attitude survey.

SPEECH   Test Results:

e.g., Goldman-Fristoe Test of Articulation (Goldman & Fristoe, 1986)

LANGUAGE—Comprehensive   Test Results:

e.g., Clinical Evaluation of Language Fundamentals-Revised (Semel, Wiig, & Secord, 1995); Informal evaluation of classroom discourse.

LANGUAGE—Vocabulary   Test Results:

e.g., Peabody Picture Vocabulary Test-Revised (Dunn & Dunn, 1997); Expressive One-Word Picture Vocabulary Test (Gardner, 1981); The Word Test-Revised, Elementary (Huisingh, Barrett, & Bowers, LoGiudice, & Orman, 1990); Informal evaluation of classroom discourse.

LANGUAGE—Pragmatics/Problem-Solving   Test Results:

e.g., Test of Problem Solving-Revised (Bowers, Jorgenson, Huisingh, Barrett, Orman, LoGiudice, 1994); Informal evaluation of classroom discourse.

LANGUAGE—Processing/Word retrieval   Test Results:

Test of Wordfinding (German, 1989); Test of Wordfinding in Discourse (German, 1991), Test of Language Processing (Richard & Hanner, 1988); Informal evaluation of classroom discourse.

FLUENCY   Test Results:

e.g., Stuttering Severity Instrument-III (1994); Informal evaluation of fluency in classroom discourse.

VOICE   Test Results:

Informal evaluation of functional difficulties; medical referral to oto-laryngologist for examinatiion of structural deviations.

AUDITORY PERCEPTION—Discrimination/Processing   Test Results:

e.g., Wepman Test of Auditory Discrimination (Reynolds & Wepman, 1987).

FAMILY/PARENT NOTES

e.g., Parent interview checklist, open discussions, parent-teacher conference notes.

TEACHER'S NOTES

e.g., Informal reading inventory, classroom reading tests, writing samples/portfolios, checklists, anecdotal notes of classroom language constructions and literacy levels.

COMMENTS/RECOMMENDATIONS:

chose many of the remediation goals cooperatively in a separated environment, occasionally the resource room, just before classroom intervention. I modified these goals daily if a boy requested changes. I judged each language contribution on its acceptability and appropriateness based on its functional value in discourse. The teacher's and students' on-the-spot reactions to each boy's comments provided additional insights into the boys' communicative competence. Moreover, ongoing conversations with the teacher about her perspectives on language constructions in the class helped me identify intersections of ideas for interventional goals and efforts.

Data Collection

I employed a range of ethnographic techniques to study each focal student's use of language in various contexts in the classroom. I also obtained descriptive information about verbal interactions and behavioral patterns in various curriculum genres through participant observations, field notes, literacy artifacts, and audiotapes of whole-class and small-group lessons and interactions. Details of the focal children's discourse strategies and communicative competence within these classroom routines provided the focus for ongoing analysis. Classroom data, collected through participant observations, reflective field notes, and audiotapes, allowed for rich characterizations of the focal children's everyday language experiences and development of strategies for using language more effectively in this classroom discourse. The process by which I gained access to classroom activities formed an integral part of this study. I documented the constructivist journey through the various forms of data collection. These forms of data collection can help classroom teachers-as-researchers to document struggles and successes of children in the classroom. I offer the specifics of procurement and use of these data here as models for teachers' studies and replications.

Audiotapes

Before the beginning of the school year, I received written permission from parents to audiotape, to write field notes, and to collect artifacts representing as many small-group lessons, peer-group conferences, whole-class conversations, and resource or pull-aside discussions as possible for the following ten months. I obtained permission and the promise of cooperation by school administrators from the district's school superintendent. The principal of the school and I discussed the goals and day-to-day expectations of the study with the classroom teachers, obtaining their verbal agreement to conduct the research. Using a small tape-recorder placed on a desk next to each focal child or on my lap, I audiotaped conversations between each boy and his teacher or peers. Although the boys could see the recorder, it was not placed in a distracting position. I could manipulate it easily without drawing the child's attention. Parents and teachers had access to audiotapes collected in the study at all times, and used them to see examples of the work I was doing and the progress that the children were making. For discussion purposes, the children could also listen to excerpts of the tapes in our meetings. Their explanations for the substance and manner of their responses in discourse helped me analyze and develop appropriate language strategies.

Field Notes from Participant Observations

To complement the information in the audiotapes, I collected field notes and expanded them after class. The field, tenor, and mode of discourse (Halliday & Hasan, 1985) let me characterize the situational context, or social environment, of the classroom language routines. These notes provided a conceptual framework for interpreting social exchanges and describing the physical set-up and nature of children's activities, thereby giving information not obvious from the tapes alone. Figure 3.2 provides examples of the format and content of field notes with contextual information.

Teachers' Evaluations

Classroom teachers' comments concerning progress throughout the school year and those recorded on the three boys' report cards provided information for triangulation of results. Discussions during informal teacher meetings, or "crisis" sessions, were also recorded. If I saw informal meetings take place in hallways or the teacher's lounge, I recorded the essence of the conversations in the daily field notes.

Literacy Artifacts

Written artifacts, such as copies of the boys' journal entries, letters to parents, and compositions, revealed how the children organized information and expressed it in written form, and let me make comparisons to oral texts. The teachers and the students themselves donated copies of reading and writing materials and products, which further elucidated the nature of the children's language in discourse.

Parental Input

Feedback from parents and family members came from parent-teacher conferences, telephone communications, contributions during professional conferences (such as an Individualized Education Program [IEP] meeting), and conversations at school functions. On a few occasions, parents sent written notes to school expressing concerns about homework or their child's communication. These informal forms of interaction were valuable because they balanced the teachers' and my own observations of the students' competencies.

FIGURE 3.2   Field Notes Format

Field Notes 1: Text Example (Mickey)

Field: Discussion is part of a Social Studies unit about families and family relationships; children are jointly looking at a page in their text illustrating several family interaction routines.

Tenor: Social distance is maximal between Mickey and the classroom teacher, low between him and me; hierarchical organization for question-answer breaks down occasionally, without penalty from the teacher.

Mode: Oral language follows a question-answer routine initiated by the teacher; visual cues are provided by the pictures that accompany the text.

The classroom teacher is trying to be helpful when she points to the page that is the focus of attention for the whole class. She has been aware that Mickey has difficulty with language during his participation in classroom discourse, but has assumed that the problem was mostly attentional. She seems more focused on the questions she needs to ask Mickey than on the individual students' responses, thereby missing the number of people in the family in the picture. Mickey seems uncomfortable with the result of the interaction, as well. The teacher has corrected her mistake in counting the number of family members but has not acknowledged Mickey's original response as being accurate. He seems frustrated by his knowledge of the correct responses and his reluctance, or inability, to answer more quickly. Mickey scowls to himself as the teacher moves on to another question and another student's response.

Field Notes 2: Text Example (Vincent)

Field: In-classroom activity; all children were gathered on the rug listening to one child presenter as he described the specifics of his research report on Sweden.

Tenor: The student assumes the teacher's hierarchical role, but interaction does not assume IRE structure; social distance is low.

Mode: Oral language consisted of question-answer discussion following the student presentations; a student-made poster provided visual cues.

The classroom teacher provided question prompts to keep Vincent's presentation focused on those points that she felt were the more important ones, such as the country's population, weather, and geographic location. Vincent frequently nodded yes or no instead of answering her questions verbally. Students' questions at the end of the presentation helped Vincent to provide missing information. Vincent used shorter responses than usual during this presentation, possibly indicating that he was nervous. He often looked down to his feet and the floor around him as he spoke.

Adapted from Halliday and Hasan, 1985.

Students' Contributions

The boys' oral comments and questions helped me determine their levels of understanding, classroom competencies, and social-communicative frustrations. Their inquiries and suggestions (for example, ". . . maybe you could . . . um . . . help me with my project . . . my building project . . . on Tuesday. We're . . . with them . . . having a hard time. . . . ") helped me to direct modifications in homework assignments and language and literacy expectations in the classroom.

Data Analysis

Consistent with a naturalistic form of inquiry, I collected and reviewed information frequently, looking for patterns (Lincoln & Guba, 1985; Strauss & Corbin, 1990). These patterns, grounded through field experiences within a school year's time, evolved through discussion and reflection. By means of a constant comparative method of analysis, I coded them for future reference. This book offers explanations of the nature and occurrence of specific patterns throughout, along with examples of narratives taken from classroom discourse.

Consistent with the methodology of action research through teacher inquiry, I used cycles or spirals of observation, reflection, and action (Pappas, Keifer, & Levstik, 1999; Wells, 1994) to analyze data. Ongoing formative analyses of discourse samples and descriptive field notes using a constant comparative method (Glaser & Strauss, 1967; Strauss & Corbin, 1990) revealed major patterns in the children's language difficulties. I made evaluative judgments at several levels of intervention and analysis in order to identify, support, and monitor changes in the boys' language and literacy competence. During the year, those problems that seemed to initially limit or interfere with the students' communicative competence in a particular curricular activity became the target for observation or instruction in my subsequent classroom visits. I then analyzed each student's new attempts at communicating effectively, and provided new instruction—and so on, over the course of the school year.

First, direct observation during classroom activities let me make "on-the-spot" decisions about the appropriateness of each boy's language constructions. I could then immediately introduce language-modification strategies when necessary. This approach supported the focus of the study: to base interventions on everyday classroom samples and to initiate them in the classroom when they were needed. Indications for intervention included increased signs of frustration as the boys struggled to initiate or complete a response. Feedback relating to the effectiveness of the strategy came immediately, in that the change allowed or interfered with Mickey's, Vincent's, and Henry's participation. We also discussed the impact of the changes later.

As a second level of analysis, I reviewed and coded transcribed discourse samples and the notes that accompanied them. Review of Mickey's, Vincent's, and Henry's language constructions and of the teacher's and students' antecedent and consequent comments provided insight into discourse routines that classroom members set and followed (Edwards & Mercer, 1987). Patterns emerging from an analysis of the language transcriptions became the long-term goals of the study. These situational field notes on transcriptions and informal conversations further clarified the areas in which each boy might modify language. The notes also helped the boys' teacher restructure questions and extend her student's responses. Because this school district assigned only one specialist to each school or set of schools, I made interpretations and set goals after this analysis without the input of another speech and language pathologist. Although the collegial collaboration would have helped extend discussion and strategy recommendations, the special nature of each school's community and each classroom's discourse routines limited the help of outsiders in determining the most effective intervention program for Mickey, Vincent, or Henry in his classroom.

As a third level of analysis, I reviewed informal conversations with the three focal boys, their parents, and their teachers in locations other than the classroom or my office. These important interactions were significant in that they were initiated by members of the study interested in some aspect of the boys' progress. These meetings were unscheduled and not audiotaped, but I alluded to them in the field-notes portfolio.

These three forms of analysis provided a way for me to reflect on the nature of each boy's language difficulties with a few inclusive concepts. Explanations of the nature and occurrence of specific patterns occur throughout this text, as do examples of narratives taken from classroom discourse.

4 Organizing Collaborative Relationships

In the classroom, all participants can construct knowledge together (Wells & Chang-Wells, 1992). However, placing students with difficulties in the general-education classroom without language and literacy support puts them at a distinct disadvantage owing to the language demands in pedagogical discourse and these students' problems with information-seeking strategies (Donahue, 1994; Silliman & Wilkenson, 1991). Discourse participation generally requires fast, competitive, and focused verbal responses. Special and regular educators each have expertise that can assist and support struggling students. To accommodate individual differences and needs, educators can modify the classroom environment through collaborative teaming (Friend & Cook, 1992), or use of consultation or cooperative teaching approaches (Coufal, 1993; Falk-Ross, 1995; Friend & Bursuck, 1999; Meyen, Vergason, & Whelan, 1996). This chapter suggests teaching strategies for meeting the language and literacy needs of students with language difficulties. It also provides collaborative models that teachers and speech and language pathologists can use to implement inclusive, situated language and literacy support for students with special needs.

One model that organizes the necessary elements into a clear sequence is that described by Prelock, Miller, and Reed (1993). They developed the model as they established collaborative partnerships for a language-in-the-classroom (LIC) program. Prelock and her colleagues built the districtwide program model around four essential components. The first building block is the identification of a transdisciplinary model for collaboration among team members. This component describes the evolving stages of relationships and assumption of responsibility among members of the special- and general-education disciplines as they gain experience and knowledge while working together (Linder, 1993; Woodruff & McGonigel, 1988). Second, these researchers acknowledge the importance of enlisting administrative support and recruiting teachers' assistance through community meetings, educational workshops, and other promotional demonstrations. Third, this approach requires in-service training for all team members and professionals, to prepare them for the changing roles and collaborative responsibilities that characterize inclusive programming. Fourth, members must organize and prepare collaborative intervention programs to accommodate all students in the classroom, including those with special needs.

Building Administrative Supports

The support of school administrators constitutes a key component in the initiation of programmatic changes for classroom-based language and literacy instruction. As leaders and decision-makers for the school's or district's policies, administrators set instructional goals and desired educational outcomes for students, provide resources and professional development for teachers, and fund new programs and innovative changes for each school or district. These superintendents, principals, curriculum directors, program coordinators, and other school officials can ease the way for new and integrated, inclusive educational programs. Whether the targeted population will include students from within an entire school district, one particular school, or limited introduction to one classroom, these officials' cooperation and financial backing are essential (Larson & McKinley, 1989; Simon, 1979).

Legal mandates, parental and community imperatives, and knowledge of the richness of heterogeneous educational grouping can all prompt administrators to support expanded forms of education for students. For example, more and more schools are experimenting with mainstreaming, or integrating students with disabilities into general-education classrooms for at least a few classes each day (U.S. Department of Education, 2000). Moreover, preservice teacher-education programs are preparing general-education instructors to teach in inclusive settings (Lesar, Benner, Habel, & Coleman, 1997). Coteaching practices are also becoming more widely accepted as models for collaboration (Reinhiller, 1996). Looking more closely at the movement for inclusion, Kutash and Duchnowski (1997), note, "There are limitations posed by policies that affect fiscal, procedural, and personnel issues . . ." (p. 188) involved in organizing programs for inclusive programs. These researchers attribute these challenges to the limited amount of research evidence of the benefits of inclusive practices and single-discipline training of preservice teachers. In the model they propose—that is, the FUSE Project in Florida (see Silliman, Ford, Beasman, & Evans, 1999)—administrators worked closely with general educators in general and special education in developing the programs. Figure 4.1 describes these coteaching strategies.

Collaborative relationships between teachers may begin as pilot programs launched by a few interested teachers with common goals for students' education. For example, teachers may develop plans to discuss the nature of students' language and literacy difficulties, organize coteaching activities, introduce strategies for compensatory interventions, or agree to alternative assessment approaches with the approval of principals and curriculum coordinators in specific school settings. These innovations demonstrate to administrators that new programs can serve as essential parts of the educational system (Larson & McKinley, 1989). The success of these

FIGURE 4.1   Fuse Coteaching Strategies

Type	Description	Benefits
Whole Group Instruction		
One teach/one monitor	One person teaches lesson; other checks for understanding, keeping a log of needs of students with LLD.	Authentic, dynamic documentation of students' progress; keeps on task.
Cooperative learning	Children work in heterogeneous, groups; teachers/SLP monitors student progress, provides mini lessons, or works with a group.	Children learn from active participation in discussion activities, group members contribute to negotiating discussion; opportunities present for ongoing dialogue between all children and for all children to be successful.
Dialogue teaching	Two teachers teach same lesson via instructional conversations.	Allows for confirmation of lesson contents, directions, or steps in a process.
Instruct and outline	One teacher teaches content; one takes notes on board or overhead, provides an outline of lesson as is presented.	Serves as model for organizing information; makes main ideas visible and explicit; teaches outlining and note taking skills.
Shared presentation	Two teachers teach same content to two heterogeneous groups; wrap-up done with whole class.	Different material taught if one group needs additional support; teachers then reverse roles.
Small Group Instruction		
Teacher-directed centers	Learning centers assigned for children to move through; Teachers/SLPs monitor or provide mini lessons.	More involvement of children with small teacher/child ratio.
Remedial/ enrichment teaching	Both teach same lesson but one teaches an enrichment lesson and the other reteaches content.	Enhancements incorporated into future lessons; students needing additional support are provided that support.
Parallel teaching	Students are assigned to groups based on knowledge and skills; teachers teach same content to both groups of children; two lessons taught using different teaching strategies.	Functional skills taught and in classroom; more student involvement in smaller groups.

Reprinted/Adapted with permission from Silliman, E. R., Ford, C. S., Beasman, J., & Evans, D. An inclusion model for children with language learning disabilities: Building classroom partnerships, *Topics in Language Disorders, 19*(3), 1–18. © 1999 Aspen Publishers, Inc.

pilot programs can further build administrators' awareness of new and effective inclusive programming, and open the door for larger, more expansive programs.

Marketing maneuvers to increase awareness of other classroom teachers and interested parents can also help highlight the merits of potential new programs. Inservice school presentations focused on collaborative teaching and classroom-based language and literacy lessons will inform other teachers of new ways to support students (Larson & McKinley, 1989). Meetings with parent-teacher organizations to discuss opportunities for generalizing new language strategies will establish firm foundations for classroom-based support and interventions. Finally, proposals for small grants may be developed to obtain new materials and introduce innovative assessment tools that teachers can share in regular classrooms, thus gaining attention for the new programs (Wilcox, Louri, & Caswell, 1991).

Collaborative Teaching Approaches

The prime responsibility for implementing compensatory language and literacy strategies is shifting from the special educator to a shared collaboration among teacher, child, and speech and language pathologist (American Speech-Language-Hearing Association, 1996; Larson, McKinley, & Boley, 1993). By providing classroom teachers with helpful information for understanding a child's problem and suggestions for enhancing the child's language, the speech/language pathologist can empower both the teacher *and* the child.

However, the success of how these consultative programs function, hinges on the attitudes of the participants and the model of the program. More specifically, language negotiation in the classroom requires metalinguistic and metacommunicative awareness on the parts of the teachers and students in the classrooms during verbal exchanges (Falk-Ross, 1997; Wallach & Butler, 1994). Students with language difficulties benefit from encouragement and reinforcement in their struggles and successes alike. Teachers, for their part, need modeling and support in their efforts to individualize conversational styles for children. The collaborative process can help on both of these fronts. One goal of collaboration is to help teachers understand the problems they will be encountering and to suggest practical ways to approach these difficulties. Many teachers resent the extra effort they must expend to accommodate special students because they have not received sufficient information to understand the nature of the problems or to feel in control of situations in which difficulties disrupt discourse (Ross & Wax, 1993). A teacher's cooperation through consultative collaboration contributes to a successful language-support program. From a constructivist view, both general and special educators co-facilitate students' learning as they construct lessons and modify instruction to suit the needs of individual class members. Together, they immerse themselves in problem-based teaching and learning, utilizing strategies such as inquiry, reflection, and discussion to develop approaches that will heighten all students' learning (Blumenfeld, 1992).

As the student population grows increasingly diverse (U.S. Department of Education, 2000), language and literacy instruction requires creative approaches to inclusive, multicultural teaching. Curriculum-centered collaboration and innovative coteaching approaches can meet this need better than exclusive resource-room delivery can (Coufal, 1993; Falk-Ross, 1997; Meyen, Vergason, and Whelan, 1996). Vygotskian theory underlies the process through which a set of organized educational team members each use their expertise to help one another develop appropriate modifications in curriculum. These same principles apply to the development of a mentored preparation program for classroom-based language intervention in elementary schools. These children will need extra help and support in the form of learning strategies tailored to their individual needs to accomplish the goals set by teachers.

Several elements of collaborative team building characterize all successful models. These include, among all team members:

- a shared vision for desired outcomes;
- an understanding of assumptions and values;
- a common language or vocabulary for teachers', specialists', and parents' contributions;
- a building of trust and mutual respect;
- a commitment to allotting time for meetings and discussions;
- parity among members;
- a set of plans for student and team evaluation

(Falvey, 1995; McCormick, Loeb, & Schiefelbusch, 1997).

As more classroom populations include students with special education needs, coteaching approaches and implementation must match the specific needs of each classroom and school district. Thus, some language and literacy difficulties may not prove severe enough to require the presence of both a general-education and special-education teacher in the classroom. Rather, a team of teachers may develop strategies for addressing these problems, and the classroom teacher will implement them. (This is referred to as collaborative consultation.) Other problems will require a form of cooperative teaching, or coteaching (Simpson & Myles, 1996). Marvin (1987) discusses a gradual growth in collaborative work through stages of coactivity, cooperation, and coordination. The final stage is collaboration, during which teachers engage in informal networking, have a high degree of trust and respect for one another, and share responsibility for students.

Collaborative Consultation

Collaborative consultation expands on the traditional practice of consultation in schools. In general, consultation includes a series of in-depth discussions among all team members regarding approaches to remedial or compensatory instruction, organizational features, and administrative coordination (Blosser & Kratcowski, 1997; Coufal, 1993; Idol, Nevin, &Paolucci-Whitcomb, 1999; Prelock, Miller, & Reed, 1993). At the very least, consultative services should include a meeting between a special and a general educator, during which the former advises the latter concerning optimal educational approaches for a student with special needs. Collaborative consultation consists of similar discussions among many partners. The very term *collaborative consultation* acknowledges that each member of the group contributes important insights into a student's educational needs, and that, together, they develop benchmarks and supports for common goals. Many team members may participate in this process, including special- and general-education representatives, social psychological therapists, medical and professional team members, parents or guardians, and any other caretakers who could contribute. As the team members move through several stages of development, from focusing on specific goals to becoming aware of the process and collaborative style of the other participants, the effectiveness of the interventions also increases (Blalock, 1997; Blosser & Kratcowski, 1997).

One notable example is the triadic model of problem-solving (Idol, Nevin, & Paolucci-Whitcomb, 1999). This model has three foci: a target (for example, the student with a problem); a mediator (such as a teacher with means for identifying the problem in the classroom); and a consultant (that is, the specialist, second teacher, or principal with knowledge about solving the problem). The triadic model also includes specifics of negotiation and shared participation (Coufal, 1993) and aspects of planning (Prelock, Miller, & Reed, 1993). Equally important, the model includes the child in the problem-solving discussions. Students provide significant insight and ideas into their own educational needs (Thousand, Villa, & Nevin, 1994; Vaughn, Schumm, & Kouzekanani, 1993).

Teacher-Assistance Teams

Teacher-assistance teams (TATs) comprise teachers who want to help one another solve problems they encounter in the classroom with students having special needs. Often prereferral, the team meets to brainstorm ideas for how they might modify instruction (Lewis & Doorlag, 1999). Through structured workshops, TATs can also help school faculty members and the principal become familiar with student behavior and needs, assess classroom situations, conduct evaluations, set goals, plan activities, develop strategies, and design ongoing activities. Special consultants can support a TAT's efforts (Chalfant, Pysh, & Moultrie, 1979).

Cooperative (Co-) Teaching Models

Coteaching occurs when at least two educators share the instructional activities in the same classroom. The teachers may both be regular educators, or one may be a specialist in language or learning disabilities. They may divide the responsibilities according to a variety of models, consisting of individual instruction, small-group work, or whole-class lecture. The educators may follow the same lesson plan or introduce parallel activities. As its central characteristic, coteaching entails team instruction. Educational professionals with diverse but complementary skills collaborate to include all students in the general-education curriculum (Bauwens & Hourcade, 1997; Blosser & Kratcowski, 1997; Friend & Bursuck, 2002).

Coteaching today takes many forms. Lynne Cook and Marilyn Friend (1996) describe five of the more common approaches: (1) *one teaches, one supports* (one teacher leads the class while another helps individual students), (2) *station teaching* (teachers share the job of helping students as they work in small clusters), (3) *parallel teaching* (teachers present different material to different groups of students, whether for remedial or supplemental teaching), (4) *alternative teaching* (the class divides into one large group and one small group for purposes of preteaching material, introduction of enrichment activities, or remediation and support), and (5) *team teaching* (both teachers have equal responsibilities for instruction of all students) (Friend & Barsuck, 2002). Figure 4.2 illustrates these approaches.

Research studies investigating coteaching between special- and general-educational staff members have proliferated in public and private school systems in recent years (Blosser & Kratcowski, 1997; Prelock, Miller, & Reed, 1993; Walther-Thomas, 1996; Walther-Thomas, Kovinek, & McLaughlin, 1999). Indeed, students have grown accustomed to having more than one teacher lead the classroom activity for varying time periods throughout the day or week. These coteaching approaches rest on educational assumptions that emphasize the merging of expertise and knowledge among educational specialists (Friend & Cook, 1992; Friend & Barsuck, 1999). Figure 4.3 depicts the organization of coteaching approaches.

There are several variations on the teacher-specialist interactions that facilitate coteaching in the classroom. Silliman, Ford, Beasman, & Evans (1999) describe approaches for supporting students with language learning disabilities. These researchers specify instructional responsibilities within the broad approaches developed by Friend and Bursuck (2002). Silliman et al. distinguish between *shared presentation* (which Friend and Bursuck call *parallel teaching*), in which two teachers divide the class in half to teach the same content using the same teaching strategies, and *parallel teaching,* in which the teachers divide the class based on their knowledge and skills and then teach the same content using different teaching strategies. They also describe a form of whole-group instruction known as *dialogue teaching,* in which two teachers use instructional conversations to teach the same lessons, allowing for ". . . confirmation of lesson content, directions, or steps in a process" (p. 5). Yet another approach, *instruct and outline,* is a specific form of Friend's and Bursuck's *team teaching,* during which one teacher presents content while the other provides a visual reproduction in the form of notes. Silliman and her colleagues further distinguish between *cooperative learning,* which features opportunities for dialogue among all children in a heterogeneous group, and the smaller groups in *teacher-directed centers,* which provide a smaller teacher-to-child ratio. (Friend and Bursack call this latter approach *station teaching.*)

FIGURE 4.2   Coteaching Approaches

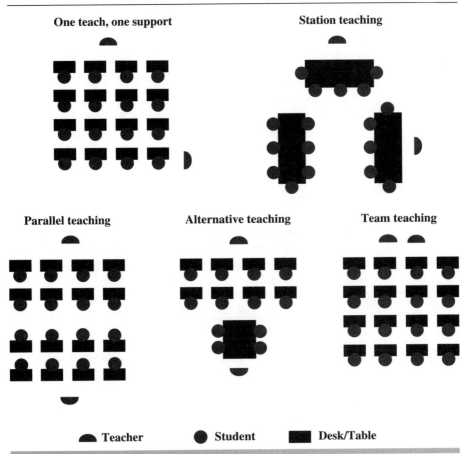

One teach, one support

Station teaching

Parallel teaching

Alternative teaching

Team teaching

Teacher   Student   Desk/Table

From Friend, M. & Bursuck, W. D., *Including students with special needs: A practical guide for class-room teachers.* © 1999 by Allyn & Bacon. Reprinted/Adapted by permission.

Another model for language support developed by Dohan and Schultz (1998), adapted from Elksnin and Capilouto (1994), includes two approaches. In each, the two teachers eventually teach all the students in one class period; that is, each teaches different content and then they switch groups (approach three), and both teachers share the lecture material (approach seven). In each of these models, the special- and general-education teachers collaborate to determine the approach or combination of approaches that will be most effective for the student(s) with language and literacy difficulties, most appropriate for the classroom environment, and most comfortable for the two teachers.

FIGURE 4.3   Changes in Classroom Members' Responsibilities

	Traditional	**Holistic**
Classroom Teachers		
Strategies:	Remedial behaviors are developed outside the classroom.	Usable cues are embedded in meaningful classroom discourse.
Language:	Discourse routines are rigidly enforced.	Reflective clarification loosens the structure of the scripts.
Motivation:	Use external attribution for remedial solutions.	Use internal attribution for strategic solutions.
Students		
Strategies:	Remedial activities are contrived in a resource setting.	"Choose and use" strategies are selected in the classroom.
Language:	Predictable patterns of langauge discourage participation.	Variations on patterns allow more freedom to respond.
Motivation:	Use external attribution for solution of problems.	Use internal attribution for solution of problems.
Speech-Language Pathologists		
Strategies:	Rules and repetition	Classroom collaborator
Language:	Contrived routines	Discussion and feedback
Motivation:	Use external attribution for solution of problems.	Use internal attribution for solution of problems.

Data are limited as to the frequency of use of one coteaching model over another. However, a survey completed by Beck and Dennis (1997) indicated that speech and language pathologists do not always use the model that they think is most appropriate; that is, team teaching. Instead, they feel pressure to use alternative teaching modes, such as small-group remedial work with only students having language difficulties. To provide more collaborative roles within inclusive education, researchers are exploring more equitable models (Falk-Ross, 1997; Reinhiller, 1996). Further guidance for speech-language pathologists developing classroom-based programs for language intervention will come with future studies of different service-delivery models.

In the cases of the three focal students in this study, I first approached the superintendent of schools for the district for permission to initiate the new approach to language intervention and to use the data collected in the process for research purposes. After reviewing a proposal for the research study and meeting with his advisors, he provided suggestions for implementing the program that were added to the methodology. The contact with the principal of the school in which the research was situated proved more collaborative. The principal and I met specifically to develop a plan that would support students with language difficulties *and* reflect the school's policies. When the principal understood that all students' names would be masked from public knowledge and that the information would not jeopardize the privacy of the students' families, he recommended several teachers with whom I could confer. I used a conference with the classroom teacher to organize the meeting times, specify the individualized educational goals, and explain the ongoing collection of data. Each of these meetings played an important part in the development of our own inclusive model of language support in the classroom.

Gaining Access to the Classroom

Implementing expansions of traditional models of language and literacy intervention programs still presents many hurdles. First, classroom teachers and speech and language pathologists may not be aware of coteaching models and may not be comfortable with collaboration. Studies of the perceptions of general-education teachers revealed that they do not feel they have adequate knowledge or skills for developing appropriate curriculum modifications for children with disabilities (Coates, 1989; Ross & Wax, 1993). Moreover, these teachers often appear to resent their new responsibilities and perceived added workload (Ross & Wax, 1993).

Second, teachers and speech and language pathologists need to develop strategies for transitioning into team-teaching pairings of increased parity. Language specialists may not have time to visit classrooms when they have high caseloads. They may need to introduce only a few new classroom-based intervention programs each year as the teachers acclimate to the more inclusive models of classroom-based teaching.

Third, speech and language pathologists and general educators need to jointly develop learning experiences that meet the Individualized Education Program goals of individual students within everyday classroom routines. Research studies of inclusive classrooms have revealed that even when children are identified as having special needs in the general-education classroom, they do not always receive individualized attention or appropriate curriculum modifications (Baker & Zigmond, 1990; McIntosh, Vaughn, Schumm, Haager, & Lee, 1994). Conversations with all team members in each student's program need to occur before the student's placement in the classroom and frequently during the school year. To overcome these problems, discussions with teachers, introductions of models, and suggestions for collaboration must precede preparations for classroom placements.

Models and Mentors

Teachers need modeling and support in their efforts to individualize instruction. In many cases, they may not have received adequate preparation to provide meaningful instruction to students with disabilities (Kearney & Durand, 1992). In other cases, they have not experienced the advantages of inclusive programs and may not be convinced of their applicability in the general-education classroom (Coates, 1989; Ross & Wax, 1993). District- or schoolwide in-service presentations provide effective means for professional development of practicing teachers in the area of inclusive models (e.g., Prelock, Miller, & Reed, 1993). In addition, preservice teacher-education programs have prepared teachers for educational approaches appropriate for inclusive settings (e.g., Lesar, Benner, Habel, & Coleman, 1997). However, changes in teaching practice occur slowly. To develop teachers' interest, motivation, and expertise in applying modifications for children with language and literacy difficulties, teachers must increase exposure to the practice through models in the classroom. To support these experiences, speech/language pathologists may provide teachers with research literature or a list of related reading materials. Armed with these resources, teachers can manage their own learning and contributions as they engage in collaborative relationships through successive stages of understanding (Bloom, Perlmutter, & Burrell, 1999; Lesar, Benner, Habel, & Coleman, 1997; Prelock, Miller, & Reed, 1993).

Either prospective member of a collaborative team may introduce models in the general-education classroom. For example, teachers may request a demonstration of a form of coteaching for instruction, or speech and language pathologists may volunteer to assist in the classroom during a reading or writing lesson. Both parties discuss the specific sequence of events and responsibilities of each member before the class and evaluate the results in a later meeting. These collaborative events may take place periodically during the several months preceding the initial placements of students, or they may occur each week as a trial period. Coteaching partners can come in the guise of invited guest speakers, assistants for special projects, ability group leaders, or individual student advocates. In addition, all participants in coteaching models need to feel that they are equals in their working relationships and interactions.

In the programs formed for the three focal students in this study, I initiated classroom visits on special occasions during the spring semester before the beginning of the study to introduce coteaching and collaborative models of compensatory language instruction to the classroom teachers. As the study evolved, each model, with the exception of *team teaching,* was used at various times throughout the school year. The *one teach, one support* and *station-teaching* models were used most frequently for language intervention within literacy activities. *Alternative teaching* and *parallel teaching* occurred less frequently in all classrooms. Discussions with teachers concerning the specifics of the study and the details of each student's language and literacy needs occurred just before the start of the school year, as student placements in classrooms were assigned. The teachers' experiences with, and attitudes toward, coteaching and classroom-based approaches to language support proved to be mixed. These variations, in turn, created differences in each of the language and literacy programs, as will become clearer in the development of each individual case-study.

Defining Roles and Responsibilities

Within the community of learners that compose a classroom, each member plays an important role in defining the educational environment. These roles are generally implicit, set early in the school year through a combination of the teacher's model and historical precedents of classroom dynamics (Edwards & Mercer, 1987). For example, the nature of language routines, the types of literacy activities, and the organization of the desks and chairs signal who may lead, follow, and control all aspects of learning. Students' educational achievement is often tied to how well their learning styles match those of the classroom teacher's instructional routines. In traditional classrooms, students having special language and literacy needs receive remedial assistance in placements outside the classroom. Thus, they have little impact on existing classroom routines.

In cases of classroom-based intervention programs for these students, both the teacher and speech and language specialist collaboratively develop new routines and responsibilities. Special educators also organize collaborative teams to share responsibilities and to support both the students who meet the strict requirements of IDEA as well as those who do not have statistically significant language problems. Professional and team responsibilities and personal characteristics guide educators' roles (Friend & Bursuck, 1999; Rankin & Aksamit, 1994). These team members may serve as core players (that is, they play direct roles in the focal student's program design and implementation) and supportive players (when their participation is less frequent and tangential) as they advise or collaborate periodically throughout the school year (McCormick, Loeb, & Schiefelbusch, 1997; Rainforth, York, & MacDonald, 1992). The responsibilities of the team members and classroom students generally evolve throughout the school year as trust builds among the members and the needs of students change. These new roles often require a higher-than-usual level of metalinguistic awareness on the part of each participant, as occurred during this study of three boys' progress in general-education classrooms. Enabling each member to develop this awareness became a part of the intervention program as well.

Teachers as Facilitators and Guides

The language teachers use during lessons and interactive activities may promote or discourage students' participation in classroom discourse and engagement in literacy experiences. Consistent with a Vygotskian perspective, teachers also guide students' progress in developing understandings and internalizing new knowledge. They support and foster students' own language constructions within the social experiences of the classroom. This last role is especially important, because schools comprise such diverse student populations in terms of language backgrounds and abilities. When working with students having special language and literacy needs, teachers are encouraged to collaborate with speech and language pathologists to clarify goals for classroom intervention protocol, such as seating arrangements, modified instructional procedures, and adapted materials. Teaching assistants or paraprofessionals need to familiarize themselves with modification strategies that they may independently apply within the teacher's planned activities.

Specialists as Models and Resources

The role of the speech and language pathologist in the coteaching pair is not always clearly defined. Some overlap may arise between the roles of the classroom teacher, who initiates basic content and introduces it into learning activities, and that of the speech and language pathologist, who develops appropriate teaching and learning strategies for students with language-based problems in reading and writing. The speech and language pathologist provides a model for the teacher(s) and students for strengthening an undeveloped skill and helping them reach common understandings within classroom lessons. Through collaborating with teachers and parents in and out of the classroom, the speech and language pathologist also develops curricular modifications to address each student's needs. Language specialists need to identify themselves as important members of the school's educational staff—that is, as members of a team whose work will have a vital impact on children who need intensive remedial language services.

Students as Participants and Collaborators

All students in inclusive classrooms benefit from introductions to the new educators, such as the speech and language pathologist, who become an active part of the classroom. Students learn to use both regular and special teachers as resources for learning, and participate in activities that both educators developed collaboratively. These activities often pair students with language and literacy difficulties with more regularly achieving peers, or "buddies," for mentoring in taking notes, remembering procedural steps, and completing tasks. Peer tutors assist in coconstruction of knowledge in small-group work and paired-reading activities in the classroom. Students with difficulties can also collaborate with teachers by explaining what they need to participate in discourse and achieve in literacy activities and self-evaluations.

Changing Roles in Classroom Interaction

As more and more classrooms and then schools have explored classroom-based intervention programs, roles and responsibilities have evolved. Autonomous decision-making by regular and special educators concerning evaluation and instruction of students with special language and literacy needs has given way to collaborative problem-solving by all team members, including the students themselves (Friend & Barsuck, 1999; Lesar, Benner, Habel, & Coleman, 1997; McCormick, Loeb, & Schiefelbusch, 1997). This change begins with a growing awareness of new strategies for supporting students' special needs, grows to participation in collaborative programs, and eventually expands into initiation of novel approaches for inclusive education. The changes are noticeable in all areas of educational planning, as the focused case studies of Mickey, Vincent, and Henry will reveal. Typically, in the case studies, the evolution of roles and responsibilities transformed each member of the classroom, whether teachers, specialists, or students. (See Figure 4.4.)

FIGURE 4.4   Changes in Classroom Members' Roles

	Before Classroom-Based Strategy Intervention	After Classroom-Based Strategy Intervention
Classroom Teachers		
Self-Image:	Leader	Classroom collaborator
Strategies:	Hit-or-miss compensatory strategies	Educated guesses for language support
Language:	General discourse routines	Reflective clarification
Emotional:	Less control	More control
Motivation:	External attributions	Internal attributions
Students		
Self-Image:	Mistake-maker/respondent	Language participant
Strategies:	Practice and leave	"Choose and use"
Language:	Predictable patterns	Risk-taker
Emotional:	Follower	Leader
Motivation:	External attribution of problems	Internal attribution of problems
Speech-Language Pathologists		
Self-Image:	Resource teacher	Classroom collaborator
Strategies:	Rules and repetition	Real, usable cues
Language:	Contrived routines	Discussion and feedback
Emotional:	Therapist, frustrated	Facilitator, less frustrated
Motivation:	External attributions of problems	Internal attributions of problems

A collaborative organization of intervention services requires a model that values students' individual efforts toward construction of language and literacy strategies. To build these strategies, all teachers must begin by emphasizing students' learning strengths, as opposed to deficits, and share expectations for success. Teachers and students also benefit from initial discussions to introduce new programs. In the particular case studies of Mickey, Vincent, and Henry, the speech and language specialist explained the changes that would occur in location and form of language remediation to each child at the beginning of the school year.

Decisions to initiate discussions inside the classroom or to hold occasional resource-room meetings were based on the needs of the children and the limitations of the classroom. For example, because of the physical organization of a particular class and its rules for quiet, independent work at individualized desks, I sometimes explained and negoiated new strategies with the boys in other parts of the classroom, in the hallway, or in the resource room, although this last occurred only rarely. Sometimes, moving instruction away from the center of classroom activity reduced disruption for everyone involved. The teacher and I also decided the type and frequency of the cueing and clueing strategies during the classroom routines.

In terms of visibility, I began as a participant observer, generally located along the perimeters of the class. If I remained still, sitting and watching the class, I sometimes drew attention from some students. These youngsters seemed self-conscious about their responses, probably because they wondered whether I was listening for any errors they may make. If I kept quietly busy, perhaps rearranging papers and books in the back or side of the room, I seemed to create less distraction, and the classroom discourse would return to a more typical style. When I sat next to one child in the same seat for several visits in a row, the focal student and his peers would later seem distracted when a student who had been ill during my previous visits occupied my former seat. Thus I found it best to sit near a focal student in a different position each time. Although the students wanted to know why I was working in their classroom, they slowly accepted my presence. My explanation was that a second teacher's (or speech and language pathologist's) help in the classroom activities was part of their school responsibilities, like that of other classroom helpers who are present in the classroom.

Following this first phase of study, all the children became less guarded, in general. The business of remediating the focal children's language difficulties to support their developing communicative competence in the classroom began, then, with fewer obstacles.

5 Building Strategies
for Language and
Literacy Learning

Children need much guidance and verbal feedback from more knowledgeable adults or peers when they first learn the intricacies of any skill or strategy (Rogoff, 1990; Vygotsky, 1978; Wertsch, 1985). The suggestions for building strategies for language and literacy learning that follow rest on this premise that learning is interactive and collaborative, enhanced by social environments such as the everyday classroom. Moreover, the strategies described herein have a "building" nature; that is, new information is added to students' present ability level, whatever that may be. Teachers and speech and language pathologists support students in their attempts to accomplish successively difficult tasks until they can independently initiate and complete them (Palinscar & Brown, 1983; Vygotsky, 1978). Classroom-based language and literacy intervention programs, such as those involving cueing strategies and modifications in discourse routines, provide opportunities for all educators to contribute to this building process.

The term *building* also underscores the enabling nature of new-strategy introduction. Students formulate and modify their own hypotheses of language rules and literacy conventions by following the models they observe in their social environments (Goodman, 1986; Teale & Sulzby, 1986; Vygotsky, 1978). A student-centered approach to collaborative development of supportive cueing and learning techniques strengthens the communication-competence and achievement benchmarks in the classroom. Children learn best when they have a connection to the activity or conversation, and when their interests are considered in its organization (Dewey, 1990).

Guiding Principles for Instructional Strategies

Educational programs vary according to the individual needs of each student, the teaching materials available in the classroom, and the discourse that characterizes verbal interaction for teaching and learning events. However, several core principles must guide the intervention strategies used to support students with language and literacy difficulties. These principles help ensure that students' language and literacy competencies develop in ways consistent with a social-constructivist approach; that is, through meaningful interactions and mentored practice using language within everyday class activities. These core principles draw from research developed for an integrated approach to language and literacy instruction and are supported by experiences working with Mickey, Vincent, and Henry. They include:

■ *Use a balanced approach in evaluating language and literacy skills and strategies.*

   This approach includes dynamic, or supported, assessment to discover achievement potential (Olswang & Bain, 1991), informal evaluation of oral language samples and classroom observation (e.g., running records and oral interviews) to determine the impact of disorder, and formal standardized tests to estimate the nature and extent of the difficulty. Ongoing evaluation and documentation of students' use of learning strategies consists of documentation of strategies that students use in the classroom most frequently and how often they ask for help.

   Evaluation materials include end-of-chapter tests, spelling quizzes, writing samples, and teacher-made checklists for all academic subjects. These materials help teachers and language specialists restructure individual education programs. Classroom teachers, responsible for students' smooth transitions through everyday activities, may compile progress reports that would guide modifications and interventions, and include them in the development of an academic portfolio. The portfolios reflect the problems and processes in a student's thinking and achieving and give educators, parents, administrators, and other specialists a chance to share observations. Modifications in evaluation forms, such as provision of orally administered assessments or reduction of homework-assignment length, can help teachers gain more reliable insight into the nature of conceptual understanding by students with literacy learning problems. All members of the collaborative team monitor students' grades as the report card periods progress.

■ *Follow an integrated model of instruction within the classroom.*

   A balanced model of language and literacy learning provides for a wide variety of materials (audiotapes, pictures, everyday objects, tradebooks, artistic works, etc.) and a wide variety of teaching methods (dyadic interaction, coaching, questioning, reciprocal instruction (Routman, 1991). An optimal model for enhancing language and literacy development integrates reading, writing, listening, and talking together—it involves a whole-language approach to learning (Edelsky, Altwerger, & Flores, 1991; Goodman, 1986). Classroom language interventionists may fall into a tutoring trap; in other words, they may repeat or reteach an isolated skill in the same manner as the original lesson, without connecting it to a meaningful activity or modifying it as needed. Instead, language specialists must view language skill as more than mastery of syntactic or pragmatic functions; indeed, as part of the entire situation or context of language (Norris, 1997).

■ *Develop metalinguistic awareness of phonology and language, and meta-communicative awareness of discourse routines.*

Intervention programs that focus on developing metalinguistic skills help children show greater progress in reading achievement than they do for those who have not received this explicit instruction (Menyuk & Chesnick, 1997). Language form, content, and use vary with the situational context in which a language construction is embedded (Halliday & Hasan, 1985; Hymes, 1970). Using reading activities as communicative contexts for language intervention develops the children's organization of more complex discourse structure and helps them grasp the semantic complexity of the utterances within the narratives (Hoffman, 1997).

■ *Expand the form of language routines that accompany literacy activities.*

Teachers need to accept longer explanations and constructions, student-initiated questions and comments, topic digressions, and open discussions. Modeling of word, phrase, or sentence expansions prepares students to apply more effective language and literacy constructions in classroom discourse. The complexity of the act of reading builds on the domains of oral language but requires a variation on pragmatic strategies, even for students who have average language abilities (Snow, 1994). Students with communication disorders who receive language intervention in the classroom (LIC) evidence more intelligible and complete oral language than those who received more traditional, individual instruction outside the classroom (Bland & Prelock, 1995). Teachers must give students the "space" they need to process and respond to classroom discourse. They can do this by lengthening the "wait time" in a way that students *and* teachers respect. Students who have difficulties with expressive word retrieval often require more time to process and respond. Thus teachers can provide extra information, shaping questions, and answer choices. Teachers can also expand language constructions by devising questions that allow multiword responses, as opposed to the limited structure provided by the initiation-response-evaulation (I.R.E.) format. These techniques encourage students to modify their comments with additional words (e.g., adjectives, adverbs) and explanations for their responses. Explanations then help teachers and peers understand why a student answered as he did and give teachers and other students an opportunity to react to his thinking.

■ *Create a manageable number of goals that will contribute to progress in a cooperative and collaborative manner.*

In the study described in this book, team members defined goals using the federally mandated Individual Education Program goals and our own general impressions of reasonable foci. In any intervention, participants should choose long-term targets that will not change during the school year. However, short-term goals and classroom activities may shift as students reach successive levels of development as measured by academic evaluation, teaching and learning strategies, and social participation.

■ *Use brief, focused comments to remind students of cues/rules/targets before and during the intervention period.*

Be sure to highlight specific areas of focus for each intervention period. Remember to model oral and written strategies by performing these before and during classroom activities with the student in an authentic manner. Introduce classroom scripts. These may take the form of an "aside" or a quiet introduction as the speech and language pathologist sits down beside a child. Cueing activities may include visual, verbal, and tactile clues—agreed upon before intervention—during classroom discourse routines and activities. These would include providing clues for when to use particular strategies, as a preview and exposure to future information. They would also include situating the reading content in a larger context of purpose or time frame.

■ *Embed cueing strategies into classroom discourse and activities.*

Use a mix of presentation forms and let students choose strategies for generation of responses, especially in language and literacy formats. This approach lets students participate in individualized ways. Modify classroom activities and educational materials using additional or similar teaching strategies as those offered to all other classroom members. Examples include shortened assignments or longer time periods in which to complete tasks, and individual or small-group instruction in development of specific language or literacy skills and strategies. Language specialists present new information within a separated, but not necessarily resource, setting. These settings include alternative teaching in which coteachers present individualized instruction in an alcove or in the hallway, close to the other students yet away from distractions and which are not disruptive to the other class members. For example, a classroom teacher can review use of necessary vocabulary terms as part of each language-intervention period or make comments that help the student track the topic under discussion.

The use of cards listing frequently used words, i.e., easily accessible "word banks," possibly affixed to the student's desk, can support word recognition and spelling. Notes reminding the student of cues, such as the development of questioning strategies, support self-monitoring of his own reading. Teachers can also affix written notes and cue words to students' desks to guide their actions for task completion. Classroom teachers may draw students into discussions by using language probes to elicit appropriate responses and questions. These probes might include prompts, such as rephrasing a question or providing extra information to cue word retrieval, or physical cues such as an action or picture. By expanding on small-group reading organizations used for ability groups within the classroom, teachers can assign peer buddies to each student. Not all students are comfortable listening to peers' help, because youngsters may not be as patient as adults. However, peers' unique perspective on assigned work often provides valuable insight.

■ *Modify classroom activities.*

   Teachers, in collaboration with the language specialist, can modify classroom activities and assignments by reducing the quantity of work in less conspicuous ways—e.g., possibly eliminating some written problems or oral questions in each category of homework or topic of discussion. In this way, the reduction may not be obvious to the other students. Teachers can also adjust the quality of required tasks, directing students to use different steps to complete specific assignments, but ending with the same outcome as the original assignment. This technique may simplify the number of repetition, in an assignment but leaves the content intact. Students can also follow specific scripts to answer questions for practice assignments, consistent with curriculum genres.

■ *Change seating arrangements.*

   Changes in seating arrangements, such as placing a student closer to the center of the classroom when the teacher moves around during recitations, can help keep the student as close to the teacher as possible. Seating arrangements may change periodically for new group associations, but the student should remain near the teacher to best benefit from the teaching and learning experience.

■ *Elicit social participation through verbal comments during reading-response discussions and language-arts activities.*

   Language use and literacy learning develop through social processes. Students must take part in classroom discussions and reading and writing activities to observe others' behavior, acquire new information, practice and revise language and literacy forms, respond to text and interpretations, and apply these skills and strategies to their own needs. With cueing from teachers, students who have language or literacy difficulties can better communicate their ideas, albeit in often atypical language forms. Mediation with peers at music, gym, lunch, field trips, auditorium presentations, and special schoolwide activities enhances students' peer interaction and socialization. Often, peers require guidance to support the attempts of struggling students. The teacher's interventions into peer-directed conversations should be infrequent but should model the ways both students might voice opinions or needs in small-group discussions. If these experiences create stress for students, adult should step in. Using individual conferencing to introduce a review of routine classroom discourse scripts, students learn specific pragmatic language for entering into activity events. These scripts may include comments for initiating interaction and for maintaining conversation through turn-taking. In the case studies that follow, the language specialist used individual conferencing to develop a gestural cueing system that could help students make specific social moves in action or language participation.

Classroom Scheduling

When children are grouped together by classroom, they can remind each other about times for lessons, support each other in their language efforts, and retain classroom membership. Youngsters who have language and literacy difficulties are supported individually or in small groups as follows:

- Individually within the same classroom during coaching and cueing language-support intervention (approximately one hour's time, several times per week);
- Individually or in small groups during peripherally situated lessons (approximately fifteen to twenty minutes, several times per week);
- In small groups or as a whole group outside the classroom for approximately thirty minutes, when necessary.

Teachers can keep disruptions to classroom discourse and activities to a minimum by using cueing strategies that are consistent with classroom routines and teaching goals. More specifically, they can use visual and tactile strategies during relatively quiet periods in the classroom, such as during teacher-directed recitation and question-answer periods. Verbal cues may prove effective when a low noise level is acceptable in the classroom, such as during small-group work and verbally interactive discourse. Peripheral conferencing allows for more focused interaction between the student and speech and language pathologist, aide, or teacher, as do other conferencing activities within the classroom.

Teacher-Student Interaction

Side-by-Side Coaching

Side-by-side coaching is intervention within the classroom. The speech-language pathologist (or paraprofessional aide) sits next to or directly behind the student who has difficulties. He or she uses individual cueing—visual, gestural, or tactile—and modeling to help the child participate competently in discourse. The language pathologist can help students locate clues for language and literacy learning in the room, such as pictures in books, or in questions being presented, such as from a worksheet. Classroom cueing strategies that support participation in literacy routines include language-processing prompts, such as additional time for responses, repetition of questions or comments in similar form, and question prompts, and additional information to help situate the information; for instance, providing a word in a phrase as a model (Richard & Hanner, 1987).

A highly supportive form of intervention and assistance, side-by-side coaching is recommended for students whose cognitive level compares with that of the other students in the classroom and who is not frustrated by classroom dynamics. Disruptions to classroom discourse and activities can be kept to a minimum by using cueing strategies that are consistent with classroom routines and teaching goals. For example, visual and tactile strategies are used during relatively quiet periods in the classrooms, such as during teacher-directed recitation and question-answer period. Verbal cues are used when a low noise level was acceptable in the classroom, such as when small group work and verbally interactive discourse were being used. Before using cueing, teachers should collaborate with the specialist to prepare an informal script of events to occur. The role of the speech and language pathologist is to encourage and support the students' language constructions. Direct and indirect instruction can help him or her enhance these support strategies.

Peripheral Conferencing

Peripheral conferencing occurs between the language pathologist, learning specialist, or teacher's aide just to the side of classroom desks and activities. This form of conferencing lets students review vocabulary terms to be used in the following lesson, go over strategies to be used, and practice strategies following a model. Feedback and student-assessment may also take place during these discussions. Conferencing helps focus interactions between a student and speech and language pathologist, aide, or teacher. It can occur in alcoves, back rooms, or in the hall just outside the classroom, where the student can still hear the din of classroom conversation and activity. Frequently, conferencing occurs when students are joining or leaving organized activity groups. Language instruction in this setting takes the form of constructive feedback concerning just-completed discourse or in anticipation of routines to follow. Students can initiate questions or rehearse language during these moments, which last approximately ten minutes. Peripheral conferencing, also called pull-asides, can be especially helpful when discussions in the classroom would be disruptive or when privacy is necessary.

Resource Assistance

In a separated or out-of-classroom location, resource assistance allows for remedial work that requires concentrated attention, such as formal testing, individual analysis or synthesis of a series of task elements, or oral rehearsal of language or literacy exercises. Resource support is used at the beginning of the school year for individual testing periods and for setting goals, organizing problem-solving strategies, and collaboratively developing meaningful cues to be used in the classroom. These sessions may consist of both direct and indirect instruction. They usually last thirty minutes or more. After a few weeks into the school semester, this form of support becomes less frequent.

FIGURE 5.1   Guiding Principles

- Use a balanced approach in evaluating language and literacy skills and strategies.

- Follow an integrated model of instruction within the classroom.

- Develop metalinguistic awareness of phonology, language, and metacommunicative awareness of discourse routines.

- Expand the form of language routines that accompany literacy activities.

- Create a manageable number of goals that we could contribute to in a cooperative and collaborative manner.

- Use brief, focused comments to remind students of cues/rules/targets before and during the intervention period.

- Embed cueing strategies into classroom discourse and activities.

- Modify classroom activities.

- Change seating arrangements.

- Elicit social participation through verbal comments during reading-response discussions and language-arts activities.

Examples of Students' Changing Roles in Classroom Interaction

The experiences of Mickey, Vincent, and Henry as the new program was initiated in many ways resembled the reactions of most children as they participate in new inclusive programs. As the school year began, I explained to each child the changes that would occur during language remediation. Because the children were not yet accustomed to my extended presence in the classroom, each child shared his ideas concerning where I might sit, how I might provide clues, and how comfortable he felt with the changes in the traditional routine. For example, Vincent felt that "it would be good" for me to join him in the classroom as long as I "talked real quietly and whispered the answer in [his] ear." Henry was not as comfortable, explaining that "it would be okay [for me] to come in [the classroom], but the teacher really does most of the talking." He reported that he didn't really have any problems telling what he knew or thought in class, and could not offer any suggestions as to how I might cue him or help him when he had language difficulties. Mickey, however, thought "it would be good to have a helper because there's so much stuff in first grade . . . and she doesn't get it [when he talks]." I made my classroom observations, participated at approximately the same time each week, and planned an individual schedule for each student. At times, teachers made the usual adjustments for curricular reasons or to accommodate schoolwide special events.

During classroom observations, I sat near the student or in the back of the room. I conducted individual interviews with the boys in quiet spots around the school, such as in the library, a secluded alcove in the hallway, or in the speech re-source room. Observation and, later, interaction with each child extended to at least ninety minutes each week during the school year, in a variety of learning contexts.

As I have indicated, before this study began I had experienced a growing frustration with the lack of transfer of new skills and strategies from special-education resource rooms into regular classrooms. The process of role negotiation introduced forms of collaboration that had not previously been encountered (or confronted) because the responsibilities of regular-education teachers and students had traditionally been separate from those involved in special-education programs. Thus, the teacher-student relationship and language routines in these two general programs had diverged. To bring remediation work into the classrooms, the roles of the participants and the language strategies that each used would needed to change.

As the intervention program began in September, I told the children that this year's language therapy would consist of mainly classroom visits to develop their verbal communication skills. All were surprised to see me in the classroom and were apprehensive about receiving help in this context. Children, in general, are sensitive to variation in their routines and participation in daily activities. Rules concerning who may lead in conversations and who may sit at desk arrangements are set early in the school year by teachers as they consider the individual needs of the children in the class. Deviations in these rules and routines often create trepidation for children.

As their first hurdle, the boys had to explain my presence in the classroom to peers, which in their view suggested that they needed some help. Mickey didn't explain my presence; he was used to receiving extra help and attention from teachers in his classroom. Vincent usually shrugged and stated that I was "a friend," although he didn't seem to believe this at first. Henry muttered quickly that we would be working on language together. The other children commented to each other that this was a good idea, considering his disfluent language style.

I closely observed the responses of the boys' peers, because Mickey, Vincent, and Henry would need their support in conversations. Most of the children in the classrooms needed a few weeks to adapt to the presence of a new adult in the classroom. As a member of the school staff, I was a familiar *face* to most of the youngsters, but not a familiar *member* in the classroom. That is, my participation in classroom activities and routines didn't fit the usual description of a teacher leading the class, or of an aide assisting children as directed by the teacher, or of a parent doing odd jobs. My responsibilities in a particular classroom clearly centered on the focal child, whether I was observing his use of language or helping him to facilitate his language during discourse. This role prompted some children in each class to feel that my giving "special help" to the boys provided them with an unfair advantage. In other words, the other children wanted help as well.

To help all the students, including Mickey, Vincent, and Henry, understand that I was not giving "answers" but offering strategies for finding the appropriate answers, I agreed to provide help or constructive feedback to any child or small group during breaks in teaching routines. Later in the year, I overheard a few students helping peers by providing strategies rather than an exact answer, possibly following my model. The children were learning that the *process* of solving a problem is just as important as the answer, probably because the changing IRE format used in the classrooms fostered this idea. This was just as important a discovery for the children with language difficulties as it was for their peers. Having a language teacher and helper, such as myself, in the room to support the efforts of those children who needed help became more natural. Eventually, all the children relaxed.

6 Developing Student and Classroom Profiles

All educational programs and research studies begin with a gathering of historical and baseline data from which the researchers can develop hypotheses and organize an intervention. In the case of our year-long study, the first step lasted three months. During this time, I created profiles of each student and his respective classroom language routines using historical files and collaborative discussions with classroom teachers. These profiles, in turn, helped me and the teachers define individual starting points for classroom-based language-support strategies.

Providing a Historical Review

Interviews with former and present teachers indicated that all three children had one set of language characteristics in common—expressive language problems, specifically manifested in difficulty or delay in accessing words during discourse. Their teachers noted that Mickey, Vincent, and Henry paused extensively between words, made inaccurate but related word substitutions, and restarted sentences frequently. Based on the teachers' descriptions and my own observations of the children in their classrooms, I concluded that their language problems fell into the category of word-retrieval disorders (German, 1992; Johnson & Myklebust, 1967; Wiig & Semel, 1984), also referred to as disruptions (Dollaghan & Campbell, 1992) or, most recently, mazes (Owens, 1995).

Word-Retrieval Difficulties

Word-retrieval difficulties take the form of problems a speaker may have in trying to recall familiar words during conversation. Until recently, the terms *word retrieval* and *word finding* referred only to a small number of naming substitutions in an individual's language, often linked to neurological damage (Barton, Maruszewski, & Urrea, 1969; Benson & Geschwind, 1969; Kaplan, Goodglass, & Weintraub, 1976). However, studies of these disruptions have increased in number and focus, revealing complex models of the phenomenon. Descriptions of word-retrieval difficulties in the research literature categorize the salient characteristics as:

- response latencies prior to production in the form of delays or pauses greater than six seconds,
- time fillers ("um," "ah," etc.) and phonemic cues ("s . . . ssa . . . sailboat"),
- semantic or phonologically based word substitutions in the form of synonyms ("cloak" for "cape"), semantic relations ("fork" for "knife"), phonological similarities or malopropisms ("code" for "comb"),
- functional attribution ("plays music" for a specific instrument name),
- insertions ("I have a . . . you know what it is"),
- overuse of unclear referents such as pronouns and anaphoric referents ("that," "there") and empty words ("thing," "whatcha-ma-call-it"),
- word or phrase reformulations, also called revisions ("He is, they are going"),
- repetitions ("We took the cookies, took the cookies, home"), and
- perseverative use of words, phrases, or clauses.

These behaviors, as they occur in normal conversations, do not always reveal a disorder. However, if they become frequent, they can disrupt exchanges and frustrate the speaker. More often, a variety of these difficulties crop up in the speaker's language. For example, a child might say, "The two babies . . . no, uh, cubs . . . are playing in there . . . in the box . . . they're in the cage." In this language sample, the child has used a word reformulation ("babies . . . no, uh, cubs"), an unclear referent with a revision("in there . . . in the box"), and a semantically based word substitution ("box" for "cage"). Often, secondary behaviors, such as gesturing and subvocalizing, may accompany the verbal problems (German, 1992). Word-retrieval problems may occur in isolation, but generally they are part of a larger combination comprising other language or learning problems as well. Numerous research studies have alluded to the significance of word-retrieval behaviors in children's discourse competencies. These studies used experimental tasks to simulate classroom language activities and interactions (Donahue, 1985; German, 1987; German & Simon, 1991). Researchers interested in understanding young children's reading delays (Johnson & Myklebust, 1967; Wiig & Semel, 1976; Wolf, 1982) and writing problems (Wiig & Semel, 1984; deHirsch, 1969) have also discussed the role of word-retrieval difficulties in classroom literacy learning. Nevertheless, the observation of these problems in naturalistic classroom settings has not been well documented.

Collecting Descriptive Information

Observations and Referral Data

Amid busy classroom activities, as an observer, I had to identify typical routines within the classroom and the related discourse patterns that accompanied these routines. While determining these routines and patterns, I also had to identify the successes and difficulties each child was experiencing while trying to participate in them. I accomplished this mostly through classroom observations and individual interviews with each child. Moreover, the three students' teachers were asked to describe the students' communicative competence in classroom-specific needs as the teachers perceived them and the students,' peers,' and teachers' own reactions to these difficulties. They each completed an informal language-behavior scale (Richard & Hanner, 1988). These protocols included observations, referrals, interviews, and formal and informal testing. The consideration of all forms of evaluation taken together formed a profile that helped identify the student's language knowledge and patterns of use.

In some state guidelines, students must lag approximately one standard deviation below the average norm in a specific area of language, and this lag must clearly adversely affect school achievement, in order for him or her to qualify for a language-intervention program. Traditionally, evidence of a significant lag in specific areas of language development has depended on a student's performance on standardized measurement instruments. These standardized test results, in general, have provided only a small piece of the complex puzzle regarding children's language and literacy difficulties. Less formal, more authentic forms of evaluation—such as curriculum-based approaches, student observation, and performance-based project completion—provide more useful information about children's ability to use language in real, everyday school activities.

To arrive at a complete, balanced assessment of students' language and literacy achievement and potential in the classroom, the speech and language pathologist and all learning specialists should consider several elements when obtaining useful information:

- Appropriateness of evaluation method
- Sensitivity to individual development
- Connection to classroom instruction

According to Tierney (1998), effective assessment emerges from the classroom rather than being imposed on it. It is also client centered and reciprocal, ensuring fairness to the individual, and includes developmental and long-term goals. The choices for assessment vary from the more formal, externally developed standardized test formats to those more authentic, performance-based classroom assessments. Each is valued differently by team members within the testing environment. Each format has different advantages and disadvantages for students.

Standardized Tests

Norm-referenced forms of evaluation, standardized tests compare students' achievements with those of other students chosen nationally. These tests allow large-scale comparisons among school districts, state schools, and national norms. Their results help determine local and federal financial assistance, educational support, and achievement recognition. Some researchers have suggested that this close link between the financial and emotional well-being of schools may indicate the need to carefully weigh the results of standardized achievement tests. As critics have pointed out, these tests may be culturally biased, do not allow for flexibility in timing or teacher-student interaction, and are developed outside the school. Therefore, their results may not help teachers provide effective classroom instruction. The results of standardized assessment protocols reflect isolated skills in narrowly defined environments. These formal tests offer some valuable information, but they do not help teachers evaluate everyday, nontesting conversational exchanges. Yet frequent changes in the structure of social routines and exchanges in the classroom affect the anxiety, motivation, and success of each child. Standardized tests can't measure the susceptibility of children's word-retrieval difficulties to these changes.

In the case studies of Mickey, Vincent, and Henry, results of standardized language testing provided information indicating possible borderline problems with word processing or retrieval. These problems might have stemmed from other language difficulties, such as mild fluency disorder, weak semantic understanding, or inappropriate pragmatic application. In each case, the stimulus questions and pictures in the formal tests did not replicate the language routines typical of classroom discourse or the language functions required in everyday classroom activities. And in each case, remediation directed at the suspected problems revealed by these tests in previous years had not significantly helped these children. The evaluation and compensatory strategies would need to be context-specific and draw from everyday difficulties in authentic classroom experiences. Results of these tests and the informal evaluations that accompanied them appear in Chapters 7, 8, and 9, which trace Mickey's, Vincent's, and Henry's progress throughout the year.

Alternative Authentic Assessment

Authentic assessment approaches provide more student-centered evaluation, in the form of curriculum-based tasks, classroom projects, performance and presentation assignments, and portfolio development. Observations, checklists, and interviews may also fall into this category. For example, parents and teachers were interviewed for their impressions of the focal children. Ongoing informal discussions with each classroom teacher about each child's communicative competence, achievement levels, social skills, general progress, and any other concerns the teacher might have had regarding the student's behavior in her classroom were also recorded. Conversations with each child's parents concerning their knowledge of these same issues occurred during parent-teacher conference days and at other times, as appropriate. These less formal data-gathering methods provide more than a product; they are windows into the ways in which students construct knowledge. Information gained from these alternative assessments more clearly points out the direction for instruction and support in language and literacy development. Moreover, teachers and parents can directly use this information. Because these assessments are informal and flexible, classroom teachers can administer them often, documenting progress or core weaknesses in students' language and literacy skills and strategies.

Authentic assessment methods do have a disadvantage: They don't help the tester to directly compare each student's performance with larger groups of students. However, some researchers and practitioners might argue that the individual nature of this form of assessment is its strength, and that evaluators can balance results through triangulation using several different forms of authentic assessment.

Dynamic Assessment

Dynamic-assessment approaches also contribute valuable information concerning how well a students can solve problems with guided help from an instructor or aide. By investigating how a student learns with a small amount of assistance, evaluators can determine that student's potential for learning and change. This approach, which entails interactions between students and experienced adults, provides insight into students' cognitive processes and models for learning (Campione, 1989; Feuerstein, 1980; Olswang & Bain, 1991).

Dynamic assessment differentiates between the performance of two students on the same task and bridges evaluation and instruction. For example, during an evaluation, two children in the class may not relate the details of a narrative text sample. However, after the teacher provides a few helpful prompts about the story elements, one child proves able to relate the information while the other does not. The disadvantage of dynamic assessment lies in rigorous comparisons between groups of students, because the tester has not matched the mentoring and support that each student receives. Again, whether this constitutes a problem depends on the goal of the evaluation.

Evaluating Students' Language and Literacy Needs

I chose a qualitative research approach to study Mickey's, Vincent's, and Henry's expressive language difficulties. In my view, this approach helped me and their teachers gain an in-depth understanding of the boys' constructions within the social context of their classroom interactions and the influence that these interactions had on the students' literacy strategies. These three case studies provide examples. It's important that we identify the presence of difficulties and set meaningful and useful goals for remediation. However, it's even more important to discover how these problems actually affect each child and then to collaborate to resolve the difficulty. In these descriptive case studies, the collection of language samples from classroom discourse captured a variety of spontaneous constructions. That is, they reflected the many social, emotional, and cultural influences that shape children's language behaviors with peers and teachers. In fact, the number of language disruptions produced by the speaker may be less important than the form such disruptions take and their impact on the listener (Dollaghan & Campbell, 1992). Classroom-based decisions concerning the level of children's language competence primarily on these nonstandardized, informal observations.

All three boys in this study attended regular-education classrooms full-time, with specific individual education program (IEP) goals for language improvements. Each teacher's descriptions indicated that she thought the child in her class had problems with word retrieval. Historical data suggested that each boy had average receptive language knowledge as estimated by the Peabody Picture Vocabulary Test—Revised (Dunn & Dunn, 1981) and the receptive portion of the Clinical Evaluation of Language Functions—Revised (Semel, Wiig, & Secord, 1995). More-over, the boys showed average cognitive level estimated by the Weschler Intelli-gence Scale for Children—III, which is normed on a population similar to the children's socioeconomic status (SES). Finally, survey forms filled out by the class-room teacher indicated word-retrieval difficulties (Richard & Hanner, 1988). The boys' scores on three quantitative word-finding tests, Clinical Evaluation of Lan-guage Functions (Semel & Wiig, 1980), Test of Wordfinding (German, 1986), and Test of Wordfinding in Discourse (German, 1991), were not necessary for eligibility in the remediation program because they did not directly reflect classroom perfor-mance. However, as the speech and language pathologist, I obtained them for com-parative information. Below-age-level reading or writing skills, as judged by the classroom teacher and reading measurement tests (such as Gates-McGinitie and se-lected reading inventories), also made up part of each child's history. Each boy thus had a personal profile of language difficulties in the classroom.

Case Studies in Classroom-Based Intervention

7 Mickey: A First Grader

Student Profile

The youngest child in this study, Mickey was short and shy. His kindergarten teacher during the previous school year, and several preschool teachers before her, had made verbal and written references to his quiet play and limited participation in group discussions. Even summer camp counselors had noticed that Mickey's comments and questions to adults and peers were frequently difficult to understand. He would often pause for several seconds in trying to retrieve a word, offering related terms or digressing. His language struck his teachers and parents as immature. Mickey's developmental and medical histories were unremarkable, with the exception of his allergies to several common products, such as milk and eggs. By restricting his diet to alternative foods that he ate at home and in school, Mickey did not require special medication to counteract the small amounts of these substances that remained in his foods. He did not require special medication for any other illnesses or problems.

Mickey's first formal language testing took place just before his kindergarten year, as part of the entrance requirements. Screening results indicated that Mickey's articulation of sounds and incorrect use of past-tense verb forms were at the low end of age expectancies but were developmentally appropriate. His scores on receptive vocabulary tests were more than one standard deviation below the average performance of other children his age. Although Mickey's parents did not observe language problems at home, the scores qualified Mickey for special-education services. He was included in a small-group resource-assistance language program that aimed to enrich vocabulary skills and turn-taking in conversations. Although Mickey's vocabulary knowledge improved in the resource room, his language constructions in the classroom still reflected expressive problems. These struggles stemmed primarily from word-retrieval difficulties, according to his teacher's descriptions and my own evaluations.

Mickey's standard score on the Test of Word Finding ranked below the norms for the test. His age was the lowest in the standardized sample and his lack of cooperation—that is, his random participation in the assessment tasks—deemed the results invalid. On the Test of Wordfinding, Mickey's score fell below the norms in the test manuals. The nature of his language became abstract, not consistent with the identification and labeling requirements of the test. Because the test protocol limited the use of questions by the examiner after the initial directives, Mickey's narrative response was unfocused. Figure 7.1 shows the results of his speech and language evaluation.

Classroom and Discourse Routines

Mickey's classroom teacher and the afternoon teacher's aide described him as a quiet and self-absorbed student. He generally watched his teachers as they addressed the class as a whole, but his gaze moved to his desk, to the side wall, or to the floor when he responded to individual teachers or other children. He usually sat at his desk completing unfinished worksheets, or followed several steps behind as he and his classmates went to recess or lunch. Mickey's rate of speaking and general pace in motor movements were slow but carefully executed. His curious set of determined behaviors set him apart from the other members of the class. For example, his unhurried approach to verbal and motor tasks was accompanied by his determination to complete each thought or worksheet he had started. This inclination created awkward, extended pauses as the teacher or other children waited for Mickey's measured response. When the teacher repeatedly asked the class to put away one set of materials in preparation for a new activity, Mickey frequently continued his work. If he couldn't present his oral responses to questions in what the teacher felt was a "reasonable time," she would call on another child to answer. However, Mickey would continue talking as the next child began, or he would raise his hand again and, when called on, continue his original response. Often, in the midst of ongoing classroom discourse, he subvocalized answers and commented about related and unrelated topics to himself.

Mickey was one of twenty-four children in his class. His first-grade classroom was divided into four activity areas, each used for a variety of purposes. There was a rug area, complete with a sofa and a student leader's chair that provided a cozy-corner listening and reading area. A second area, in another corner of the room, featured a small semicircle of chairs for more formal, teacher-led reading instruction with not more than eight students. A central, third, area contained the students' chairs and desks, arranged in groups of four and five to allow for peer collaboration. The fourth area had places for exhibiting special-interest objects, such as shells or butterflies. These objects, displayed on long tables in the remaining corners of the classroom, were available for students to touch and explore. The language used in this last area consisted of informal questions and observations among peers or between students and the teacher.

Mickey's teacher, Ms. Lucas, strived to develop the children's emergent literacy skills in meaningful ways: for example, through informal exploration of the many types and genres of books she made available in the classroom library, and through a rich environment of printed materials on the walls, doors, and desks. Still, she organized the class into rigid ability groups for reading lessons. Moreover, she

FIGURE 7.1 Speech and Language Assessment Data

Student's Name _____Mickey_____   Date _____September_____
Student's Homeroom ____Ms. Lucas____   Age/Grade ___6 years, 6 months, 1st___

STUDENT INTERVIEW
Mickey explained that he liked leaving the classroom for the resource room; he wasn't sure how I could help him in the classroom since his impression was that, "You're not allowed to talk." He felt that, for him, ". . . it's not an easy thing to tell something [or participate, in the classroom]."

SPEECH	Test Results:
Results from articulation testing in previous years:	Substitutions of w/r, d,f/th.
Informal deep testing of speech sounds in words:	50% mastery w/r (all positions)
	50% mastery f/th (final position)
	65% mastery of d/th (medial position)

LANGUAGE—Comprehensive	Test Results:
Clinical Evaluation of Language Functions	
Receptive Language	Standard Score: 74
Expressive Language	Standard Score: 72

LANGUAGE—Vocabulary	Test Results:
Peabody Picture Vocabulary Test-R, Form M	Standard Score: 82
Expressive One-Word Picture Vocabulary Test	Standard Score: 96

LANGUAGE—Pragmatics/Problem-Solving
Not tested. No problems noted.

LANGUAGE—Processing/Word retrieval	Test Results:
Language Processing Behavioral Checklist	At-Risk Classification
Test of Wordfinding	Standard Score: below norms listed on table

FLUENCY
Informal evaluation revealed no problems with fluency.

VOICE
Comments for classroom teachers: "Needs to speak up."
Voice is quiet; occasional subvocalizing in classroom.

AUDITORY PERCEPTION—Discrimination/Processing
Medical history of chronic otitis media with myringotomy.

FAMILY/PARENT NOTES
Concerns relating to socialization skills and achievement levels. A neuropsychological evaluation performed by an independent testing service indicated verbal information and reasoning to be intact, language behaviors reflect latencies and language processing difficulties when responding to questions.

(continued)

FIGURE 7.1 *(continued)*

TEACHER'S NOTES

Teacher commented that Mickey cries easily (~3 times per week), has "low endurance for work," and blinks a lot.

COMMENTS/RECOMMENDATIONS:

Initiate classroom-based language and literacy intervention program with initial transitional period.

---

used basal materials and worksheets and organized her teaching around a teacher-dominated IRE (initiation-response-evaluation) discourse format.

Mickey appreciated the large variety of reading materials in his classroom library. He often commented on the bulletin boards and read words aloud from books and posters. Each week, Ms. Lucas printed a new riddle or joke on colorful posterboard and taped it to the classroom door as a reading and language challenge. By the end of the week, Mickey knew the joke, even if he didn't understand it. In addition, each child had an opportunity once a month to read his or her favorite book aloud to the class. Mickey always enjoyed this role, anticipating it several days in advance and smiling broadly as he read and showed pictures to his peers. Although serious in demeanor during organized reading tasks, Mickey laughed easily as he read aloud during his time as "author" or "class reader." During student read-aloud time, he often imitated the teacher's IRE style of presentation by asking his peers questions about what he had already read and what might come next. However, his pauses and occasional digressions often interrupted his delivery and made it difficult for listeners to follow the original story line. Mickey's previous and present teachers, his parents, and I knew he would need extra help in developing language strategies to communicate competently in the classroom.

Dynamic Assessment Phase of the Program

During the previous school year—Mickey's kindergarten year—he and I had worked almost exclusively on one language goal: his receptive and expressive vocabulary development. We worked with one other child in a resource-room setting. Although Mickey's score on vocabulary tests improved, the classroom teacher and I noticed from weekly observations that his language contributions in the classroom changed little. During the first three months of this school year, I gathered information about Mickey's everyday language needs in the classroom and his typical language constructions in classroom discourse. I followed Mickey in his classroom activities as a participant observer and spoke to him individually about difficult situations. A clearer and very different portrait of Mickey's language strengths and weaknesses presented itself.

After informally consulting with Mickeyís classroom teacher, Ms. Lucas, it was decided that remediation goals would need to be developed for three sets of difficulties:

1. Increase Mickey's participation in classroom discourse, because Mickey grew confused and frustrated when others misunderstood his comments.
2. Develop strategies for retrieving words, because his slow processing and phrase reformulations caused him to miss his full turn to speak.
3. Improve general problem solving so that Mickey could discover ways to gain the teacher's attention and thereby contribute to discourse and receive help when necessary.

Participation in Classroom Routines

Mickey's slow retrieval of information often limited his participation in conversation, because the teacher would answer for him or continue on to another student. The transcription in Example 7.1 shows how these behaviors appeared in classroom discourse. The field of discourse, or situational context, portrayed in this example is a social-studies lesson that includes interaction between the teacher and another student and then with Mickey. The tenor of discourse between the teacher and Mickey was informal, positive, and relaxed. However, Mickey began to perceive his answers as incomplete or incorrect, because the teacher would move on to another student before he could revise his response. I sat next to Mickey at an empty desk in his usual grouping of four students. (See Appendix A for details on transcription format.)

EXAMPLE 7.1   (September)

1	T:	What else can you tell by the picture? [The teacher notices that Mickey is turning the pages; she walks to his desk, and touches the correct page and picture.]
2	S:	They're playing songs. And the mom is playing a thing like a violin and he's playing a tambor . . . tambor . . .
3	T:	. . . ine.
4	S:	And another thing . . . the moccas.
5	T:	The maracas.
///		(Other children respond.)
6	T:	Mickey, can you tell me how many people are in the picture? Look over on page nineteen. Tell me how many people are in any of those pictures.
7	M:	Um. That has one . . . [After three seconds, he appears to have finished counting to himself, but he has still not completed his answer.]
8	T:	One has four. OK. Do you think that's a big family or a small family?
9	M:	Small.

10	T:	Small, OK. [T starts to call on another child, then Mickey interrupts to try again to give a full response.]
11	M:	That one's five. [Actually there are five people represented in the picture, not four as the teacher had mistakenly noted. T doesn't acknowledge Mickey's answer and calls on another student.]
12	T:	Alan, can you tell me how many are in the next one?
13	A:	Three.
14	T:	OK. We have three and five on that page. ["Five" acknowledges Mickey's correction of the teacher's earlier comments.]

As Ms. Lucas began to ask questions about a specific picture in the social-studies book (line 1 in the transcript), she assumed that Mickey was not attending appropriately and tried to direct his attention to the picture by pointing. Although this is a helpful strategy, she was not aware that Mickey often flipped through previous pictures and text to gain additional cueing information before answering. When she tried to pull him into the discourse by asking him a question, he was slow to think and formulate an answer (line 7), so she completed it for him (line 8). She gave him another chance to answer, but this time asked in a more structured form; that is, a choice question for him to choose big or small family (line 8). Mickey used the safe, short response she set up for him (line 9). But he then returned to the question about the number of people in the picture that she had previously answered for him in order to complete it himself (line 11).

Mickey's return to his first question both interrupted the strict IRE-like format of this routine and served to correct the teacher's original answer. Although Mickey's answer was correct, his "turn" to speak had passed and the response was not acknowledged. The teacher skipped over him as she called on Alan, emphasizing Mickey's mistake in calling out (line 12). Nevertheless she finally did acknowledge his answer as she summarized the children's comments (line 14).

Mickey participated in some way in all classroom activities, but at his own pace and in his own deliberate way. He was slower than the other students at reading, writing, and oral interaction. He would "warm-up" to oral language games, such as choral responses, just as the activity was about to end, joining in completely for just the last stanza or verse. Interactional exchanges challenged Mickey, because he did not feel comfortable with quick, short responses to questions posed by the teacher. When he felt hurried, he had trouble retrieving an appropriate answer within the allotted time, often giving an extended, associated response. The teacher or listener often needed to ask Mickey for further explanations to understand his meaning. Mickey, in turn, interpreted these requests as criticism and became reluctant to participate in discourse, as Example 7.2 shows. This discourse excerpt was a continuation of the lesson described in Example 7.1. The field remained the same, but the tenor became slightly more formal and tense as the teacher struggled with Mickey's responses and sought clarification.

EXAMPLE 7.2   (September)

1	T:	How about the bottom picture? What's that family doing down there? Gary?
2	G:	The two little babies are fighting with their dad.
3	T:	Fighting with their dad, you think?
		[The children in the picture appear to be playing with their father.]
4	S2:	I think they like it.
5	S3:	Ha, ha. No.
6	T:	Yeah. It's usually more of a playing. A kind of a rustling, tussling, rolling in the grass. Any of you do that with your mom or dad? [There is a lot of noise as kids agree and react by talking among themselves.]
7	M:	[Mickey turns around to face me.] I do that with my dad.
8	F:	You rustle and tussle?
9	M:	[nods yes]
10	T:	Do you think they're having fun?
11	Ss:	[excluding M] Y E S!!!
12	T:	Mickey, do you think those little kids are having fun down there in the grass?
13	M:	Yep.
14	T:	What tells you they're having fun?
15	M:	[M speaks quietly and slowly.] They're . . . on the ground and like . . . that baby is like . . . like playing on . . . they're done.
16	T:	They're doing what?
17	M:	They're . . . done . . . with their mom.
18	T:	[Teacher uses a frustrated voice.] How can you tell they're having fun?
19	M:	[no response]
20	T:	Can you tell from the picture? She [the illustrator] give any little clues?
21	M:	[no response]
22	T:	Look at one of the child's [sic] faces.
23	M:	S . . . s . . . smiling?
24	T:	Smiles, yes. People smile when they're having fun. Absolutely. Have you ever rolled around in the grass with your dad?
25	Ss:	Yes. Oh yeah. [Other short, affirmative responses erupt from many students.]
26	T:	I'm asking Mickey. You have? Did you have fun? Did you like it?
27	M:	I didn't . . . I did. [Mickey seems to start to answer one way but then changes his response.]
28	T:	So then you can maybe guess that these kids were having fun, too.
29	M:	I was . . . I was in the grass and I was . . . like . . . I was . . .
30	T:	[interrupting] When you were what?
31	M:	When I was trying to tackle my dad down . . .
32	T:	Ohhh. Sure. Learning how to play football. OK. (T shifts attention to the whole class.) We'll continue on page twenty.

In Example 7.2, Mickey demonstrated that he had information to contribute to the teacher's question and that he wanted to answer by sharing his comment with me (line 7). Ms. Lucas observed us talking and tried to include Mickey in the class's task (line 10) by directly asking . . . him the question she had directed to the class. After his short response (line 13), she re-asked the question in a more structured form that required more details and a longer response. Because this was the beginning of the school year, and the beginning of the intervention study, Ms. Lucas wanted me to see how Mickey answered in class—to observe the mismatches in question-answer form that had frustrated her. Mickey's response (line 15) was less than competent as he struggled to describe the picture within a perceived limited time slot and competitive conversation from classmates. He completed his thought to his own satisfaction and repeated the end of it (line 17) but not clearly enough to satisfy Ms. Lucas. She tried to reformulate the question several times (lines 16, 18, 20) but without changing the structure of the question and without providing any additional information to help cue his answer. Until she asked him to look at the children's faces (line 22), Mickey did not respond to her questions. He was not sure what she wanted as an answer, and her language was not helping him to find an answer. Ms. Lucas and Mickey were both trying very hard to communicate, but both were becoming frustrated.

During an informal conversation between classes, Ms. Lucas explained that she wanted Mickey to succeed in his language contributions. She wanted to provide him with positive feedback for entering the discourse. This was why, she told me later, she returned to her original question (line 24); she hoped for a simple, complete answer to end their discussion. Mickey did not accommodate her; his answer was not clear (line 27), and the struggle continued for both participants. Later he explained to me that he wanted to clarify for Ms. Lucas that he wasn't just "rustling" with his dad. He "was playing tackle football but it looked like rustling, so both answers were good" (referring to lines 27 and 31).

In a traditional resource-assistance language program, these same language difficulties would not show up as clearly. That's because Mickey would probably not have the same difficulties sharing his experiences, owing to the longer allowance made for response time and language revision. The resource room's typical communication dyad (specialist and student) does not lead to the frustration that become apparent in the above example. Although the more relaxed nature of the resource room is more comforting to the student, it does not provide practice in the real, everyday conversations that occur between teachers and students.

In general, teachers and specialists had found it difficult to assess Mickey's achievement in school. He "tested" below age level on standardized vocabulary knowledge and comprehension tasks. However, all evaluators agreed, based on their own observations, that these scores were not valid for Mickey, and that his general knowledge appeared accurate and age appropriate. He handed in worksheets later than his teacher expected, but the work he completed was generally acceptable, according to her informal comments and report-card entries. He had difficulty explaining a concept completely, or describing an experience to a naive listener. Nevertheless, he used vocal nuances and gestures that suggested he felt he had logically, and even amusingly, related all the information. His comments, such as, "She thinks

I don't know it," indicated that he was aware of the teacher's frustrations with him and was sensitive about his academic performance. His anxiety was noticeable to a psychologist whom Mickey had begun to visit, and the therapist decided to put Mickey on the anti-depressant, Imipramine, six months into the school year.

To help Mickey, I needed to review for him the need for his participation in classroom activities and heighten his awareness of which behaviors constituted participation, such as listening and talking. Mickey's lack of verbal participation in his first-grade class affected his overall performance, because discourse with the teacher played an important role in the transfer of academic information. For example, because most children in this class could not yet fluently read written directions on worksheets, Ms. Lucas explained the instructions before the children completed the written portions. These worksheets required Mickey to respond in isolated, one-word productions, an activity that made his word-retrieval problems more obvious. The teacher gave the children at least five worksheets each day. Mickey felt overwhelmed and failed to complete the work in the allotted time. He asked for and received special permission to bring the unfinished work home to complete with his mother's help.

Often, Mickey showed his discomfort in talking—which became especially noticeable when he had word-retrieval difficulties—by breaking eye contact with listeners. His evasive glances may have helped him to avoid the impact of others' impatience or amusement. However, this lack of direct eye contact may have also prevented him from picking up visual cues that might have helped him continue talking more fluently. That is, maintaining eye contact with listeners could have cued listeners to help him along. Example 7.3 relates one of Mickey and my early conferencing, or peripheral conferencing, discussions about Mickey's need to maintain eye contact during interactional exchanges. Mickey and I were joined by another classmate, Joe, who also needed information concerning the importance of maintaining frequent eye contact with the teacher. The tenor of discourse during this conferencing was less formal than that of classroom instruction. However, it was mainly teacher-directed and included lecture material as well as questions, the more common mode of discourse. Both children felt comfortable enough in our modified question-answer discussion that they could interrupt to add or redirect the conversation at any time.

EXAMPLE 7.3   (October)

1	F:	I'd like to talk today about "listening" and "talking." There's one thing that's very, very important. And I want to show you about it. Joe, could you turn around? Here we go. You [Joe] start to tell me something and, Mickey, you tell me what I'm doing that's not so good to do when we're talking. Something that shows that I'm not really listening carefully. Watch me. Now, [Joe,] what would you like to talk about?
2	J:	Nothing.

3	F:	OK, Mickey, you tell me something and Joe, you watch what I do.
4	M:	You know what happened to . . . [not intelligible]?
5	F:	[I'm purposefully looking all around the room but not at Mickey.]
6	M:	[tries to keep talking but is distracted by my actions, then stops]
7	F:	What am I doing wrong, Joe?
8	M:	I know. [He imitates my head movements.]
9	F:	It shows that I am not really a good listener.
10	J:	You are moving your head around.
11	F:	[I look back and forth between the boys.] When I'm speaking, I like someone to look right at me and that means that they're listening. Now I'm going to tell you something that I haven't told anybody yet. Look at me and I'll tell you. [Both boys look up at me.] I LOVE pumpkin pie. [I look directly at each boy; both smile.] Now [Mickey,] you can tell us something you haven't told anyone yet. We'll all watch you.
12	M:	I'll tell something about Stranger Danger. There's someone at the land company over there, someone who is arguing . . . and fighting with someone . . . and someone did it again . . . and my mom said, "Go away" and he went to . . . and she . . . went away. Sometimes people are bad. [During this response Mickey's visual focus slowly moves from Joe and myself to other parts of the room.]
13	F:	OK. It's important when you're talking, to look at the person also.
14	M:	[using appropriate eye contact with Joe and myself] If a teacher is giving directions about pieces of [unintelligible word] or [unintelligible word] whatever . . . and then [He demonstrates, looking all around, not attending]. Oh. Oh . . . look at that!
15	F:	I see you looking all around. Would that work?
16	M:	[shakes his head back and forth]
17	F:	"N" "o" spells no! You have to look right at the person and then one, you show that you're paying attention—you want to learn it, two, you're showing that your interest is right there.

In Example 7.3, our peripheral conferencing began with a focus statement encouraging eye contact between the speaker and listener in the classroom (line 1). To emphasize the importance of these, I chose to demonstrate the opposite behavior (line 5), which Mickey often exhibits.

Mickey noticed the problem and identified it using imitative head gestures (line 8). After I first modeled the "wrong" behavior by looking around as I spoke, and then modeled "better" behavior by looking directly at each child as I spoke (line 11), I gave him the chance to practice it himself (line 12). During Mickey's first comments, he did not use appropriate eye contact. As expected, his language became less fluent when he turned away from me and talked about Stranger Danger (line 12). After a verbal reminder (line 13), he shared good eye contact with me during his explanation and then demonstrated his understanding of inappropriate behavior.

During Mickey's example of a teacher giving directions, he experienced two word-retrieval difficulties. In the first, he used a muffled voice (line 4); in the second, an unintelligible word (line 14). Both times, he produced unclear substitutions for the desired words. Probably to avoid any more problems, and to continue the "turn," he changed his communication to gestural moves (lines 8 and 14).

Mickey's use of gestures and physical actions to substitute for linguistic explanations is characteristic of children with expressive language problems. His efforts to continue communicating were admirable. To encourage them, I did not ask him to clarify his words. Instead, I interpreted his actions, modeling words for him and helping him to restate a form of the rule for eye contact (lines 9, 10, 15). Mickey frequently used restatements of newly acquired "rules" we developed together by explaining them in his own words to teachers and peers.

A second set of problems that stemmed from Mickey's language difficulties included his reluctance to ask clarifying questions in the classroom and his awkward attempts to get help with reading and writing tasks through questioning. The form of the questions was not important as the goal; Mickey had demonstrated his knowledge of syntactic rules for forming a question. The problem derived from his difficulties with delayed word retrieval and slow language formulation, both of which prevented his timely entrance into ongoing discourse. Mickey needed encouragement to initiate questions. Therefore, practice in smaller group settings, such as in the peripheral-conferencing meetings, let me investigate his sensitivity to working on this metalinguistic task.

Example 7.4 presents an example of Mickey's difficulties formulating questions. This excerpt of conversation was taken from one of our conferencing, or peripheral conferencing, discussions. During these discussions, I encouraged Mickey to ask me questions about my Thanksgiving weekend. The classroom teacher had been discussing this topic with the children before my arrival to the discussion. Mickey had made facial expressions indicating his interest in the other students' activities, but he had not volunteered any information of his own or asked follow-up questions, as had the other students. One other classmate, Joe, accompanied us in our peripheral-conferencing meeting because he also needed help participating in classroom discourse, although for different reasons. Having a peer to share the discussion seemed to make the social atmosphere, or tenor of discourse, more comfortable and let each boy benefit from the other's question-answer forms. Another characteristic of the tenor was that the boys were allowed to initiate questions. I hoped that, through modeling and practice, Mickey and Joe would learn to modify their comments and questions to the more acceptable form of IRE in the classroom.

EXAMPLE 7.4   (November)

1	F:	Your turn, Mickey.
2	M:	Oh. Uh . . . Did your . . . did your . . . momma [This word was almost blurted out, typical of behaviors noted when a speaker finally "finds" the word he was

		trying to retrieve and typical of Mickey's language] cook the turkeys r . . . uhhhh . . . [He shrugs his shoulders.]
3	F:	Did my mom cook the turkeys?
4	M:	[nods yes]
5	F:	No, my mother did not. I cooked my own turkey.
6	M:	You cooked it?
7	F:	Mmm hmm. I cooked it for my mother and my family.
8	M:	Oh.
9	F:	That was a good question. I liked the way you asked.
///		
10	F:	Can you [Joe] ask me a question?
11	J:	When did you come to dinner?
12	F:	I went into my house to get it ready at about noon.
13	M:	[quietly to himself] When's noon? [louder] When's noon?
14	F:	Good question. I went into the house at noon, which is exactly twelve o'clock in the middle of the day. Noon is at lunchtime in the day. Mickey, you can ask another question.

In Example 7.4, Mickey felt encouraged to increase his use of questions in a modified form of classroom discourse; that is, a relatively contrived activity within the context of the classroom. In this attempt to question me (line 2), Mickey showed word-retrieval difficulties. He had trouble finding the noun "momma" and the verb "cook." He later used gestures instead of saying a final word to complete his question in line 2. Mickey's responses during this short meeting introduced several issues for discussion.

First, the everyday classroom language routines did not encourage question formulation by children except in very specific cases. That is, the teacher usually presented information through recitations to large groups and led conversations through her own questions in small groups. Children generally initiated questions only for clarification purposes. Most children were reluctant to ask questions; perhaps they felt that doing so would make them appear uncertain or inattentive. Through this remediation goal, I encouraged Mickey to make himself vulnerable by asking the teacher or speaker for more information or explanation. Although he did not find this task easy, he needed to probe for details so he could better prepare for the comprehension questions that the teacher would direct to the class at the end of a content unit or reading chapter. Thus, in Example 7.4, Mickey practiced posing questions for further information.

A second issue concerned the nature of the questions Mickey tried to ask. Questions in discourse in Mickey's classroom were most often factual, literal questions concerning specific textual material. Mickey demonstrated that he understood this routine when he led the discussion during "author's chair" one day in his classroom. This question format was not too difficult for him, because it required familiar, simple language. Following several practice sessions in peripheral-conferencing meetings within the classroom similar to that in Example 7.4, Mickey felt confident enough to try using these during classroom discourse. More frequently, however, he used questions to make personal connections with the content or author of the text. He did this in separate individual conversations. For example, he would ask me whether I had a dog or animal like the one in the story he had read, and whether I would do with it what the main character did. He would then give his opinions of the actions ("I think he could have . . .") and evaluate the author's perspective ("He didn't know much about dogs because . . ."). His questions, serving as lead-ins to more evaluative comments, did not come easily to him. Nor did the teacher accept them easily during reading lessons. However, this was how Mickey preferred to interact during class discussions. I asked him to ask at least one of each type of question during each lesson, so that he could participate and share what he felt about the information in his books. Moreover, he could gather numerous important details and use them to predict and answer questions.

A third issue involved the stilted nature of practicing asking questions. Although the questioning activity might seem contrived in Example 7.4, each question seemed to begin a short exchange (approximately four turns or moves) for Mickey. I pointed this out to him on several occasions. That is, I explained that if he could get into the conversation, he could add or clarify information and practice the language strategies he was learning. This activity also encouraged him to pose more, which let me gather a better sampling of his (and the other boy's) language use.

Existing Strategies for Language Use

Word-retrieval difficulties often arise from weak semantic organization abilities. Therefore, I reviewed and enriched vocabulary taken from classroom talk whenever possible. Mickey used the words in the same context as he observed them in classroom discourse. These review discussions occurred usually on the same day that we heard them in the classroom, so that Mickey could get familiar with them for when the teacher continued or extended the discussions the next day.

In many instances, especially at the beginning of the school year, Mickey felt overwhelmed by the pace of the school day, the number of other children in his classroom, and the amount of work his teacher asked him to do. He did not ask questions, but rather mumbled to himself as he shifted papers on his desk. After he began seeing his psychologist, Mickey's parents, his classroom teacher, and I agreed that he occasionally needed and preferred a less distracting environment in which to question and verbally interact. Therefore, during the first few months of school, Mickey and another student in the class, usually Joe, would occasionally invite friends to accompany them in the form of a "mini-class." We conducted these sessions in the resource room. I usually led the content of these meetings, using information gained from observations of Mickey's language difficulties in the classroom. As his classroom interactional skills improved, these smaller classes became less frequent and in-classroom help dominated.

Example 7.5 provides a sampling of a resource-room pre-reading activity. The information gained in the resource room would not directly apply to skills Mickey would use in the larger classroom, but it provided clues for how I might help Mickey enter classroom discourse, and it gave me opportunities to assess his classroom abilities. In this case, we played a game of categorization using pictures. The oral language followed a routine: I provided and asked for clues to categorizing words, and the boys used the information to construct responses. This excerpt describes part of the discussion associated with choosing pictures of things that are found outdoors. I suggested strategies using imagery and associations to help Mickey compensate for word-retrieval difficulties. The tenor was relaxed and allowed for expanded language routines and more fluent language constructions by Mickey. I later shared these observations with the classroom teacher.

EXAMPLE 7.5   Phase I (October)

1	F:	Geyser. Do you see what this is [to Mickey]? A geyser. That's water or liquid that spurts up from inside the earth in the ground because there's so much energy pushing it. So much gas and energy pushing the water up. OK. What would you find outside, Mickey?
2	M:	You find . . .
3	F:	Remember these are categories of things that you find outside. If we were mapping, we would put them on the board in little circles.
4	M:	[Mickey chooses a picture and labels it.] [Postal] letters.
5	F:	Do you find letters outside?
6	M:	Yes.
7	F:	Well, I think you find letters, these are mail letters, at the post office or in your mailbox.
8	M:	Not the letters that you count one, two, three.
9	F:	One, two, three are numbers. Do you mean letters like A, B, C?
10	M:	Like A, B, C. But it's just . . . it's a letter like when you read it. They mail something to you?
11	F:	Right. Well, that wouldn't be outside. You would find them in your home. Try something else that you would find outside.
12	M:	[M picks a card with a picture of something he felt went outside.] Um . . . um . . . [He can't seem to name the picture of a lobster.]
13	F:	What's that?
14	M:	I don't know. But it is something outside.
15	F:	How do you know it's outside? What is it? Tell me something about it. That will help you remember the word.
16	M:	I'm thinking that you could just say that . . .
17	F:	Is it a plant or an animal?
18	M:	Ah. An animal.
19	F:	Is it like a dog or like a fish?
20	M:	Like a fish.
21	F:	OK. Do you know what it's called yet?
22	M:	[pointing to the word and picture of the lobster] That's the word but . . .

23	F:	That's the word. That would give you help. If you look at the sounds, it would help you. [no answer from Mickey] It goes like this [I "pinch" my fingers together]. What could it be?
24	M:	[shouts as he figures it out] Lobster?
25	F:	Yeah. Good for you. I helped you with the sign, the gesture.
26	M:	A lobster does that. [He imitates the "pinching" of fingers.]
27	F:	Help yourself with those gestures. Help yourself. A lobster's outside. Good for you.
28	J:	Rrriverrrr.
29	F:	River. Good "r's." Good "r" in the beginning and good "r" at the end.
30	M:	"R's" everyplace.
31	F:	Can you find something that's outside? It's Mickey's turn again.
32	M:	. . . um . . . What you see what's outside?
33	F:	That's the question. What is outside? Something that's outside.
34	M:	Thunder?
35	F:	[nodding yes] Where's thunder? Where is thunder and lightning? [M doesn't respond, so I point upward.]
36	M:	Out.
37	F:	It's outside, where outside?
38	M:	In . . .
39	F:	[I give him a phrase to help him retrieve the word.] Up in . . .
40	M:	The sky!
41	F:	OK.

In Example 7.5, Mickey showed that he had developed some strategies for helping himself to retrieve words, but he needed the help of a teacher's probes to complete his efforts. For example, Mickey's first problem occurred when he tried to identify "letters" (line 2). He tried to remember the word by looking at the picture longer—a visual cue. When I provided him with additional information (line 3), he successfully retrieved the word he wanted. His attempt at word play with the word "letters" (lines 8–10) probably came from his efforts to differentiate the meanings of the word in his mind and possibly to show the extent of his knowledge—something he rarely had an opportunity to do. This example supported my observations that word play was an important strategy that Mickey used naturally and one that I could develop to help him retrieve words in the classroom. Eventually, Mickey's teacher could share in this supportive relationship and use of cues.

In Mickey's second and third attempts to retrieve a word, he exhibited a willingness to try, but he needed to develop and expand his repertoire of strategies. When Mickey could not name the picture of the "lobster" (line 12), he tried to cue himself with repetition of given information; for example, that "it is something outside" (line 14). As seen in line 16, he tried to use a longer phrase ("I'm thinking that you could just say that . . ."). I helped him in two ways. First, I asked whether the object was a plant or animal, then a dog or fish, to which he responded correctly (lines 17–20). Still not being able to say what it is, he tried to read the word under the picture, with little success (lines 21–22). Finally my gestural cue of pinching (line 23) helped him name the word himself. Later, my extensions and partial word helped foster his retrieval of "sky," where thunder and lightning are (lines 35 and 40).

In Example 7.6, I targeted vocabulary knowledge. In this sample, Mickey and Joe were looking at picture cards of Pilgrim figures and foods, as a follow-up to discussions about these in the classroom earlier that day. I asked the boys to describe the pictures to each other. Mickey initially experienced word confusion and ultimately engaged in word play. The tenor of discourse during this lesson was teacher-directed, but the question-answer banter was more supportive of Mickey's language constructions than in traditional classroom discourse.

EXAMPLE 7.6   (November)

1	F:	[referring to a picture of a typical Thanksgiving dinner] Turkey and cranberries.
2	M:	Crayon berries?
3	F:	Not crayon berries . . . We don't color them in . . . It's cranberries. They taste kind of tart, or funny, so you eat them with something, like turkey.
4	M:	Cranberries. They're red. I never had them.

///

5	F:	"Dressing" . . . or stuffing. Why do you think they call it "dressing"? Do they dress the turkey up? Does he wear shoes and a jacket?
6	M/J:	[Both boys shake their heads "no" without an oral reaction; they are not watching me or attending.]
7	F:	Stuffing is called dressing because you put shoes and a tie on it, is that right?
8	M:	[laughing] Noooooo.
9	F:	No. Now you're listening. OK. The stuffing is called "dressing." There are different kinds of dressing. There's dressing that is called stuffing on Thanksgiving, and then there's salad dressing, and then there's Joe, dressing in the morning. They're not the same.
10	M/J:	Oh no . . . no. No.
11	F:	Here's my question; this one is for Mickey. How is dressing different from turkey skin?
12	M:	Uh. I don't know what dressing's like.
13	F:	It's stuffing.
14	M:	Oh, stuffing?
15	F:	Yes. How is dressing different than turkey skin?
16	M:	Oh. Because is . . . it . . . it's . . . it's made out of squares and . . . and skin . . . actually is made flat, like pieces.
17	F:	On the turkey? You think the turkey is made flat?
18	M:	[laughing] No.
19	F:	The skin is on the . . .
20	M:	. . . is out.
21	F:	. . . outside.
22	M:	Outside the turkey and you take it off.

23	F:	Where is the dressing? Where is the stuffing? [We jointly look at the picture of the turkey showing the stuffing protruding from the inside.]
24	J:	I don't know.
25	F:	It's on the . . .
26	M:	It's on the chair!
27	F:	. . . inside. That's why they call it stuffing, because you stuff it into the turkey. In the store they take out all of the insides of the turkey and you stuff it into the turkey, and then it cooks and cooks and gets all the juices and it tastes really excellent.
28	M/J:	[Both boys are bidding for a chance to tell their own stories with "oh's" and "yeah, yeah's.")
29	F:	You have questions?
30	J:	I would like to say something.
31	M:	[quietly] What is dressing?
32	F:	Joe?
33	J:	[He begins a short narration about his father waking up this morning. It's unrelated to the vocabulary topic, but this is understood to be acceptable during this informal meeting. He ends; we all nod.]
34	F:	[to Mickey] What is dressing? It's bread and seasonings. Bread and seasonings.
35	M:	[He asks an unrelated question about a poster in the room. I answer but try to return to the topic of "stuffing."] I would like you to pay attention one more minute. Stuffing is bread and seasonings. You can take little pieces of bread and chop them up and season it. What does that mean, "season it"? Throw it out in the fall and spring and winter?
36	M/J:	[laughing again] NOOOO!
37	F:	What does it mean to season it?
38	M/J:	[no response, then laughing]
39	F:	Some words have two meanings. "Dressing" has two or three meanings, and "seasoning" . . . Seasons are what comes four times of the year. *Seasoning* means you give it a special flavor just like different times of the year have, special flavors. Some are cold, some are warm, some are medium, and some have snow. So you take a little bit of it, something specific or special for it, like paprika or cinnamon or onion or garlic, salt. And you put in on and that's the dressing.
40	M/J:	[pointing to a language game I brought] What's the name of *that* game? [The boys attempt to change the conversation again to the game; but the therapist ends the discussion to return them to their regular classroom; the time allotted for small-group; talk is over.]
41	F:	Time to stop now. You all did a good job of talking. Thank you.
42	M:	You're welcome. And dressing doesn't mean a tie.
43	F:	No. That's not what dressing is.
44	M:	And you don't color crayon-berries.
45	F:	No. We made a lot of jokes today; that was fun.
46	M/J:	Yeah.
47	M:	And you put on the seasons.
48	F:	No, not that season.

The words reviewed in the classroom-aside discussion transcribed in Example 7.6—specifically, "dressing" (lines 5–15), "stuffing" (lines 1–4), "cranberries," and "seasoning" (lines 34–39)—were frequently used in the classroom at this time of the school year. Mickey and his friend would need to be familiar with, and possibly use, these words to talk about and compare experiences in conversations. As the transcription shows, Mickey had no problem identifying these words, as evidenced in my question asking if "dressing" is something you wear (line 7). Providing descriptions and comparisons (lines 11–16) concerning these words proved more difficult, as revealed by Mickey's use of "out" for "outside" (line 20) and "flat" for "thin" (line 16).

Mickey seemed to enjoy word-play activities, exemplified by his repeated attempts to change word expectations in a joking manner. For example, he changed the word "cranberries" to "crayon berries" (line 2), and "seasoning" to "season" (line 35). He also changed the context of "where is the dressing" (line 23) from its location in the turkey to the location of the *picture* of the turkey with dressing, which had fallen onto a nearby chair (line 26). Strengthening categorical skills and vocabulary knowledge would help Mickey anticipate topics and content to be covered in class. Armed with this new awareness, he could feel more confident about entering discourse.

As another common difficulty, children with word-retrieval problems have trouble answering questions that require one-word responses, owing in part to the isolated context of the necessary word. However, this response form is typical of the IRE format that most teachers—like Mickey's—use. They often ask literal, "pseudo" questions (that is, questions to which they already know the answers) in classroom language routines. Mickey needed strategies that would help him participate in these routines, because many teachers in his future classrooms would use this format. In previous meetings, I had recommended to Mickey that he include his responses within a larger context of words, such as a phrase or whole sentences. For example, as an answer to the question, "Who was the first president of the United States?" Mickey could answer, "The first president was George Washington," or "It was George Washington," or "I think George Washington." He was reluctant to change the form of what he felt was the expected answer—a one- or two-word response—because he thought his teacher would judge it as incorrect. Mickey and I had remarked to his teachers that it would be easier for him to use longer phrases when responding to questions. Mickey became less anxious when his teachers reassured him that they would appreciate any correct answer, regardless of the form. However, Mickey found it hard to remember to apply this strategy during classroom discourse. The strategies for working through problems with questions or comments requiring one-word responses were presented to Mickey and Joe (see line 4) in aside discussions, as in Example 7.7, when I was reminding them to use these strategies. The tenor of instruction was informal and mostly a form of recitation, but with less social distance between teacher and student.

EXAMPLE 7.7 (October)

1   F: You'll get used to a school. And you'll get used to teachers. But even though, you have to start off with a new person [each year] and you have to remember your own strategies for answering quickly. Some teachers want you to answer with one word. But if you're used to saying it with a couple of words, you can still use that strategy. That's a secret for you. For example, if your teacher says, "Who is a little mouse that has big ears? There's a whole vacation area made and named after him." You would say, "Mickey Mouse." But what if it's hard to remember the name? You would say, "Ummm . . . Umm . . ." Then maybe you could say, "The mouse's name is Mickey." You could say a whole phrase. Can you try that sometimes?

2   M: Uh oh . . . not if I forget it.

3   F: I know [it's hard]. But you have to use the whole phrase. Remember, use a longer sentence and it helps you remember the word you need.

///

4   F: What I was saying was when you're in school with your teachers I need you boys to use the extra secret strategies that we've worked on: using longer sentences, participating more, and staying on topic. There's a lot of talking in class. If you raise your hand, you're a part of it.

In Example 7.7, a language strategy that slightly altered the language expectations of the teacher worried Mickey (line 2). My modeling a longer phrase helped him understand how he might add words within the confines of the usual language routine (line 1). He could now think about and attempt the strategy in class when he was ready to risk the change.

Fostering Problem-Solving

Mickey felt extremely sensitive about how others reacted to his language. He knew that he frequently understood the information presented to him and had the answers to the teachers' questions, yet he felt frustrated that the teacher and students were misinterpreting his comments and finishing sentences for him. He seemed to withdraw from classroom discourse and made fewer attempts to verbally problem-solve.

Teachers' oral reports and filed notes of classroom observations indicated that Mickey had learned to deliberately dodge questions and avoid participating in discourse with the teacher. For example, if he waited long enough, his teachers would notice his problem and then try to solve it for him. Or if he forgot a pencil and didn't want to ask a peer, he just sat quietly until the teacher noticed that he wasn't writing and lent him a pencil. He needed reminders that he could help himself with acts and words, rather than depending on the teacher's observations. He also had to determine when asking for help was appropriate. Fostering his problem-solving specific to language use became an additional goal.

Example 7.8 illustrates the typical approach that Mickey employed to complete his work. This sample centers on his attempts to do an overdue math worksheet that had two parts. The result of the first step, finding the mathematically derived answer, determined the second step, coloring in geometric shapes on the worksheet. Mickey could explain the answers to the math problem, and had already written in several sums, but he wasn't careful about matching the color-code key. Earlier in the day, he and his teacher had discussed the inaccuracies in his work, but he still didn't understand the problem. The tenor of that earlier discussion was not comfortable enough for Mickey to approach the teacher for further explanation. Still, he needed to learn to problem-solve, in a parallel fashion, during situations in which he required assistance.

EXAMPLE 7.8   (November)

1	F:	Watch what you're doing. Look at what you're doing. What color are you making it?
2	M:	Blue.
3	F:	Oh, you're coloring in two parts, in two [different] colors?
4	M:	No. That's blue and that's blue, it's just that that's [first blue] blue-green 'cause I don't . . . don't have a [plain] blue.
5	F:	I could give you blue. You could ask.
6	M:	Oh.
7	F:	I can give you blue. Just don't use the same color [pointing to the blue-green that he has used to substitute for regular, navy blue, and which is similar in color to the green he has used for another set of answers] or it will be confusing [and marked as incorrect by the teacher].
8	M:	No. Because it's gonna be the balloon [with numbers that add to five]. It's supposed to be . . . Mrs. Lucas said it's supposed to be the same color [for the same sums].
9	F:	Right. You need another blue. This [a navy-blue crayon from my crayon basket] is the same color as this [pointing to his first set of colored-in spaces]. Finish it in blue so it matches [the others]. I know that's what you meant to do. You said you were out of the one crayon so you did it in that [blue-green] color, but it would be a good idea to . . . What do you think would be a better idea? I don't want to tell you. I want to see what you think. What would be the best idea if you came up here and you didn't have the right crayon; what's a different thing you could do?
10	M:	Just ask if you have one?
11	F:	That's exactly right. One good thing is to do your very best and substitute another color for it and get the job done. The other way to solve the problem would be to ask me or a friend. Sometimes I think you're so used to working by yourself that you don't ask the teacher for the help that you need. She would be

pleased to help you. Do you know that? You're a good student and you know how to ask nicely. You do your work well. So ask for help more often.

In Example 7.8, Mickey knew he had used a crayon color that was different from his first (line 4). But he did not consider asking the teacher or another student to lend him one (line 6) even though lending occurred frequently in the classroom. He didn't follow up my comments to him suggesting that he ask for help (lines 5 and 7) until I gave him a choice of solutions (line 9). His compensatory strategy of using a closely related color for his original crayon was appropriate. However, it represented his difficulty in using language to solve simpler problems, such as borrowing a crayon or asking for help. Possibly, he wanted to avoid talking.

Summary

Mickey wanted to participate in classroom discourse, as evidenced by his animated body language and voice when he read aloud to the class and by his awkward but determined attempts to connect classroom topics to his home experiences. In smaller groups of students, and in less competitive discourse contexts, such as the resource-room and peripheral-conferencing meetings, Mickey proved more verbal and asked more questions in order to interact. Initially, he seemed to enjoy the busy atmosphere and learning environment of the first-grade classroom—he smiled as he colored math worksheets and investigated the science exhibit near his desk.

Yet Mickey was becoming discouraged by his frustrating language experiences and the teacher's difficulty understanding his contributions. He muttered under his breath during ongoing discourse, broke eye contact with other speakers or listeners, and withdraw from classroom language routines. He needed additional strategies to build his confidence in his ability to competently contribute to classroom discourse and to gain help and clarification on everyday problems. By staying in the classroom, I could target and remediate his problems with language pace and word naming as they occurred in the everyday discourse routines.

Mickey, his peers, and his teacher seemed to acclimate to my presence in the classroom, as indicated by fewer references from classroom members to my seating arrangements and to my quiet talking with Mickey during class. Mickey's peers asked me more questions than during previous visits during reading and small-group activities. This change in the classroom members' behavior had taken several months of modeling language activities and goal-setting decisions. Now we could actively begin working toward realizing Mickey's goals and to giving his language more focus. The classroom atmosphere itself became more animated as the December holidays approached and would remain so when the children returned from vacations with stories to share. The classroom teacher and I had set three goals with Mickey for the remaining school months because he struggled with a large range of social and language problems. Opportunities for me to provide Mickey with classroom-based language support would now be abundant.

Intervention Phase of the
Language Support Program

Mickey received my language-support services on four days every week, for approximately thirty minutes per visit. The time we spent together building language strategies was divided between morning and afternoon sessions. How Mickey received help, whether through in-class, peripheral-conferencing discussions, or occasional resource-room tutoring, depended on the classroom activity, Mickey's anxiety level, and the teacher's recommendation. Following the early period of acclimation, Mickey's anxiety seemed to ease and the teacher's help increased, as documented in field notes and teachers' progress notes. Thus, this new period of active intervention, which began for Mickey in December of the school year, consisted mostly of classroom and peripheral-conferencing interactions. There were three general periods of time during which I helped Mickey in class.

1. During morning visits, I would join Mickey's small-group (eight children), teacher-led oral reading class. The children and teacher alternated reading aloud from a basal series. During this time the students sat on chairs in a semicircle, engaging in a set of established language routines. For example, the teacher initiated and controlled questions concerning the comprehension and interpretation of the reading material following an IRE pattern, with few exceptions. These questions were evenly divided between those directed at one particular student and those that were open to volunteers. The children's answers most often consisted of one-word responses or short phrases. In this group-reading activity, participation was mandatory. However, Mickey attempted to avoid participation by reducing eye contact with the teacher and commenting on tangential topics. The teacher misinterpreted these behaviors, concluding that Mickey didn't understand the content and had an immature attitude, as indicated by her informal comments and notes on his second report card.

2. In the afternoon, just after the lunch and recess hour, the whole class sat on a large rug or sofa in a corner of the room and shared in an informal, student-led read-aloud program called "author's chair." Participation in this activity was optional; students could choose to remain at their desks to complete unfinished worksheets instead. For the first few months of the school year, Mickey chose to use this afternoon time to work at his desk rather than to listen to a child reader. He and I used this time to discuss his school participation, to evaluate his language patterns, and to set goals for classroom discourse. I also introduced remedial strategies were first introduced at his desk in the classroom.

3. Later in the afternoon, the teacher held a whole-class, combined recitation and discussion period for topics in science or social studies. These classes usually required more formal classroom behavior, such as hand-raising to answer a

question posed by the teacher, discourse following strict IRE language routines, quick-paced language interactions and competitive bids for teacher selection. By December of the school year, Mickey attended to the teacher's recitation but avoided participating in classroom discourse. When Ms. Lucas solicited his response, he either shrugged his shoulders to pass his turn (an acceptable response) or he attempted his answer in a way that did not conform to the routine established by the teacher. For example, Mrs. Lucas interpeted his response "If I thought about it, I guess I would say . . ." as an unacceptable answer—a stall tactic—and his turn to speak ended.

All three of the intervention goals collaboratively set for Mickey in the first months of the observation and assessment phase—increases in strategy use for discourse participation, word retrieval, and problem-solving—were targeted for instruction in some degree during each of my visits to his classroom. The amount of help he needed to use these strategies, his proficiency in retrieving words during responses, and his competency in entering classroom language routines began to change as the school year unfolded.

Changes in Language Support

Two sets of changes in language guidance were expected to occur for Mickey. The first consisted of moving the prime site for language remediation and support from the resource room to the classroom. Because all eyes were on the teacher at these instructional times, the children and the teacher noticed when I entered the room and sat by Mickey. After several weeks, the novelty of my presence passed for most of the children and for the teacher. Mickey, however, seemed to feel the difference more strongly. He'd sometimes place his forefinger to his lips ("Shush!") to stop me from commenting or clueing him in the direction of an answer. At times, he'd only glance at me sideways to acknowledge my presence. Yet after two months of sharing conversations in the class, he, too, became used to my efforts. He found it helpful when I would reorganize the teacher's question into a form he could use more successfully.

The second, and more challenging, change occurred in the form and amount of language assistance that Mickey would need to accomplish the goals set for him earlier in the study. Usually sitting in an empty desk next to Mickey in the classroom, I could observe and participate as the students and teacher engaged in discourse. At times, Mickey became almost "paralyzed" when called on to answer, even when he had selected the correct answer. His word-retrieval problems and slow speaking pace prompted me to find ways to model, facilitate, or cue him to respond and participate.

Example 7.9 shows early efforts to assist Mickey in his participation. The discourse in this example occurred during a social-studies activity, as the children completed a worksheet on mother/baby pairs along with their teacher. The interaction between teacher and students followed the traditional IRE format as the lesson began, but my model for cueing reminded Ms. Lucas to provide extra language support in the form of cues and encouragement.

EXAMPLE 7.9   (December)

1	T:	[directing this question to Mickey] Which picture goes with the baby? Which number down?
2	M:	[doesn't answer]
3	F:	[whispering near his ear] Mickey, which picture are we on?
4	M:	Here [gesturing toward the picture], the baby [tadpole].
5	F:	Which one down? [I trace my finger down the line of pictures to cue his answer.]
6	T:	Which one goes with the tadpole?
7	F:	[I follow his finger and again touch the choice he made.] Tell this one.
8	M:	[raises his hand quickly, although the teacher was waiting patiently for his answer]
9	T:	Mickey?
10	M:	The frog.
11	T:	Good. And what number is that?
12	M:	[He pauses, his finger still on the picture of the frog. I touch the numbers 1, 2, 3, 4, and 5, cueing him as I put the numbers in a silent but mental count.] Five.
13	T:	What number is that in ordinal numbers [names]? Like "first," "second,". . .
14	M:	[Mickey counts visibly in his head, mouthing the numbers. At "fifth," he stops and looks around.]
15	F:	[I touch the numbers and quietly count.] First, second, third, fourth, fifth.
16	M:	[in unison with me] Fifth.
17	F:	Tell fifth.
18	M:	Um . . . fifth.
19	T:	OK.
20	M:	[Speaking more loudly, interrupting to repeat using the phrase.] It's he . . . um . . . fifth.
21	T:	Fifth. That's right! It was a little hard there, but you kept trying.

Facilitation cues in the above example included two instances of rephrased question cues in lines 3 and 5, and two instances of scaffolding comments (for example, prompting with the verbal directive, "Tell it" in lines 7 and 17, and providing numbers in lines 12 and 15). Each cue aimed to help Mickey retrieve a verbal response appropriate to the discourse occurring in the classroom at that time. Equally important, the modeling opportunities helped the teacher individualize her discourse routines so that Mickey could participate along with his peers. By contrast, the individual practice sessions in the resource room, which had attempted to duplicate this classroom environment, had proved less useful.

In Example 7.9, Ms. Lucas tried to support Mickey's responses by giving additional information. She added the adjective "ordinal" to the word "number" to give additional information (line 13). She also began the rote counting of ordinal numbers, beginning with "first," to give Mickey an additional context from which to retrieve the information.

This part of the class's reading lesson seemed to provide a positive experience for Mickey, for several reasons. First, he provided four appropriate answers to the teacher's questions (lines 4, 10, and 12), answers he would not have been able to provide alone in these contexts. Second, he had a taste of contributing to the classroom discourse, which empowered him to reenter it with a louder and expanded version of his response (line 20). Third, the teacher's reinforcement (line 21) and his own perception of a successful experience helped him stay focused during the rest of the activity, as noted in field notes of classroom observations.

For a few more weeks, Mickey still needed external cueing from me or from the teacher. For example, he continued to enter and exit routine language conversations with our help, but used these mostly in his own classroom and with us. On one occasion, shown in Example 7.10, Mickey tried to enter a fast-paced language exchange led by a substitute teacher during a social-studies lesson but was unaccustomed to her cues. In this example, the children and substitute teacher were reading from a social-studies text and describing pictures of different groups of people wearing uniforms. The teacher's questions formed part of a larger discussion of community members and cultural groups.

EXAMPLE 7.10   (February)

1	T:	OK. Let's look. Look at what these girls are doing. Tell me what they're doing and why they have special clothes on. Oh, that's a whole bunch of questions. What they're doing . . . why they have special clothes on . . . OK, Peter, give it a shot.
2	P:	They're playing a game.
3	T:	Exactly. What game are they playing?
4	F:	[to Mickey, observing that he is subvocalizing] Do you have something to say?
5	M:	[nods "yes" to me]
6	F:	[after a brief pause, a cue is provided] Why do they have special clothes on?
7	P:	Basketball.
8	T:	They're playing basketball. He gets it. Nails it on the head. Do you know which team these girls are on?
9	S:	I know.
10	F:	You know, too. Those are what kind of clothes?
11	M:	[raises his hand slightly]
12	T:	Look! One team is wearing purple uniforms; one team is wearing white, and so they know which team they're on.
13	M:	[directs his comment to me] That is which [team]?
14	F:	That's the question. Tell the answer to the question. [We are both touching the picture to help cue the word. The children are very animated in the background, calling out answers and raising hands to answer.]

15	T:	Next picture. What's going on in this picture? And what kind of uniform do these young men have on? Two questions.
16	S1:	That's easy.
17	T:	Yes, ma'am?
18	S1:	They're in a parade?
19	T:	They're in a parade. . . . um . . . Sort of a parade. And why do you think they have on a uniform?
20	S2:	Because they like doing different subjects and all.
21	T:	What do you think? Did anybody ever have or see an older brother who had a uniform like this? Everybody think real hard. What might this uniform be? [Mickey's hand is raised.] Mickey, what might this uniform be? Got a thought?
22	M:	Ummmm . . .
23	S3:	I got a thought.
24	T:	[to Mickey] What were you thinking when you raised your hand? Did you have a thought?
25	M:	[very quietly] Uh . . . could it be . . . uh . . . policemen?
26	T:	I didn't hear you, hon. Just tell me again what you said; I couldn't hear you.
27	M:	Umm . . . a . . . uh . . . um . . . it's . . .
28	T:	Do you think these men are going to work in those uniforms? Are they on their way to work?
29	Ss:	NOOOOO.
30	M:	NOOOOO.
31	T:	She told us she thought they were marching in a parade. Why do you think these guys wear these uniforms?
32	M:	Um . . .
33	T:	Remember, uniforms, they all have to look alike. That's what a uniform does. Look alike. Shows people we're on the same team.
34	M:	[pauses to find an answer]
35	T:	Somebody help Mickey think about this.
36	S4:	It's a camp order.
37	T:	This is not a camp in this particular picture. It doesn't look like they're at camp.
38	S5:	Yeah. It doesn't.
39	T:	What kind of guys are they? I need a name.
40	S5:	Cub Scouts.
41	T:	OK. They're the grown-up version of the Cub Scouts.

In this example, Mickey had limited success constructing responses to the new teacher's questions. My language guidance, consisting of question prompts (line 4), refocusing comments (lines 6 and 10), visual and gestural cues (line 14), helped focus his attention on the teacher's questions and encouraged him to attempt a response. The substitute teacher offered comments in the form of several scaffolding attempts (re-asking her question in line 22, giving him a second chance to re-structure his answer in line 26, providing additional information in line 33, and asking for help from the class in line 35). Mickey could not provide an appropriate answer, perhaps intimidated by her comments. If the teacher had provided additional wait time for a response or requested that he, "Tell more about that," the discourse routine might have "opened up" beyond the boundaries that literal questions create, and Mickey might have contributed additional comments. In his personal comments to me during an informal moment, Mickey explained his disappointment in this setback—"I'm doing it again." However, he achieved more successes when he accepted my support, and became more fluent in later discourse exchanges, according to the substitute teacher's account. It would take more time to build a trusting relationship with a new teacher.

Language facilitation did not always take the form of verbal reminders and graphic cues. Often my physical presence triggered a carryover from peripheral-conferencing discussions and resource-room mini-lessons and provided a form of emotional support. Teachers' and parents' comments indicated that Mickey worked—that is, read, wrote, listened, and talked—more attentively and appropriately in the presence of an adult. His need for adult guidance and reassurance was obvious in his frequent visits to the secretary or nurse for general complaints. Mickey's classroom teacher commented frequently that his participation improved in quantity and quality when I was "close by" in the classroom. After several months of working with him during Phase Two of the study, she observed that "it all seemed to click" for him when I visited the classroom. I strengthened this emotional encouragement by telling him that I was informing his teacher of his successes in more individualized language activities. Thus, he knew that she had positive impressions of his potential for classroom discourse. This support-by-advocacy became important to Mickey, as evidenced by the "get-down-to-business" attitude he assumed when I entered the classroom.

However, Mickey could benefit from my assistance even without close proximity to me. On one occasion, I left his side to help another student in the classroom. As I was working with the second student, I looked across the room and saw Mickey with his hand raised, ready to answer a question but looking at me for some sign of approval. I gave him a "thumbs up" sign, and he turned his attention back to the group. Though the teacher didn't call on him to answer in that instance, he remained enthusiastic. When the teacher asked again for a volunteer to answer a comprehension question, he looked toward me for approval, this time with his hand raised but bent at the elbow. As I nodded and raised my eyebrows in approval, he straightened his hand and answered correctly. This behavior once more provided evidence that language help provided directly in the classroom was more beneficial than lessons taught out of the classroom.

Collaborative consultation with the classroom teacher thus also played a part in strategies to scaffold Mickey's participation in discourse routines. Because Ms. Lucas generally controlled the flow of the classroom language routines, I asked her in December to try to include these language-facilitation cues when directing comments to Mickey. This was a new responsibility for her and difficult for her to remember to implement during discourse. Often when I was in the room to help Mickey, she called on him whether he raised his hand or not, knowing I would further instruct him in new strategies for language use. Examples of Ms. Lucas's efforts to use the language-processing remediation techniques appear in many of the language examples already provided. (See Example 7.1, where she allowed a longer pause for Mickey's answer than she usually allowed for the other children in the class; Example 7.9 for an illustration of stimulus repetition as she rephrased the word "baby" with "tadpole" in line 6 and re-asked a two-part question in separate parts in lines 1, 6, and 11.)

In addition to helping Mickey use new language strategies, I suggested that the teacher use foreshadowing to help Mickey attend, prepare, and rehearse, if necessary, a reading or response that he would be required to provide. In Example 7.11, a group of eight children were completing a crossword puzzle in response to worksheet comprehension questions that followed a reading of text from their basal reader. The teacher used forewarning as a language cue to further help Mickey prepare his response. Although this may seem like a simple task, Ms. Lucas had to consider this remark as she taught the other students and listened to their responses. She thus needed a metacommunicative awareness of the flow of discourse.

EXAMPLE 7.11   (April)

1	T:	We are on number three. Read for the class . . . who haven't I heard from? Alex.
2	A:	WHAT DID HE [author] WRITE?
3	T:	[As Alex is reading aloud, T leans over to Mickey and whispers, forewarning his turn.] Mickey, I'm going to ask you to read this one [touches number four]. What did he write, Jill?
4	J:	Poems.
5	T:	Poems, good. He might have written one play. That was number three. OK. Number four. Read for the class, Mickey.
6	M:	HE WROTE ABOUT THE "BLANK" OF BLACK PEOPLE.
7	T:	What was missing in that answer? Yes, Mickey?
8	M:	Rights, yes.

The use of a forewarning cue (line 3) helped Mickey focus, organize, and retrieve words by giving him time to rehearse and review information that answering would require. This provision of additional time before his turn eliminated the anxiety that usually would build in him with the teacher's random assignment of readers during the lesson. I introduced this strategy to him using more structured material, or the text, before using it with Mickey as Ms. Lucas would ask him a question or assign a task during a literacy activity.

As Mickey showed improvement in discourse participation and seemed more comfortable conversing in classroom activities, I decreased the amount of time I spent sitting next to him. Instead, I moved farther away to other areas within the classroom. I made this change partly to motivate Mickey to initiate questions and comments independently and partly in response to his decreasing need for language support. He often looked around the room to check whether I was watching and listening for his answers. I was. My verbal language cueing grew less frequent during this time.

Changes in Use of Language Strategies

As this second phase of the study began, Mickey still did not use strategies for word retrieval independently. In December, he depended on modeling and cueing to retrieve words, as in Example 7.9, when I counted quietly to help him to retrieve number names. In both of these instances, I sought to clarify the word's context—in the number-name case, providing the previous words in sequential order. I had explained to Mickey other ways to clarify context, including placing the word in a phrase rather than answering in a short response. He tried to do this in Example 7.9, when he stretched his answer "Fifth" to "It's the . . . um . . . fifth."

His responses to the teacher's questions often required more than labeling and locating one- or two-word responses. Sometimes the children had to provide longer descriptive responses and supportive details to demonstrate their critical thinking and comprehension processing. However, Mickey's difficulties in retrieving words limited the fluency of his discourse in this regard. In Example 7.12, Mickey needed to organize and retrieve information about what objects typically characterize a classroom in order to respond appropriately to the teacher's question. The discourse occurred during a small-group reading lesson in the morning. The children were previewing the pictures in a story about a child's experience in school. The teacher's aim in this lesson was to help students learn to identify contextual clues from the pictures for improved reading fluency. She accepted and helped reshape Mickey's partial answers in a supportive and positive way.

EXAMPLE 7.12   (December)

1	T:	Turn to page twelve. Looking at the two pictures. Where do you think they're at? Are they at home?
2	C:	[in unison] At school.
3	T:	How do you know they're at school?
4	S1:	Because they're at school; they're in a classroom.
5	T:	Kinda looks like a classroom. What clues in that picture tell you that it looks like a classroom? Mickey? Look at that page's picture for me. What's in it that tells Ryan it's a classroom?
6	F:	[Mickey stares at the page that contains a picture of a typical classroom and tries to find words to identify pictures of classroom artifacts. I point to visual clues by tracing across the page's pictures with my finger.]
7	M:	Because . . . um . . . there's . . . there's tables . . . and lots of chairs . . .
8	T:	Tables and lots of chairs . . . You don't have tables and lots of chairs at home?
9	M:	No.
10	T:	Not that many, right?
11	M:	No.
12	T:	Or not that many in the same room. Donald, what else?

Mickey seemed to need to focus on the additional information provided by my nonverbal gesturing toward the page's visual cues to generate a response. Note that the teacher now had learned to provide these clues or cues—namely, she encouraged him to look at the pictures (line 5).

In this example, Mickey's language use changed from frustrating pauses to slightly disfluent phrase reformulations. These reformulations kept his response moving and afforded him some control as he answered (line 7). This shows an improvement in his language use because it let him become more of a participant in the discussion. Moreover, it let the teacher respond to his comment about "tables and chairs" (lines 8 and 10) and provide feedback. Mickey also demonstrated that he knew an appropriate answer, which the teacher had doubted at the beginning of the school year.

Example 7.13 also shows Mickey developing an awareness of helping himself retrieve words and participate in discourse. In this example, the field of discourse consisted of an interaction in a small-group reading class. The teacher and children took turns reading a poem aloud, then identified words with similar-sounding endings. The tenor of the discourse, i.e., the relationship between the speakers, remained informal as Ms. Lucas became aware of Mickey's attempts to participate, and she supported his efforts by calling on him after a few inappropriate interruptions. Ms. Lucas accomplished two goals as she led the students' responses: The IRE pattern that she had set remained intact, and she modeled for Mickey the more appropriate time to respond; that is, after the question cue.

EXAMPLE 7.13   (January)

1	T:	[referring to the written text] Look at the endings [as I read along]: "IN EARLY SPRING DO THE RAINDROPS SING? ON THE FOURTH OF JULY AS THEY DRIPPY-DROP-DROP FROM THE TIPPY-TOP-TOP, DO THEY TRICKLE DOWN THE BRANCHES OF THE PEAR TREE? ON THE FOURTH OF JULY AS THE RAINDROPS FLY ARE THEY RED, WHITE, AND BLUE? DO THEY YANKEE-DOODLE-DOO? WHEN VACATION ENDS AND SCHOOL BEGINS, DO THE RAINDROPS CRY AS THEY SAY GOODBYE? WHEN WINTER COMES AND NUMBS THE THUMBS, DO THE RAINDROPS FLAKE? DO THEY SHIVER DO THEY SHAKE?"
///		[Several children read aloud until the poem is finished.]
2	F:	[I touch each ending as Mickey follows along. He reads silently but uses his finger to guide himself. In this case, I also whisper the final words in unison with Mickey to emphasize them for him.]
3	T:	What do you think? Did you like the poem? Did you hear any words that sounded alike?
4	M:	[He selects two words by touching them—"cry" and "bye." He raises his hand to answer. The teacher chooses another child who has raised her hand after Mickey. Mickey is visibly disappointed, sighing aloud.]
5	S1:	"Cry" and "bye."

6	M:	[loudly] Yep. I was thinking of that.
7	S2:	"July" and "fly."
8	M:	Yep.
9	T:	Mickey, did you find a rhyming pair?
10	M:	[nods with his finger touching two words] "NUMBS" and "THUMBS."
11	T:	And "comes" at the end of the sentence before it.

In this example, the teacher read aloud from parts of a poem in Mickey's basal reader to model the rhyming style, carefully stopping at the end of each line to accentuate the final sounds (line 1). During the follow-up discussion, Mickey called out his agreement with an answer whether or not he'd been appointed by the teacher (lines 6 and 8), indicating his desire to participate. He needed extra time to cue himself by seeing the word on paper and by listening to his voice as he repeated the words, but he grew only mildly frustrated as he checked his answer against those of others. Mickey had identified the rhythm of the poem and planned his response. When the teacher finally called on him for examples, he was ready with an answer.

During these months, I was available to help cue Mickey's word-retrieval strategies. Toward the end of the school year, he didn't always need my assistance. He was beginning to experiment with different strategies that we had discussed and that were improving his construction of competent responses in discourse. His avoidance of words he thought he could not retrieve became less frequent, and his comments were more appropriate to the topic of conversation.

In Example 7.14, Mickey participated in his daily reading-group lesson without my active help, though he was aware of my presence in the room. This activity occurred during an in-classroom, small-group reading lesson, the topic of which was the inflection used in rhyming patterns. The teacher read parts of the poem aloud to the students, they read it back in several individual turns, then the teacher read another portion, and so on until the poem was completed. Vocabulary words were introduced and reviewed as necessary during the readings. The tenor of discourse was informal; Ms. Lucas posed open questions that invited long and varied constructions. This format also let students exchange comments between responses to her questions, and Mickey's contributions were appropriate.

EXAMPLE 7.14 (March)

1	S1:	FAME.
2	T:	No, that's not fame. There's an "r" in here.
3	S1:	FARM.
4	T:	What's a farm?
5	M:	[He volunteers this information along with the other children, but his definition is lost in the noise. He raises his voice and stays in the bidding until they stop to listen to his definition.] It's . . . there's animals . . . it's where a farmer takes care of his animals.

6	T:	[T reads aloud from the text so the children will find a pattern. She tells them to listen for the pattern, which is an up and then down inflection, typical of poem readings.]
7	M:	[tilts his head from side to side as the teacher reads, in time to the teacher's reading]
8	T:	What did you notice about the words? Did you notice anything about the words?
9	S3:	They rhyme.
10	T:	Anybody else notice rhyming words?
11	M:	[among other students' voices] Yep.
12	S4:	It's kind of a sleepy morning.
13	T:	Yes. It's kind of a sleepy morning. But a lot of the animals are up and about. What I notice about the words as I read the story is I go up and down. It kind of has a rhythm to it.
14	S5:	[referring to the picture in the text] Hey, this looks real!
15	M:	Yep. Looks real but this is easy to do [meaning easy to draw].
16	T:	OK. We're going to read together.
17	M:	[aloud with the class] PAGE 10. A MORNING IN FALL. [As the children read, Mickey's voice is as loud as, if not louder, than most of the others. He follows and guides his own reading with his finger.]
18	T:	Who can find rhyming words?
19	M:	[raises hand confidently] "Hill," "still."
20	T:	OK. "Hill," "still." Where are those words on those lines?
21	M:	It would be on the end.
22	T:	End of those lines. Everyone see that? See the words "hill" and "still" on the end of those lines? Those are rhyming words.

Mickey's answers in this example came in the form of phrases or sentences. He cued himself for one-word responses, i.e., the rhyming words, by touching and reading them (line 17). Because he had been listening to the conversation about the pictures in the text, he offered his opinions (line 15) as well as required answers. He read aloud easily—as long as he used his finger to guide himself across the page, and he seemed to enjoy hearing his own voice.

Mickey had clearly learned to attend to the teachers' comments as a way to get a "jump" on the upcoming language exchanges. Unlike with his delay in giving examples of rhyming words in earlier readings (such as in Example 7.13), Mickey now followed along in the reading from the earliest mention of the concept "rhyme," and anticipated the teacher's request for examples. Mickey provided these examples early in the discussion of rhymes (line 19), possibly remembering his frustration during a previous lesson with similar goals. For Mickey, this was an assertive move. As his teacher explained his answer to the other class members, he was pleased with his success. In this short series of language routines he had been able to switch to a different correct answer as the lesson began (line 5) and to show his understanding of rhymes (line 20).

Changes in Discourse Participation

Mickey had participated minimally in classroom discourse routines as he began school in September, improving only slightly by December. After March, he began to progress in the number and competence of his language contributions.

In Example 7.9, line 20, Mickey's voice became louder as he repeated his answer for emphasis. He began volunteering to answer in Examples 7.10 (lines 22 and 25, during a worksheet activity and line 38, to describe a picture), and 7.13 (line 4, in search of rhyming endings). Mickey started to call out answers in Example 7.13 (lines 6 and 8, as he agrees with a student's answer) and 7.14 (line 5, as he defines "farm"). As his confidence grew, his attention to discourse routines became more focused. Mickey began to try to enter language routines in the classroom.

The children in Mickey's class began to notice his attempts to participate. They tried to use the same techniques that I had been modeling in the classroom. For example, they provided additional information, more time, and question prompts to help their friend stay in the conversation and competently share his thoughts. In Example 7.15, Mickey read aloud to the class as they sat on the large rug in the classroom. He was the storyteller, leading and responding to peers' comments. The tenor was informal during the reading, listening, and talking activities, but Mickey was very aware of being the "leader" and reader for the day.

EXAMPLE 7.15   (February)

1	M:	It's called Beef Stew. [He looks to me for acknowledgment.]
2	F:	Beef Stew.
3	S1:	[not hearing Mickey] Finish up the name of it.
4	M:	I already did.
5	S2:	Louder.
6	S3:	Hold it up.
7	F:	[pointing at the child who commented; telling M] Hold it up so they can see.
8	M:	[showing it to the class] Guys . . .
9	F:	OK, enough.
10	S4:	That's enough. Just show it one time, like this, and you're done [demonstrates how to show the picture in a wide semicircle so everyone can see] or if someone says they didn't see it, you hold it more [time].
11	M:	[starts reading, his voice barely audible; children are not attending well]
12	F:	I can't hear it very well. You're reading it so quietly, but you have a great voice.
13	M:	[reads more loudly] "HE WOKE UP. HE SMELLED SOMETHING GOOD. WHAT WAS THAT GOOD SMELL?"
14	S2:	What's the boy's name?
15	M:	Nicky. Danny, sit down. [M continues to read slowly in a loud, animated voice. The children lose interest and begin shifting in their seats and talking to one another. M attempts to regain control over his audience in the way he had noticed the teacher always did; that is, initiating directions.]

16	S3:	Sit down. Someone might come.

16   S3:   Sit down. Someone might come.

17   M: [repeats S3's comments] Someone might come. Stop. Just stop. Please?
              [Children sit down.] Thank you. All the way. What did I say? [He holds up two
              fingers, the sign for "be quiet."] What's that sound?

18   S2:   That's good. Not a sound.

19   M: [reading aloud] "AT LUNCH NICKY WENT TO SIT WITH". . . um . . .
              [looks to a girl in the class for help]

20   S4:   [reads the word for him] "CARLA."

21   M: "FOR CARLA."

In this example, Mickey had received his turn to sit and read aloud in the classroom's "author's chair." Although Mickey, as the reader, was allowed to present his book in any way he chose, the children volunteered to guide his oral presentation in a more appropriate, more routine arrangement. For example, the class members provided positive encouragement. Two students showed Mickey how to display the book after he read a portion (lines 6 and 10), while others helped him read difficult words (line 20). Mickey demonstrated that he was familiar with the language routine his teacher had used often; that is, initiation, response, and follow-up comments. He used these as he shared his story text (lines 1, 4, 11, and 13) and asserted his leadership through language (lines 16 and 18).

Before this reading, Mickey had struggled while sharing stories with the other children. This time, he had rehearsed with this story book at home before bringing it to school. The practice helped him retrieve words more fluently. He welcomed the help from his peers, as well. The emotional support of his teachers and peers strengthened his self-cueing with pictures and led to this successful language experience.

For the rest of the reading, Mickey slowed down occasionally when he had trouble with a word. He asked for help from the girl in the class who, in his words, "knew all the words," and continued to read. He seemed comfortable reading and leading the group, and was not embarrassed or nervous about asking for help with problem words. Near the end of this reading, the teacher informed Mickey that the allotted time for his reading was nearly over, and that he could complete the book the next day. Mickey was slightly upset by this announcement. The smile left his face, he stared ahead for several seconds, and then he began to read faster than before. The teacher repeated her comments, but Mickey continued reading quickly. The students called out in support of Mickey—he had only two pages left. He smiled broadly at the encouragement, the teacher relented, and Mickey finished his book with a large sigh. His determination to finish reflected a positive change in his confidence level and in his language abilities.

Now, when Mickey chose to participate in discourse routines, his determination to continue for more than one turn became noticeable. In Example 7.16, Mickey read from a basal selection. He then contributed to the children's efforts to corroborate their predictions concerning a portion of a story they were reading. This activity was part of the daily small-group basal-reading lesson. The students were answering the teacher's questions near the end of the story to determine whether their predictions about a girl's collecting pieces of yarn were appropriate. In the story, the girl, Sarah, helped a bird to build a nest as colorful as a rainbow.

EXAMPLE 7.16 (April)

1	M:	[reading aloud] "SHE WENT OUTSIDE TO PLAY WITH". . . [He looks at the word. If he has begun a verbal attempt at decoding, it is not audible to the teacher. Probably assuming the word too difficult for him, she says it to encourage him to repeat it.]
2	T:	[providing the word for M] "PETER". . .
3	M:	[reading aloud] "PETER AND". . ."ANN" [This attempt to decode is quicker and more audible, although a wait time of another few seconds might have let him finish the last syllable.]
4	T:	[corrects M] . . . "ANNA." "ANNA."
5	M:	[reading aloud] "ANNA. I AM LOOK . . . KEEPING SOME STRING IN A BOX, SAID SARAH. I HAVE SOME PURPLE STRING IN MY". . .
6	T:	[is talking to another child during some of the reading, but turns quickly to provide the word for M] . . . "POCKET."
7	M:	. . ."POCKET. YOU MAY HAVE IT, SAID PETER. ARE YOU KEEPING STRING, AN . . . ANNA?"
8	T:	[correcting M] "SAID ANNA."
9	M:	. . ."SAID ANNA."
10	F:	[I make the gesture for "stretch it out," indicating that M should keep his words in phrases as often as possible. Then I whisper to him.] I can sit back here now. [I move farther behind M to give him a little more independence and less assistance.]
11	T:	[cueing him to continue reading] "WHAT". . .
12	M:	. . ."SAID ANNA. WHAT ARE YOU DO . . . GOING TO DO WITH ALL THAT STRING? WILL YOU . . . WILL YOU CAAAA". . .
13	T:	[correcting] "YOUR". . .
14	M:	. . ."YOUR CAT PLAY . . . PLAY WITH IT? NO, SAID SARAH. YOU'LL SEE."
///		[Another student in the class continues reading.]
15	T:	We found out some things. We're trying to become good predictors, good detectives, thinking about what might happen by what we find out in the story. We've eliminated some of them. She's not going to use [the string] to wrap a box. She's not going to use it to fly a kite. Those are things to rule out. Does anybody have a different idea about what she will use it for?
16	S1:	No.
17	T:	Want to still go with wrapping it around blocks, or make a rainbow out of the string?
18	S2:	Yeah.
19	T:	[noticing Mickey reviewing the pages with some excitement] Mickey?

20	M:	Uh . . . Well, not . . . not about making a . . . a rainbow . . . making a rainbow next to the trees. [M is referring to not eliminating the rainbow prediction from the possibilities.]
21	T:	All right, now. Let's return to our page and continue reading.
22	M:	"LOOK, SAID SARAH. OH, MY, SAID SARAH'S DAD. THE STRING HELPED A BIRD MAKE HER NEST, SARAH'S MOTHER SAID, AND LOOK! THE BIRD MADE A RAINBOW FOR SARAH." [M is pleased with his reading; he reads loudly and fairly fluently.]
23	T:	The nest was the rainbow.
24	S2:	Why did Sarah ask everybody for string?
25	T:	Why did she do that? [M's hand goes up quickly and confidently.] Mickey?
26	M:	She wanted a . . . uh . . . bird to . . . to take it and make it out of a rainbow nest.
27	T:	Help a bird out, that's right. Did you [class] ever do that, help out little animals?
28	M:	[He is not called on, but feels comfortable enough to enter the conversation.] Yeah, I . . . I . . . I had extra bread so I gave to the birds. The birds . . . [is still talking, pleased to have the "floor" again to tell his stories and gain the attention of the other students]
29	T:	[ignoring M's added comments because he had continued "out of turn"] Yes, Alex.
30	A:	[not audible]
31	T:	Jimmy, would you read the next question number four, please? OK.
32	J:	[stumbles through] What was Sarah's rainbow?
33	M:	The string.
34	T:	No, the string wasn't Sarah's rainbow. Remember we talked about this.
35	M:	[loudly] Oh! . . . The mom [doesn't get to finish saying that the mom had said the answer in the text]
36	T:	SHHHHHHH. There are still people trying to think.
37	M:	Oh . . . I know . . . Oh . . . [His hand is raised high.]
38	T:	What was Sarah's rainbow?
39	M:	I know . . .
40	T:	Jill?
41	J:	The nest.
42	T:	Do you agree with that?
43	Ss:	Yes.

Mickey actively monitored his own language participation throughout the above reading lesson, both in his own reading aloud and in the discourse. He was monitoring his language when he repeated his reading miscues in phrases, placing these words in context (lines 12 and 14) rather than repeating them alone after the teacher. His responses proved "bumpy" at times, as he slowed down to retrieve words and use time fillers (such as, "um," lines 20, 28, and 37), but, he volunteered and kept himself moving along. He waited for an "opening" to add that his prediction—that Sarah was saving the string for the birds to build a rainbow—was not yet ruled out (line 21). As he read aloud, he gained confidence and spoke more loudly (line 23). By the end of his turn, he was fluently reading vocabulary words that had posed problems for him before. In fact, near the end of this part of the lesson, Mickey actively added a comment in response to the teacher's question, without Ms. Lucas's appointing him (line 29). He was participating and growing more successful as the lesson continued. This pattern was observed in many other language routines throughout the day.

As Example 7.17 illustrates, Mickey was learning how to use word-retrieval strategies to his advantage in the classroom. On this day, Mickey was taking part in a small-group basal-reading lesson. The teacher had listed new vocabulary words on a page from the large basal workbook on an easel near the children's chairs. She introduced new vocabulary words taken from the text in a prereading lesson.

EXAMPLE 7.17 (May)

1	T:	I know most of you know this word [pointing to a word on the board].
2	C:	[in unison] Blue.
3	T:	Yes, blue. Blue's a what?
4	C:	[in unison] Color.
5	T:	Good. Let's read our sentence together.
6	C:	"JANE CANNOT FIND HER BLUE CAT."
7	T:	Very good.
8	C:	"JANE'S" . . .
9	T:	[stops the reading] Jane's? . . . Who remembers? Why is there an apostrophe "s" there? What did we learn yesterday? [Every child's hand is raised, including Mickey's.] I like the way everyone's hands went up. [to me]: Boy, they learned this well. Mickey?
10	M:	That . . . it means that it belongs to someone?
11	T:	[nods yes] And who's going to be that someone?
12	M:	um . . . Jane?
13	T:	Jane. We're going to have something that tells us something belongs to Jane. Is that what you would say?
14	S1:	Yes.
15	T:	So, let's find out what belongs to Jane.
16	Ss:	[in unison] "HAVE YOU SEEN JANE'S CAT?"
17	T:	What is it that belongs to Jane?
18	S2:	Blue cat.
///		[T explains several other words to the children.]
19	T:	What's this word?
20	Ss:	"BOX." [T points to a sentence that follows it.] "JANE LOOKED FOR HER CAT IN THE BOX."
21	T:	That "x" sound at the end of box, what [other] letters make up that sound? If you didn't know it was "x," what letters does it sound like? Jimmy?
22	J:	"S."
23	T:	There's an "s." Any other letters that might go with that? [Only a few hands go up, Mickey's included.] Mickey?

24	M:	"K?"
25	T:	"K." There's one other.
26	S3:	[calls out] "C."
27	T:	"C," "K," "S." That's right.
28	M:	[aloud] "C," "K," "S"?
29	T:	[nods "yes"] What's this [word]?
30	S:	"ONE."
31	T:	What kind of "one" is that? Is that the "one" like "I won the race"? Or is that the "one" like "I am one year old"?
32	S5:	I am one year old.
33	T:	OK. So it's the number one, isn't it?
34	M:	[volunteers aloud] It's like this, "I have one apple; one apple thing."
35	T:	Right, the number, meaning you have one of something.

At the end of this example (lines 29–35), Mickey showed that he knew he needed additional time to answer. He waited until there was an opening in the discourse exchange and then added his own example (line 34) to show that he understood the material and could contribute to the discussion. Early on, he also checked his own understanding of information (the spelling of the "sounds" of "cks" and "ks" for the "x" in "box"), by calling out loud (line 28). He was becoming an active learner, monitoring his comprehension by using examples throughout his discourse participation. Although confident in his language attempts, he still checked my location several times in the room, probably more for assurance than for help.

Figure 7.2 shows the results of the more formal, end-of-the-year speech-and-language evaluation, which reveal changes in Mickey's language and literacy constructions. Mickey's scores indicated some improvement in each area of language competenices over approximately eight months, using normative data. For example, his scores on language comprehension and receptive vocabulary came within two points of the results from his September test results. These changes suggest that Mickey's language knowledge and comprehension were still age appropriate in content, but interrupted less frequently by word-retrieval difficulties. Some new tests were added to the battery, such as the Test of Problem-Solving and the Language-Processing Test, both of which suggested age-appropriate levels of performance. Classroom observations by the speech and language pathologist, parents, and teacher, as noted in the case study, revealed room for further development in these areas. Mickey's progress may not have been stellar, but it was forward moving and empowering.

Summary.   As illustrated by the examples above, Mickey was beginning the "handover" phase of learning to use his language more competently in the classroom. More and more, according to his teacher's comments and my classroom field notes, he was taking an active, effective role in using new language strategies to express and share what he knew or wanted to know. For example, he often changed his discourse contributions to conform with the classroom routines by answering within a time period closer to that expected by his peers and teacher. He adapted his

FIGURE 7.2   Speech and Language Assessment Protocol

Student's Name _____ Mickey _____   Date _____ May _____

Student's Homeroom _____ Ms. Lucas _____   Age/Grade __ 7 years, 2 months, 1st grade __

STUDENT INTERVIEW

Mickey commented, as a summary for his progress during the school year, "I like to read . . . a lot . . . of stories about things. I talk OK . . . in my class. It's a little hard."

SPEECH	Test Results:
Informal Deep Testing of speech sounds in words:	75% mastery of /r/ (initial)
	70% mastery of /r/ (final), f/th
	(final) d/th (medial)

LANGUAGE—Comprehensive	Test Results:
Clinical Evaluation of Language Functions—	
Revised	
Receptive Language:	Standard Score: 87
Expressive Score:	Standard Score: 82

LANGUAGE—Vocabulary	Test Results:
Peabody Picture Vocabulary Test, Form L	Standard Score: 90
Expressive One-Word Picture Vocabulary Test	Standard Score: 125

LANGUAGE—Pragmatics/Problem-Solving	Test Results:
Test of Problem Solving	Standard Score: 50 (mean score of
	50)

LANGUAGE—Processing/Word retrieval	Test Results:
Language Processing Test	Standard Score: 48 (mean score of
	50)
Test of Wordfinding in Discourse	
Language Productivity	Standard Score: 105
Wordfinding Behaviors	Standard Score: 80

FLUENCY

Informal evaluation indicates average levels for age and grade.

VOICE

Uses soft voice; often mumbles (or rehearses language) to himself.

AUDITORY PERCEPTION—Discrimination/Processing

Fewer episodes of ear infections than during previous year, according to parent's report.

FAMILY/PARENT NOTES

Concerns relating to problems with abstraction and critical thinking.

TEACHER'S NOTES

Concerns relating to problems with abstraction and critical thinking. Literacy achievement still lags, but by approximately 6 months. Composite score on Iowa Test of Basic Skills indicated percentiles on achievement to be: verbal ability, 52; nonverbal ability, 72.

COMMENTS/RECOMMENDATIONS:

Continue classroom-based language and literacy intervention services.

language style to include phrases in place of one-word responses when he experienced difficulty with word retrieval. He also became a willing participant in classroom discourse, which was a large part of learning and sharing knowledge in school.

Not all Mickey's language was fluent, but he began using strategies to move through most language difficulties. And, his word-retrieval difficulties became more manageable and less frequent. Mickey had shown improvement in each of the targeted goals—development of word-retrieval strategies, participation in classroom discourse, and attempts at problem-solving—as he discovered ways to join the classroom routines more often and in a more focused manner during the last six months of the school year. He would require language support in the classroom during the next school year. However, he had made gains in language strategies that had not been seen in previous years, as evidenced by teachers' written comments on final report cards, parents' verbal remarks at IEP Annual Review meetings, and specialists' formal and informal results from testing.

Mickey's social and emotional struggles would need further attention in order for educators to address his needs in classroom literacy activities and peer interactions. Continued communication with medical specialists and the school psychologist would direct the nature of additional support services. Frequent consultation with parents and family members by school faculty would also help him generalize new strategies beyond the boundaries of the school and provide feedback concerning his progress.

8 Vincent: A Second Grader

Student Profile

Vincent was first identified as being at risk for developmental language problems at age three and a half, during a school-district preschool screening service. He participated in a parent-child readiness program in the early childhood department of the school one morning each week, for a year and a half. He was then retested during the school district's prekindergarten screening program. At that time his scores on tests of vocabulary, language, and auditory memory skills were below age level, and he cried easily during the evaluations. Results of tests for academic readiness and motor skills did not indicate any other problems. Based on these results, Vincent was included in a one-year developmental (retention) kindergarten class. Although he was not originally recommended for special-education services as he entered regular kindergarten classes, his weak performance in classroom discussions qualified him for participation in a language-resource program focused on developing syntactic strategies for classroom discourse.

Vincent did not require or receive medication for any special problems aside from common illnesses until the spring semester of the school year. A pediatrician prescribed Ritalin to help control Vincent's apparent hyperactivity, but the symptoms persisted.

Vincent was an affectionate child, living with his older sister and his birth parents. He was as independent as his young peers and interacted well in small groups. When he progressed to the first grade, teachers again noted his language problems, mostly in the area of grammar confusions. He began having word-retrieval difficulties near the end of his first-grade year, when his speech intelligibility and language productivity increased enough for his teachers to notice problems in communication. Figure 8.1 shows his early speech and language evaluation.

Classroom and Discourse Routines

Teachers described Vincent as quiet and shy, in the classroom of twenty-three children. His second-grade classroom was usually bustling with activity. The children

FIGURE 8.1   Speech and Language Assessment Protocol

Student's Name ____Vincent____	Date ____September____
Student's Homeroom ____Ms. Olsen____	Age/Grade __8 years, 3 months, 2nd__

STUDENT INTERVIEW
Vincent wants to work on his speech and language problems by himself in the classroom. He admits that he forgets words but wants more time to "remember" what he wants to say. He wants me to convey this message to his teacher.

SPEECH
Informal evaluation reveals lingering [w/r] substitution (~40% frequency) in the final position in syllables.

LANGUAGE—Comprehensive	Test Results:
Clinical Evaluation of Language Functions— Revised	
Expressive Language	Standard Score: 62
Receptive Language	Standard Score: 87

LANGUAGE—Vocabulary	Test Results:
Peabody Picture Vocabulary Test-Revised, Form L	Standard Score: 79
Expressive One-Word Picture Vocabulary Test	Standard Score: 95

LANGUAGE—Pragmatics/Problem-Solving
Informal testing revealed language is weak in areas of revision, articulation, and approaches to interactional skills and question formation.

LANGUAGE—Processing/Word Retrieval	Test Results:
Test of Wordfinding	Standard Score: 87

FLUENCY
Word-retrieval difficulties are disruptive in classroom discourse.

VOICE
Occasional forcing of voice when frustrated, causing hoarseness.

AUDITORY PERCEPTION—Discrimination/Processing
Auditory screening by school nurse reveals no problems.

FAMILY/PARENT NOTES
Vincent's parents are interested in having him tested for learning disabilities, beyond speech and language services. They are concerned about his low achievement despite his best efforts in school.

TEACHER'S NOTES
Vincent is in the lower reading group, i.e., primer level. He "loses attention in larger groups" and "asks for repetitions of directions" often in the classroom. Woodcock-Johnson Full Scale Test of Reading indicated the following grade equivalents: broad reading, 2 years, 1 month (SS: 91); broad written language, 1 year, 8 months (SS:89).

COMMENTS/RECOMMENDATIONS:
Initiate a classroom-based language and literacy intervention program.

understood the activity routines, and most moved around the room purposefully to complete a "job" such as returning classroom library books or adding completed assignments to portfolios. Six hermit crabs had been the center of attention and study for six weeks in the first few months of the school year. Selected children's completed work on the crabs was displayed on bulletin boards around the room for a week at a time to encourage careful attention to math concepts and writing activities.

Vincent's classroom was divided into three areas, the largest of which consisted of the students' chairs and desks. The desks, organized into groups of four, were used for "center" work and individual seat work. Classroom discourse varied as the activity shifted from teacher-led recitation and instructional discourse to peer-group interaction in math or science work. The second area involved a long, rectangular table in the back corner that was used for structured small-group activities, such as reading instruction, alternative math activities, or special art projects. Structured language routines, such as literature response meetings and teacher or peer conferencing, also occurred here. A rug area, the third area, was in the back corner of the room. Here, students engaged in informal reading, individual math activities, and informal discussions of feelings and behavior in a program called Project Charlie. The language used in this area varied but was primarily student-initiated and occurred among peers.

Acting as both an observer and a participant in this classroom, I moved with Vincent from activity to activity, often facilitating language among several children in small-group arrangements when the classroom teacher was elsewhere in the room. When the teacher, Ms. Olsen, was with us, or during classroom discussions, I supported Vincent's language in interactions with all classroom members but did not lead the discourse. After approximately three weeks, all members of the class became familiar with my presence and knew that, although I was primarily helping Vincent with language support, I was also available to answer their questions.

Dynamic Assessment Phase of the Program

During the previous school year, Vincent was enrolled in the school's speech- and language-therapy resource-assistance program, with goals to improve his poor articulation and syntactic skills. Typical of programs based in resource-room settings, Vincent made some improvements in these areas of remediation, but had very little carryover of strategies into the classroom. Compared to Mickey, Vincent had spent two more years in the classroom with less than competent expressive language strategies. Following classroom observation and individual discussions with Vincent and Ms. Olsen, I chose three goals for him: (1) developing strategies for word-retrieval difficulties that limited his language constructions, (2) increasing his participation in classroom discourse, and (3) eliminating the growling noises he made when he encountered word-retrieval difficulties.

Existing Strategies for Language Use

In the classroom, Vincent was not very talkative. Yet he still interacted with peers, socializing more often through physical closeness and gestures than verbal interaction. For example, he would stand near or within small groups of children, watching and laughing along with them and using exaggerated movements with his eyes or hands to communicate. When he did speak, he gave mostly supportive responses; for instance, "I think so, too," or "That's funny." He was more talkative with teachers than with peers, for he seemed to seek the personal feedback and assistance from informal conversations with adults. There was improvement in the quantity and quality of Vincent's oral language from previous years, but his word-retrieval difficulties persisted. At times, Vincent would begin to answer and then "forget" the words even after he purposely raised his hand to participate. After a pause, he often gave the same answer another child had already given. Associated substitutions, such as "plane" for "train" and "to" for "from," occurred frequently in his responses. Other examples of substitutions included "play" for "movie" as he related a weekend activity, "letters" for "numbers" as he referred to a math problem, and "can" for "van" as he referred to the family's means of transportation.

Example 8.1 depicts these difficulties. The teacher led a classroom discussion about old and new explorers and their discoveries; for example, Columbus discovering North America, astronauts landing on the moon, and doctors finding cures for diseases. The pattern of exchange consisted of the teacher calling on a child and then the child naming an explorer and his or her discovery. The students drew pictures to depict their understanding of a "new discovery." Vincent's discovery picture showed a space capsule in orbit. During the interaction, the teacher repeated student responses and then usually expanded on the answer to explain or correct the information in an IRE format.

EXAMPLE 8.1   (September)

1	T:	[to Vincent] What makes it a discovery?
2	V:	They went up to the sky to discover. It's going up to Earth [referring to a picture of a space capsule on the worksheet].
3	F:	[I nodded, repeating quietly to him from my seat behind him.] It is going up from Earth.
4	V:	[picking up the modification] It's going to Pluto.
5	T:	[directed toward the rest of the class, still looking for an acceptable answer] What makes it a discovery?

An analysis of Vincent's discourse in this discussion revealed several language difficulties related to word retrieval. First, in his initial response (line 2), he did not answer the teacher's question, which required a definition of "discovery" (line 1). Instead, he described a picture on the worksheet. Typically, Vincent avoided abstract definitions if he could provide a more concrete, familiar example, such as the reference to the space capsule in Example 8.1.

Second, Vincent used ambiguous pronouns, also a common strategy when a word is difficult to retrieve. At first, his use of the word "they" (line 2) seemed to refer to all discoveries named up until that point, but this was not the case. Vincent's reference was limited to the astronauts in the sky in a picture, a fact that was not clear to the rest of the class. His use of the pronoun "it" in his second response (line 4) also does not indicate his referent—his own worksheet pictures of a space capsule—to the other listeners.

Vincent's third difficulty, noticeable in other classroom discourse examples, was in naming or labeling items in one-word responses during classroom discourse. Vincent's attempts to verbally list items for his second-grade worksheets were also unproductive. The opportunity to provide these same words in a more expanded form might have helped him to succeed. However, he wasn't willing to expand his usual language pattern of short, simple utterances.

Vincent's journal writing also revealed his reluctance to use either complex forms or animation in his language constructions. He usually limited his entries to his name, one phrase or sentence, and a drawing. Example 8.2 is an excerpt from a discussion I had with him during journal-writing time. Ms. Olsen had suggested "Halloween" as a topic. In fifteen minutes, Vincent had attempted only to write his name and create a sketch of a haunted house. I sat near him and offered to help the children at his group of four desks.

EXAMPLE 8.2 (October)

1	F:	How are you doing? Writing about Halloween?
2	V:	I'm going to be a vampire.
3	S1:	I'm going to be a princess.
4	V:	I'm going to wear black and I have it up [on my neck], too [gestures a cape].
5	F:	A cape?
6	V:	[nods yes]
7	S2:	My brother is a vampire.
8	V:	And I have a turtleneck shirt. Push it way up. And a hood.
9	S1:	I'm going out with my sister.
10	V:	Me, too. And I'm gonna bite her neck. It's 'cause I have . . . [gestures "fangs"] make-believe teeth here.
///		[Other children share details about their costumes.]
11	F:	Well, write your stories down. Sounds interesting.
12	V:	[writes "Halloween is here," stops, looks around]
13	F:	You might try saying your thoughts aloud as you think them. You could talk to me or to your friend or to yourself. Saying it to someone who is listening helps.
14	V:	[points to his picture of a haunted house]

15	F:	Why this?
16	V:	Because.
17	F:	What is your story about?
18	V:	Halloween.
19	F:	And . . . ?
20	V:	Just Halloween.
21	F:	And vampires.
22	V:	[nods yes and adds a stick figure to his picture] That's a vampire. That's him. [adds a ladder] That's how he'll get up to the roof.
23	F:	Write it down.
24	V:	[thinks for a minute] I forgot it. [V then raises his hand for the classroom teacher to come to check his work. As she arrives, he just smiles, giving no introduction or comment about what he wants her to see or do.]
25	F:	[whispering to Vincent] Vincent, you could ask her to look at your picture or to look at your writing, or to check it for you.
26	V:	Miss Olsen, do you know how they [vampires] get down?
27	T:	No, Vincent, how?
28	V:	They put out their arms like this [gestures flapping] and fall down slowly.
29	T:	That's great, Vincent. [She walks to another student.]

In this example, Vincent's only word-retrieval difficulty occurred when he seemed to recall the word "fangs" as he described his Halloween costume (line 10). He substituted a gesture for the large teeth that would appear in his mouth and orally used the term "make-believe teeth" to describe them. The other children in his group nodded their understanding. He seemed relieved that no one had provided the word for him, which he would have interpreted as a correction. In this small, supportive audience, he had been more verbal than usual. However, when I asked him to write these details in his journal entry (line 11), he could add only three words (line 12). His invented spelling, which the teacher encouraged, approximated conventional spelling in his level, and his handwriting proved clear and intelligible. Therefore, these latter two variables were probably not responsible for his difficulties.

Vincent's language sometimes included unclear references to himself and to his written work. For instance, he used the pronoun "they" (line 26), which I understood to refer to "vampires" but which the teacher couldn't interpret. She politely responded to his comments but did not understand their purpose: to call attention to his journal entry. Vincent's lack of specificity caused confusion in communication during everyday classroom discourse.

Thus, although Vincent's academic achievement was average for his age, his verbal interaction during classroom events was limited and caused difficulties, as noted in Ms. Olsen's referral for special-education assistance and in parent-teacher meetings. His teacher also had concerns about his attentional focus during classroom instruction and independent work time. For example, Vincent frequently got out of his seat to sharpen a pencil, take or put away materials, or confer with peers, when the other children were listening to the teacher. To limit these distractions, I assigned Vincent several different seating placements. Vincent's parents, in close cooperation with his pediatrician, started him on a trial period of medication to improve his on-task behaviors. Subsequently, his attentional focus improved somewhat, but he still had little patience for extended periods of concentration in all areas of classroom work.

Participation in Classroom Discourse

Vincent needed to learn to seek and accept help from others. New strategies could help address his problems with word retrieval and expressive language, but the frustration Vincent had experienced in earlier incidents had left him unwilling to risk trying these. Vincent needed to practice sharing his problems through verbal means in the classroom. To help him slowly work toward this goal, I at first encouraged him to subvocalize responses, or to repeat the answer quietly to himself, and to let me, as an "outside" teacher, give him individual help in the classroom. Because Vincent showed self-conscious behavior in the form of darting head and eye movements when I sat next to him for more than five minutes, I approached Vincent for consecutively longer periods of time. For example, during Phase One, I sat near him for ten to twenty and then thirty minutes, to accustom him to having me close by.

Example 8.3 illustrates a typical early intervention in the classroom, as we learned to work together. On this day, Vincent was sitting at a long table with three other children as they sorted dry beans to match shapes on a worksheet. The math activity aimed to help the students create addition patterns involving the number nine. I tried to follow and guide Vincent's discourse with peers during this work.

EXAMPLE 8.3   (October)

1	F:	What does it say?
2	V:	[has begun to write a number problem; points to the number on the page, waits fifteen seconds, then speaks] Six.
3	F:	Good. Say it out loud. You should say it out loud to yourself. See if it's right. That way you can check it with your neighbor . . .
4	V:	[looks at me with mild irritation]
5	F:	. . . later, to see if you've made a mistake.
6	V:	[looks away and addresses the child opposite him] Andy, can I use your crayons?
7	F:	He's doing his work, too.
8	A:	[looks at me, then relents] OK, Vin.
9	V:	[seems to be having trouble writing and subvocalizing the answer to the number problem he has written]
10	F:	Say it out loud.
11	V:	Six plus three equals . . . [points to the number nine at the top of the page]

12	F:	Yes. [I point to my open mouth to cue him to say the word.]
13	V:	[shakes his head "no"]
14	F:	[I notice that he has corrected his answer.] You already wrote "seven" but you erased it?
15	V:	[nods yes]
16	F:	That's OK. When you say it out loud, you can . . . [I am about to finish saying, ". . . check yourself."]
17	V:	[holds up an eraser] I've been thinking.
18	F:	Hey. Cool. You're really organized these days, huh, Vince?
19	V:	[He smiles and nods yes.]

In this example, Vincent initially reacted to my conversation by withholding his own. He used long pauses before saying something to me (line 2), avoided me altogether by talking to another child (line 6), gestured instead of talking (lines 2 and 11), changed the topic (line 17), and used nonverbal substitutions for "yes" and "no" (lines 15, 17, and 19). When he asked for an extra crayon (line 6) even though he already had the correct materials in front of him, I concluded that his question was another way for him to avoid listening to me and to change the topic. However, his attitude was apparently changing as he listened to and followed my suggestions to "say the problem out loud" (lines 3 and 10) and to check his work (lines 3 and 14). The purpose of talking during the math activity was for him to gain feedback from me on this day and to problem-solve and gain feedback from peers at the same table on other days. Encouraging him to talk more often in these small groups would help him expand on successes he had achieved with peers in the resource room. An experience that Vincent had originally avoided—talking his way through a problem to check his answer—in this case had helped him correct his math computation and brought a smile to his face as we ended the interaction.

After the first month, Vincent began cooperating with me. He would now wave me over to his side when I entered the room and would listen to my suggestions, still deciding on his own whether to use them. He learned to consider my ideas, mulling them over for a few days before trying out a new strategy in the classroom. His choice to try these strategies in the classroom would be an important indicator of their usefulness. If he did not try to use new strategies, we discussed his reasons and developed another set.

We also worked to improve Vincent's participation in classroom discourse. He had begun to avoid entering into class discussions, shrugging or answering, "I don't know" when the teacher called on him, and changing the subject when he did choose to talk. Encouraging him to ask questions involved him in classroom discourse without his having to provide information. Example 8.4 captures a discussion between Vincent and me in the resource room, in which my major purpose was to urge him to participate more in classroom talk. In this way, we did not use the resource room in the traditional way; that is, to drill readiness skills in repetitive tasks. Rather, we used it to prepare Vincent for authentic classroom language routines.

EXAMPLE 8.4 (November)

1	F:	It's important to talk in school, to try. You're a really smart cookie.
2	V:	Uh uh [for "no"].
3	F:	You know what you're doing in school, and you do very well.
4	V:	[looks up and listens without protest]
5	F:	I think it's important for you to raise your hand and participate and try to answer as often as you can. You have very good answers. Don't you think so?
6	V:	Uh huh [for "yes"].
7	F:	Yes? What do you think is your best subject? What do you do best in school? Is it reading or science or social studies?
8	V:	Math.
9	F:	Math? Well that's easy for you, is it? That's good. That means you mostly have to write. What about something in which you talk? Like social studies, when you have to answer about why things or groups are together . . .
10	V:	Yeah!
11	F:	What about reading?
12	V:	Sort of.
13	F:	Sort of? What do you think is the best?
14	V:	Uh . . . reading group. [laughs]
15	F:	I was in your reading group. I thought you read very, very well. What about social studies? You were having a great social-studies class. You were all talking about . . . what? Uniforms? I think it was about why people wear their uniforms.
16	V:	I like science.
17	F:	Science is good. With the . . .
18	V:	. . . hermit crabs.
19	F:	Yes. Crabs.
20	V:	Now we have the grow lab.
21	F:	The what?
22	V:	Now we have the grow lab. Grow lab.
23	F:	Are the plants doing very well?
24	V:	Yeah. [pause] I don't want to take speech anymore.
25	F:	Why?
26	V:	Because it's boring.
27	F:	You only come up with the other boys, your friends, once in a while for [learning to pronounce the "er"] sound work. Most of the time I go into your room and sit there with you, right?
28	V:	Yeah. Uh huh [for "yes"].
29	F:	I don't necessarily want you to come up a lot.
30	V:	Once a week?
31	F:	When you're with your friends, you don't like talking about sounds?
32	V:	I just want to listen to the other people.
33	F:	You just like to listen to the other people. You say that all the time. You said that about Project Charlie [a social-skills program in which students are encouraged to share feelings about common problems].
34	V:	Just want to listen?

35	F:	Yes. And you said that when your [class] was doing reports.
36	V:	Listen?
37	F:	But you know, other people want to hear what you say. Plus, you learn when you participate; when you're a part of it. What do you think? Why would I say that?
38	V:	Uh . . . I don't know. Maybe, you won't learn anything?
39	F:	What do you mean?
40	V:	If you don't . . . paripate [sic].
41	F:	Participate? That means "join in."
42	V:	If you don't, you can't learn.
43	F:	Why? . . . I want you to understand it. If you think that's true, talk to me about it.
44	V:	It is true.
45	F:	How do you think you learn when you join in? How do you learn?
46	V:	I don't know.
47	F:	When you raise your hand and you say the answer. For example, if someone says, "How many fingers are on our hand?" and you raise your hand and say, "I know, I know, four!"
48	V:	No.
49	F:	Your teacher says, "Well, that's close. Why don't you count . . . oh, five?" Do you see? She can help you figure out the right answer. Then you'll always remember that it's five. Or if she says, "How many fingers are on your hand?" and you say, "Five," she'll say, "That's exactly right. That was smart of you to count them." Most questions are harder than that. But if you don't raise your hand and you think the answer is "four," but you don't answer, then she doesn't know that you don't remember how many fingers there are. She thinks you know the answer.
50	V:	I know. [nods head for "yes"]
51	F:	If you raise your hand and say, "Four," she says, "You must not have counted. Why don't we try it again?" She says it nicely.
52	V:	I go like this. [raises his hand, fingers apart]
53	F:	So you raise your hand and she sees five [fingers]. There are harder questions. I was just trying to show you. [I use several other examples to illustrate my point.] . . . If she says, "What's a chrysalis?" and you don't raise your hand, she won't know that you studied it and know it.
54	V:	[raises his hand]
55	F:	You're raising your hand? What is a chrysalis?
56	V:	[using a forced voice] A caterpillar grows a chrysalis.
57	F:	I can't hear you. You're using a different voice. It's important to use your real, regular voice if you want people to hear you well.
58	V:	[using his normal voice] A caterpillar grows it on when it wants to go out . . . out.
59	F:	A caterpillar grows it on . . . when it wants to . . . ?
60	V:	. . . grow into a butterfly.
61	F:	When it wants to grow into a butterfly. OK. A chrysalis is the outer covering . . .

62	V:	I know.
63	F:	A caterpillar covers himself with a chrysalis before he becomes a butterfly.
64	V:	I know that.
65	F:	Well, I didn't know you knew that. I thought you had it mixed up.
66	V:	I said it mixed up when you said that.
67	F:	Yeah. But then, what did I do? I helped you get it exactly right. There you go! So if I didn't help, you still would have been mixed up. That's why it's important to raise your hand and participate, not just with teachers. It's important with children also. Talk to them and share what you know. Then you can learn better. OK . . .

In this discussion, Vincent initially responded with his usual humble, yet face-saving, denial of his true cognitive skills in the classroom (line 1). His language also remained simple at first. He did not easily offer more complex language constructions because he seemed to sense that I might misunderstand or "mix-up" his comments (line 66), although he did not attribute the problems specifically to word-retrieval difficulties. As he explained, he used gestures to respond or complete a response to the teacher's questions whenever possible (lines 50 and 52). He also made it clear in these comments and in other instances that I brought up (lines 33 and 35) that he preferred to "just listen" in class, rather than to verbally contribute to conversations. As this example shows, when he used short, curt responses, he experienced few word-retrieval difficulties. He did not want to go to the resource room (lines 24 and 26). For this reason, by the end of the first few months of school, I had begun to visit with him even more often in his classroom. We ended the small-group resource-room meetings altogether.

From the above examples, audiotapes, and observations noted in field notes, I realized that with coaxing, generally in the form of praise, Vincent could contribute to a conversation. In the example above, he cautiously extended his remarks, occasionally providing more information than required; for example, when he talked about the grow lab (line 20) or provided an explanation of a chrysalis (lines 56 and 60). He needed this same language support in the classroom to increase his verbal participation in discourse and accumulate as many successes as possible. Even though I initially advanced the argument that he'd learn if he participated (line 37), he seemed to agree to it subsequently. In general, he liked to please his teacher and to demonstrate that he knew the information she might be searching for. When he considered that feedback could be helpful and important (line 66), he became more attentive to my suggestions. This more open attitude toward participating in discourse would later manifest itself as an increase in his classroom participation.

Vincent also needed some strategies that would help him answer his teacher's and peers' questions competently. I explained that answering simply, using just the words he needed at first, and then adding extra information later, would be the best way to start. I had told him to always use a phrase or sentence, not just one word alone, to make it easier. In either case, whether it was asking or answering questions, staying on topic became an important goal for Vincent.

Elimination of Related Behaviors

At a parent-teacher conference one month after school had begun, Vincent's mother voiced her concern about a new habit he had developed since September. Specifically, the teacher had reported that he was using guttural noises as he worked on writing exercises in the classroom. Vincent's mother also noted that this voice change occurred later when they discussed school work in the evenings at home. The noises seemed to stem from his frustration, and gave him a personal and fairly quiet way to either vent anger or motivate himself to perform a task. We decided to discuss our concerns with Vincent, given that the habit was audible to others, negative in connotation, and hurtful to his vocal cords. Classroom observations indicated that he used this new sound when he retrieved a word after a pause, and when he was having trouble writing fluently. In several asides, I had stressed to him that the "growling" took his mind off the answer, and that using that same effort to cue an appropriate word would help him more. He seemed to understand my explanation, and the guttural noises lessened. Still, in addition to addressing language difficulties in the classroom, modifying aspects of Vincent's voice quality became another goal for remediation.

Summary

At this point in the school year, classroom-based assessment indicated that Vincent's language problems consisted primarily of word-retrieval difficulties. He made common word substitutions and unclear referents, or "empty words." When Vincent did speak at length about his interests or tried to explain a procedure to a naive listener, the details of the narrative were difficult to ascertain. Occasionally he made the growling sound, further disrupting his message. Listeners frequently had to ask Vincent for clarification. For a second grader, these language difficulties caused considerable concern.

Vincent was aware of these problems. He reacted by using short, simple utterances to answer the teacher's questions. He developed gestures, such as shoulder shrugs and hand movements, to replace verbal responses. He left his seat often to pursue unnecessary jobs, such as sharpening pencils, and to avoid discourse participation. And he was distressed that an adult would choose to draw any more attention to his problems by sitting near him and suggesting strategies.

Vincent's goals would include participating more in classroom discourse by asking questions and using phrases or longer constructions instead of one-word responses. Developing word-retrieval strategies and eliminating negative behaviors would also require my help and that of his teacher. Vincent had already become used to my presence in his classroom. Now he would need to take risks as he learned to use these new language strategies.

Intervention Phase of the Language Support Program

I visited Vincent's classroom three times each week, in three different settings. Once or twice a week, for approximately thirty minutes in the early afternoon, I followed Vincent around the room as he initiated and completed math "tubbing" activities. During these activities, the students used different objects, stored in little plastic tubs, to solve mathematical problems and to write down the answers. Vincent proved more talkative during these activities than in larger group gatherings, often subvocalizing answers to himself, shaking his head, and self-correcting his answers. When I listened closely, I noticed that he was correcting his own number identifications; for example, "That's two, I mean three, that's a three." These might have been word-retrieval substitutions. I chose to observe him in this setting because the language interaction there represented the everyday classroom discourse in this second-grade classroom. This setting also provided opportunities for individual counseling.

Although Vincent had become used to my presence in the classroom, he was initially impatient when he tried to explain the procedures he had to follow to complete the math activity. If he had a question, he preferred to go to the classroom teacher, whom he felt had the "right" procedural answer; he asked me questions about the correctness of his answers only occasionally.

I also helped Vincent during the teacher-led content-area recitation period that followed just after the math activities. This whole-class presentation required the children to sit at their own desks as Ms. Olsen conducted a social-studies or science unit. The teacher generally chose students to respond to her comprehension questions, alternating between those who volunteered to answer and those who did not. In December, Ms. Olsen had to draw Vincent into the discourse.

Finally, I visited Vincent during journal time in the morning. The teacher suggested topics relating to upcoming holidays or current events, but also let the children choose their own topics if they had another interest. In Vincent's class, the students' writing skills and word knowledge had come far enough along that the teacher expected the children to write on their own with only periodic supervision. This was not the case for Vincent. His teacher had specifically asked me to help him with this aspect of language expression after watching him struggle with his thoughts during the study's first few months (Phase One). He rarely wrote more than a short phrase or stilted construction. His word-retrieval difficulties worsened when he tried to explain what he had related in written form.

Throughout the second phase of the study, we worked on the goals targeted earlier—developing strategies for word retrieval and discourse participation and eliminating growling and frustration-centered behaviors. Initially, Vincent was unconcerned, and rather unwilling, to talk about developing new language strategies and modifying his language use. He was clearly more interested in giving a short answer and ending his turn, not in taking part in the interaction that might follow or expanding on the teacher's or a peer's comments. However, he grew frustrated when he knew that others didn't understand his answers. Over the next six months of the intervention phase, he made important changes in how he accepted language assistance.

Changes in Language Support

In the beginning of December, Vincent sat in the front corner of the room, where the teacher could "keep an eye on him" and where he experienced fewer distractions. The location was inconspicuous, letting me move next to him without engendering much reaction from the surrounding children. Still, Vincent seemed irritated by my presence. He was used to receiving language instruction exclusively in a resource-room setting. In an effort to "blend" into the classroom and take the pressure off Vincent, I began to help all five of the other children in Vincent's seating area. He was able to observe me working with the children and see their positive reactions. This helped him view me less as a "resource-room teacher" and more as a part-time member of the classroom.

During this time, Vincent left the classroom once every two to three weeks to attend a speech and language class in the resource room with six other boys his age. His distorted production of the sound "r" had decreased his intelligibility during the previous school year and had contributed to his difficulty communicating competently. In this informally organized speech class, Vincent communicated differently than he did in the classroom. He participated in small-group conversations without frustration, although he still discouraged my efforts to improve his language form. In this small class, each child had difficulty in some aspect of language construction—a situation that may have made Vincent feel more relaxed about participating. Here, I was able to vary my question forms to reduce the quantity and degree of his word-retrieval difficulties. I used observations and recordings of his appropriate use of dialogue with peers in this setting to provide feedback and help him develop strategies for future conversations. These sessions stopped after January. This view of Vincent's capabilities also let me see how much language input he was withholding from classroom discourse.

In the classroom, Vincent remained sensitive to my more obvious forms of cueing, such as verbal instructions to help him focus and gestural clues to motivate an answer. He wanted to feel that his answers and questions were his own, which they were, and that he did not have to rush his responses. He wanted to be the only one in control of how and when he used language. I repeatedly explained my intentions to support, not supply, his language contributions.

In the second phase of the program, Vincent slowly became more confident in the classroom and in social relationships with peers as he began to accept my suggestions. His language style changed. In September it consisted of bursts of telegraphic, key words that were often out of order. By December, he began pacing his constructions more slowly and forming clearer and longer phrases. With a more fluent language style, he became less self-conscious. His attentional focus sharpened, and he stayed in conversation for several turns. He also began to use an audible voice quality. He knew that he had become more successful in his language experiences in the classroom because of the help I had given him, and now waved me over to sit next to him in class. He seemed to want the emotional encouragement more than the language cues, but I offered both during my visits.

Vincent's reluctant attitude is obvious in Example 8.5, as he first rebuffs, then uses, my suggestion for entering a discussion that followed peers' research-report presentations. The children had gathered on a large rug in the classroom, and had listened to one child describe the specifics of his research report on Sweden. The teacher then led a class discussion on the student's presentation.

EXAMPLE 8.5   (December)

1	T:	Peter, that was an excellent presentation. We all learned a lot about Sweden. Are there any questions from the class for Peter? [Hands go up all around the room.]
2	P:	Carla.
3	C:	Did you like learning about Sweden?
4	P:	Yeah. I'd heard about it before and I wanted to know more about it. Joe?
5	J:	Do you know any Swedish words?
6	P:	No, just the names of the cities.
7	F:	[leaning down to Vincent] Ask a question about Sweden. Anything will be fun.
8	V:	No.
9	F:	Try once. Think of a question for a minute or so and then ask.
10	V:	[thinking to himself] No. I can't think of it.
11	P:	Ellie?
12	E:	Did you ever visit Sweden?
13	P:	No.
14	F:	Ask about the weather. What's the weather like each day?
15	V:	I don't like the weather. [moves to another part of the rug, away from me]
16	S1:	Do you know how to yodel?
17	P:	[Tries to yodel. All the class members laugh.]
18	T:	Any other questions? [My hand is raised.] Mrs. Ross?
19	F:	What is the weather like each day in Sweden? Is it warmer or colder than in Chicago?
20	P:	The weather is colder in the mountains and it's kinda the same in the cities.
21	F:	Thank you very much.
22	T:	That's all for Peter's presentation. Who wants to be next?

///		[The next day, during the continuing series of research presentations, I do not sit next to Vincent, but I watch him carefully. He knows I'm watching, but doesn't look at me. Amy finishes her report.]
23	T:	Thank you, Amy, for your presentation on Mexico. You showed us a lot of pictures. I think we all really enjoyed it. Does anyone have questions for Amy about her report or her country? [Three children ask questions, which Amy answers.]
24	A:	[sees Vincent's hand up] Vince?
25	V:	What is the weather like during the day?
26	A:	It's warm there and people wear clothes like in summer. That's why people go there for vacation.
27	V:	[turns to me and smiles broadly]

In this example, Vincent asked the same question on weather that I had modeled earlier following Peter's report on Sweden (see lines 19, 25). This imitation was Vincent's first effort to join in what he usually considered a difficult classroom exchange. He felt anxious as he tried to construct his question (lines 10, 15), but he had clearly noticed and modeled my question.

Audiotapes of subsequent presentations revealed that Vincent asked a few other questions of the child presenters, but not more than one question per presentation. When I was in the classroom, he would catch my eye to make sure I saw and appreciated his effort. Vincent's mother called to thank me for helping him during this time, so Vincent must have reported his successes at home. I had thought he was irritated by my attempts to have him join in the questioning session, because of his physical movement away from me during the previous day's class. Instead, he had just needed extra time to follow my model and ask the question I had posed.

On days when Vincent voiced his frustration with his language difficulties and with my attempts to help him, we spent time in the classroom and in the halls for individual peripheral conferences. During these sessions, I explained that he needed to monitor his avoidance tactics and focus on the requirements in the classroom. As Vincent contributed more frequently to classroom discourse, these sessions lessened.

To address Vincent's syntactical errors, Ms. Olsen and I modeled correct constructions. These errors abated slowly, as noted in transcripts of discourse. Possibly, Vincent became less anxious about responding in class. When he managed to slow down his pace of answering, he became more careful and accurate in his choice and ordering of words. He still made some word substitutions, such as "feetprints" for "footprints," but these did not disrupt his intelligibility or keep him from competently presenting his ideas.

By March, transcripts indicated that Vincent still took his time before volunteering in classroom discourse, but often proved eager to show me that he was participating. For example, we had discussed beginning an answer with a simple response—several words that explain the gist of what he wanted to say—and then expanding the thought in the same turn or another one. Vincent often gained momentum as he joined in classroom conversations. Each successful comment reinforced his effort, as Example 8.6 shows. In this sample, the teacher and students exchange questions and answers relating to the children's interpretations of pictures.

EXAMPLE 8.6 (March)

1	T:	We are now picking up a social-studies unit because we finished the science unit. We did Chapter One, so let's open up to Chapter Two, which begins on page thirty-eight.
2	V:	[Turns to page fifty-eight, looks around, sees that he's on the wrong page. He says aloud:] What?
3	T:	Thirty-eight.
4	V:	Thirty-eight. [Changes to page thirty-eight.]
5	T:	OK. We talked about communities. The first chapter dealt mostly with learning about different kinds of land formations and directions. This chapter is going to deal with smaller communities.
///		[The lesson continues as the other students predict the sizes and types of several communities depicted in pictures in their books.]
6	V:	[Checks my reactions to his lack of responses so far. I have not touched his paper, but I make facial movements to cue him to respond to the generally easy questions. V then directs his comments toward me, in a quiet voice.] Can you stay until my bus comes [at the end of the school day]?
7	F:	[I shake my head "no" and touch my wrist watch, indicating that I don't have that much time.]
8	T:	Look at the kids riding their bikes. What kind of community do you think that is? [V's hand is raised.] Vince?
9	V:	Small. [V looks at me and then back to the teacher.]
10	T:	OK, small. Does it look kind of like our community out here?
11	V:	Hmmmm, yeah. 'Cause . . .
12	T:	Does it look like something we live in?
13	V:	[nods "yes"].
14	T:	It sure could. [V raises his hand again.] How do you know it was a small community? Vince?
15	V:	Because there's only two people.
16	T:	OK. Only two people. What are they doing?
17	V:	Riding bikes.
18	T:	Riding bikes. Do you think you could ride bikes like that in the city?
19	Ss:	NOOOOOO.
20	T:	Probably not.
21	V:	[calls out] Only if you stay close to the curb.
22	T:	OK, on the sidewalk maybe, but it looks like these kids are even in the street. Do you see the sidewalk in this picture?
23	V:	No.
24	T:	Some areas don't have sidewalks, in rural communities.
25	J:	I get to ride on my street.
26	V:	Me, too. [smiles]

Vincent chose not to participate at the beginning of this lesson, but when he realized that I would be leaving the classroom soon, he began to contribute. I attributed this change of heart to an initial period of orientation that he needed to build his confidence and to his need for language scaffolding that would end soon when I left his classroom.

Vincent first answered the teacher's question with one word (line 9), a simple response that he could control and expand. As we had discussed, this was the easiest way for him to enter a discussion. As he tried to explain his answer, he was cut off by the teacher, who again tried to help by imposing her own language. Unnerved slightly, he came back with a minimal response (the nod in line 13), but soon made another bid to respond more fully (lines 14, 15). He used phrases for the appropriate, fluent answers that followed (lines 17, 21), and avoided gestures and nods (lines 23, 26) and pronouns.

By the last few months of the school year, Vincent was using the new language strategies I had suggested to him and was participating in class discussions, as illustrated by the above example. Moreover, in most classroom situations, he worked alone and talked to himself without a teacher-helper at his side. He problem-solved and paced himself in classroom schoolwork and discourse. He was not always successful at entering conversations or at providing the right word. However, as I pointed out to him on several occasions, neither were the other children in his class. He often needed prodding to keep working on language participation and strategy development, but indirect reminders were generally sufficient to keep him aware of these goals. A large dose of praise for his accomplishments helped him begin to accept responsibility for his successes. Example 8.7, from a classroom aside meeting, shows his response to praise.

EXAMPLE 8.7   (April)

1	F:	[to Vincent] Have you been asking questions and participating in school talking?
2	V:	Yes, I did.
3	F:	Great! I know you've been answering questions. Also, I've been watching today, and I noticed lots of kids asking you questions, like, "Where are the crayons?" and "Where are the folders?" and "Could you help me pick up?" You answered so well, so clearly. And you used a good voice.
4	V:	I know.
5	F:	Maybe that's why they ask you questions now. You sound important when you answer.
6	V:	[He smiles broadly.]

Reinforcement for staying in conversations helped Vincent remember times when he appropriately interacted with teachers and peers. Building his self-monitoring skills in the classroom, where he found it most difficult to communicate competently, proved more successful than resource-room instruction. His peers were now satisfied with his answers to questions; he used fewer word substitutions, and he now finished his explanations whether or not he needed to pause for word retrieval.

I supported Vincent's increasing language skills by facilitating and contextualizing his word retrieval, modifying and modeling his language structure, and stimulating and praising his verbal contributions. His peers' positive reactions helped me. The other children easily picked up my models and helped Vincent with his writing. They also befriended him once they discovered that his shyness had been a "cover," for his word-retrieval difficulties. I also received help from Vincent's teacher, who welcomed me into the classroom and listened to my suggestions.

Ms. Olsen did not need to learn to use most of the cueing strategies. She already employed additional information, question prompts, naming, and question or stimulus repetition with all her students. However, she did not always allow an adequate amount of additional wait time for those students who needed a few extra seconds to process and answer content questions. Vincent needed this extra time to compose his responses. Although she tried to use this strategy more often, Vincent learned to answer or add comments during breaks in conversations or at the end. On several occasions, he called out that he didn't understand or that he needed Ms. Olsen to slow down. This solution worked for Vincent, because he was distracted by the silence that accompanied additional wait time.

Ms. Olsen and I met formally on only one occasion to discuss my language goals for Vincent and her reactions to them. She agreed with my foci, and we discussed ways she could integrate them into her verbal exchanges with the class. Most often, we exchanged ideas and progress reports before or after class time. In this way, we knew when Vincent was having struggles and successes, and each of us could adapt our work accordingly.

Ms. Olsen and I comfortably shared Vincent's attention in a crowded classroom of children unaccustomed to having two teachers in charge. Many children who wanted and needed my help were disappointed when I continued to stay close to Vincent. Others learned from the modeling and began to help each other. Ms. Olsen's patience and assistance became critical when seating arrangements changed or children grew distracted by my presence in the first months of this study. These experiences taught both of us new lessons in the art of collaborating gracefully.

Changes in Use of Language Strategies

Once a week, I joined Vincent during "journal time" in his classroom. For Vincent, journal writing had always been difficult. I decided to talk him through the activity and help him gain a result that he could comfortably share with the class when they occasionally called on a volunteer. The mechanics of writing (i.e., his invented spelling, letter formation, organization on the paper) and his general ideas were age appropriate, but each word required a major effort for him to create as he wrote.

The quality and quantity of his journal entries were only part of the problem; he had developed a "mental block" against the activity itself. I had suggested to him that he choose a topic, think or "imagine" it in his mind, subvocalize or mentally rehearse an intended sentence, and "keep moving." These exercises were an extension of word-retrieval strategies for fluent spoken language constructions. We had practiced these steps in the resource room during games for articulation therapy earlier in the year. I had also helped Vincent in the hallways with his journal when he seemed overly frustrated watching other children filling their pages with words.

Example 8.8 comes from an independent work period in Vincent's classroom, during which Ms. Olsen had scheduled writing conferences and journal writing. When I entered the room, Vincent was at the teacher's desk, waiting for a writing conference with her. He often lined up at her desk just to explain that he can't write any more, which was the case on this day. His teacher tried to encourage him, but briefly; she had to divide her conferencing time among all the children, and they had finished products in their hands. Vincent needed to "talk" his way through the writing, with a peer or a teacher.

EXAMPLE 8.8   (December)

1	F:	Can I help you, Vincent?
2	V:	I can't write anymore.
3	F:	Well, let's see if we can stretch it more.
4	V:	I don't know [about that]. [He sits down at his desk, looks at his journal entry, but can think of nothing to add. He has written, "I like to sleep. I go to sleep."]
5	F:	What are you thinking today?
6	V:	Nothing.
7	F:	[I silently read his journal entry.] This is interesting, what you wrote. I would love to have a whole day to sleep. I get so tired. Maybe that's because it's Friday? What do you think?
8	V:	[shrugs]
9	F:	You could write about Fridays or about being tired. But write it like you would tell about it, with more words.
10	V:	OK. [He subvocalizes his message as he adds to his entry: "I would sleep all the day. After Friday. My MOM wake me up. I so tired."]
11	F:	[I read it back aloud with syntactic corrections.]
///		[The class puts away their materials as T has instructed them. As T passes V's desk, he holds up his paper near her. She doesn't initially seem to understand the significance of that move, because he offers no salutation or question. So, she greets him.]
12	T:	Hi, Vince. How are you?
13	V:	Fine.
14	T:	You must have written quite a bit in your journal. You were writing for a long while.
15	V:	[smiles] Yeah.

My suggestions to Vincent (line 9) were meant to encourage his subvocalizing behavior as he wrote and help him extend his journal entry. His writing habits resembled his language habits; that is, he strived mightily not to err. In this sample, he began with a negative attitude, insisting that he didn't know (lines 4 and 8). But with encouragement, his attitude changed. Suggestions to focus on ideas, to rehearse (or subvocalize), and to "keep moving" remediated his word-retrieval difficulties in oral language and written work as well. It was hoped that remediation in an authentic writing context in the classroom would improve his oral and written contributions beyond their present skeletal form.

Vincent often practiced using language in the classroom by saying the answers softly to me during the verbal interactions of lessons. He did not always follow through by volunteering these answers aloud at the appropriate time to the class, probably because he did not trust his spontaneous answers quite yet. However, this verbal rehearsal was a start toward increasing his participation in classroom discourse. He learned to find clues from the other children's answers and questions, looking to me for acknowledgment that his answers were appropriate and correct. Example 8.9 depicts his use of this strategy. The classroom activity in this instance was a review and discussion of social-studies content from a text on rules and laws.

EXAMPLE 8.9 (January)

1	T:	Let's think now about what this chapter's about and talk about what we've learned so far through this chapter in social studies. [Hands go up.]
2	T:	Aaron?
3	A:	Rules.
4	T:	OK. This is all about rules. What is a rule?
5	S1:	Something you obey.
6	T:	OK. Something that you need to obey. That's another word. What does "obey" mean?
7	S1:	Laws.
8	T:	Like laws. OK.
9	V:	[His hand goes up.] I know.
10	T:	You have to obey laws, Vincent?
11	V:	Yeah.
12	T:	Certainly do. We're still trying to find out what "obey" means.
13	V:	[to me] I still think I can say it.
14	F:	Then you should give your answer.
15	S2:	[explains "obey"]
16	S2:	It's when you have a law and you have to follow it.
17	T:	Good: So we know that obey basically means things that you need to . . .
18	V:	[directed to me] . . . follow.
19	T:	Follow . . . OK? So you're going to follow . . .
20	V:	[directed to me] the laws.
21	T:	The rules or laws. We need to follow the directions or . . .
22	V:	Laws.

23	T:	Things you need to do, right. What happens when you don't follow the rules or laws?
24	V:	[Looks at me, then raises his hand.]
25	T:	Vincent?
26	V:	You may go to jail.
27	T:	Well, good. Yes.
28	S1:	You can get hurt.
29	T:	Yes, you can get hurt. We talked about that a lot.
30	S2:	You have to suffer the consequences.
31	T:	Exactly. That's what I was talking about. There are many things that would happen.
32	V:	[aloud] I don't know what she's talking about.
33	T:	You know what consequences are, right?
34	V:	[aloud] No.
35	T:	And if you don't obey you have to suffer the loss, like paying money, or missing a recess, getting a ticket or going to jail, or being grounded.
36	Ss:	[oooh's and ahhh's]
37	T:	So it's in your best interest to you to make a wise decision and follow the rules and laws wherever those rules may apply.
38	V:	[whispering to me] It's better than going to jail.
///		
39	T:	What's one of our rules for the classroom?
40	V:	[He raises his hand and then is appointed by T.] Pay attention to the person who's talking.
41	T:	How can you do that?
42	V:	By using attention rules. Looking at the person.
43	T:	Looking at the person. Paying attention to the person who's speaking.

In this example, Vincent first attempted to participate in the classroom discussion in his response to the teacher's search for a definition of "obey" (line 9). Her response, repeating the two previous students' contributions (lines 5, 7), did not help him provide an appropriate answer. Instead, she must have assumed from previous language habits in the classroom that his answer would duplicate another student's or her own response. Vincent did not correct her impressions or assert himself. Instead, he answered simply, "Yeah" (line 11), although he still wanted to attempt a definition for "obey" (line 13). Vincent first used me as a "sounding board" to provide feedback and encouragement, answering quietly to me (lines 13, 18, 20), then to himself (line 22), and then by just looking toward me (line 24). Thus, he slowly decreased his need for support and became more confident in his ability to verbally participate in the exchange. In lines 32 and 34, he even commented aloud to voice his confusion. Vincent was beginning to use new language strategies in the classroom to his advantage.

As Vincent entered the beginning of the "handover" phase in developing more competent language in the classroom, his concerns during language routines began to shift. Whereas he used to get preoccupied with the structure of what he contributed (such as a pause in fluency or use of time fillers), he now began focusing on the appropriate content of his answers (such as retrieval of the exact word he wanted). He still required help in the form of occasional peripheral conferences to discuss his language difficulties. However, his frustration, as well as tension in the classroom, eased, according to observations by Vincent, his teacher, and myself.

In Example 8.10, during an in-class reading lesson, Vincent appropriately answered several questions that the teacher had posed. The story concerned the predicament of a girl whose family lived in a lighthouse. The teacher led a lesson in reading comprehension through question-answer interaction.

EXAMPLE 8.10   (May)

1	T:	[reads aloud a description of storm clouds] What does that make you think of? What is the author trying to tell us? [She reads it a second time for emphasis.]
2	S1:	Animals?
3	T:	Animals.
4	S2:	Fire?
5	T:	Animals.
6	S3:	Lightning?
7	T:	How many say lightning? [Many hands are raised.] What is lightning part of?
8	V:	[looks up to the ceiling] The sky.
9	T:	The sky?
10	S4:	Raining.
11	T:	Raining and storming. What grumbles and growls?
12	S3:	Your stomach.
13	V:	Thunder.
14	T:	Thunder grumbles and growls. The story we're going to read, *Put the Lights on, Abby,* tells about how a young girl named Abby tried to do her father's job. I want you to think about how the author makes the story real.
///		
15	T:	What is Abby looking at?
16	S1:	She's looking at the sea.
17	T:	Where is she right now?
18	S2:	On a boat?
19	S3:	No, in a lighthouse.
20	T:	In a lighthouse? Where is a lighthouse?
21	V:	In the water.
22	T:	It's definitely in the water.
23	S3:	On a peninsula.
24	T:	Kinda on a peninsula. It's attached to the land but it's mostly on the water.
///		
25	T:	Why is the father going to leave?
26	S4:	He needs to get more food. He needs to get fish.
27	T:	Noooo.
28	V:	He needs TO GO TO TOWN [reading words from the text].
29	T:	Yeah. Why is he going to town? There's a reason.

30	V:	For food.
31	S5:	They have a radio and they'll radio for food.
32	T:	OK. We need to keep moving. They need food, and medicine, and oil to keep the lights burning. John, pick a reader. Vincent.
33	V:	[V reads slowly but smoothly; his articulation and word identification strategies are good. Only twice does T "give" him a word. He seems relaxed and confident, and makes no guttural sounds.]
34	T:	Do you think that was a hard job she had to do?
35	V:	Yeah.
36	T:	Do you think she was kind of afraid?
37	V:	Yeah. [When another child reads, Vince subvocalizes the correct word to check himself.]
38	S6:	". . . WHEN WILL PAT [This was a miscue; the correct word was "Papa"] GET BACK?" ASKED . . .
39	V:	[in a loud whisper to himself; looking at me] PAPA [for Pat]. [During this child's reading, V picks up four miscues and corrects them to himself in a barely audible whisper.]
40	V:	[Raises his hand to be picked again by a peer to read. This time he speeds up as he finishes a page of text.]
///		
41	T:	How did he know [the family was OK]?
42	V:	They were still in the lighthouse.
43	T:	How did he know they were OK?
44	V:	They were in the house.
45	T:	What did he see?
46	V:	Oh . . . the lights.
47	T:	Yes. He saw the lights in the lighthouse.

In this example, Vincent used the various strategies and cues we had discussed to participate competently in the discussion of the reading material. During the first part of the discussion, Vincent responded competently to the teacher's inquiry about the nature of lightning (lines 1, 7, 11). He answered correctly that lightning was a part of the "sky," although this was not the association that the teacher wanted. Vincent had looked up at the ceiling to "see" the lightning, a cue using imagery, to retrieve the word (line 8). Still confident, he volunteered "thunder" (line 13) in response to the additional information cue, i.e., "grumbles and growls" that the teacher provided (line 11).

In the second and third parts of the transcription, the children read aloud, looking for clues in the pictures on the pages. Vincent used the pictures as cues before giving his simple, but correct, answer that the lighthouse was "in the water" (line 21). He also used textual cues to explain why the father was leaving the lighthouse: "to go to town" (line 28). The teacher rephrased questions to help him clarify his answer—"for food" (line 30). Moreover, question prompts (lines 41, 43, 45) and additional time helped him explain that the father knew his family was well when he saw "the lights" in the lighthouse (line 46). During this language interaction, Vincent's language was simple and appropriate. He was not as easily discouraged from answering when challenged (lines 42–47) as he had been in previous months.

Changes in Discourse Participation

At the beginning of the school year, Vincent had begun to withdraw from classroom discourse routines. He needed to practice talking aloud in the classroom. To slowly work toward this, he first subvocalizes as he sought to increase his confidence. He also allowed me to help him. As Phase Two began, the most comfortable setting for our beginning collaborative efforts seemed to be the math "tubbing" activities. During each visit to his classroom, I approached him for short periods of time to accustom him to having me nearby.

In Example 8.11, Vincent wanted to enter a discourse routine but was hesitant, conferring with me for just a brief rehearsal before calling out his answer. This exchange occurred during a teacher-led math recitation in which the teacher used an overhead projector to show joined unifix cubes that represented addition problems.

EXAMPLE 8.11   (February)

1	T:	What is this math fact?
2	V:	[to me] One plus four is five.
3	F:	Tell that. That's right.
4	V:	[doesn't raise his hand]
5	T:	[rearranging the cubes] What is this math fact?
6	V:	[Calls out] Three plus two equals five.
7	T:	[surprised at the calling out, but accepts the answer] That's right.
8	T:	Who can find one "turn-around" [set]?
9	V:	[doesn't raise his hand or react]
10	S:	Two plus three and three plus two.
11	T:	Good, any others?

In this example, Vincent practiced one appropriate answer (line 2) and then vocalized another (line 6). This transitional approach let him check his response and monitor his own participation. Vincent's participation in discourse increased slowly; one or two fluent contributions per class felt reinforcing and safe to him. In this case, the visual images provided by the overhead projector served as cues, helping him to retrieve number names and vocabulary appropriately. Ms. Olsen accepted Vincent's calling out, but it was common knowledge in the classroom that students must wait for the teacher to nominate them before they answer. This introduced a pragmatic problem: knowing the rules for entering and exiting a verbal interaction. Vincent seemed to want to answer as soon as he could think of an appropriate answer.

In a peripheral conference meeting afterward, I reviewed with Vincent more appropriate strategies for joining in a conversation—such as raising his hand or using polite language. I also reiterated that his contributing to classroom conversations let the teacher know that he understood the lesson. My mini-comprehension check, in Example 8.12, verified his understanding of the math concept of "turn-arounds" and gave me a chance to encourage his continued participation.

EXAMPLE 8.12 (February)

1	F:	Good job paying attention and answering [in class].
2	V:	[nods "yes"]
3	F:	Did you understand "turn-arounds" in class?
4	V:	Yes.
5	F:	Show me an example of turn-arounds.
6	V:	[writes $5 + 0 = 5$, $0 + 5 = 5$]
7	F:	You didn't raise your hand, so I didn't know if you understood. The teacher knows who understands by who raises hands and answers. You can let her know that you understand by raising your hand and answering when she asks a question.

In Vincent's small-group reading lessons, children could add their own observations without waiting to be called on. Instead, each child chose a peer randomly, a game they called "Popcorn." This worked well because the children didn't have to wait nervously, and they had to be ready at any time to read. However, to avoid being chosen, Vincent used to hide his eyes, slouch in his chair, or "drop" an object and disappear to locate it.

On the day of the reading lesson presented in Example 8.13, and for several weeks before this, Vincent demonstrated a willingness to participate in reading turns. He entered into the discussions that the teacher initiated concerning locating the main idea of a paragraph in the text.

EXAMPLE 8.13 (April)

1	T:	The next one talks about main idea. Whenever we talk about main idea, we're talking usually about one sentence that describes what the whole paragraph is talking about. All the other sentences are details and they support the main idea. Let's read this first one together.
2	Ss:	[read all together with T leading]
3	T:	Think about that paragraph. Reread it in your head. See if you can pick out what the main idea is. One sentence tells the main idea.
4	S1:	[calls out an answer]
5	T:	That's your guess? That's a good answer, but there's one that does a better job.

6	V:	ABBY WAS A LITTLE AFRAID TO CARE FOR THE LIGHTHOUSE.
7	T:	That's right, Vincent. Very good.
8	S2:	How could that be it?
9	T:	It doesn't have to be the first sentence. It can be anywhere.
10	S2:	But there she's thinking about it. It doesn't tell how she's scared. She's thinking about it.
11	V:	[actively defending his answer] She was afraid.
12	T:	And she was alone. This [referring to his sentence choice] explains it [the theme] the best.

Clearly, Vincent's ability to answer competently and confidently was building, evidenced by his defense of his answer (line 11). In this example, he didn't wait to be selected or appointed by the teacher; he volunteered his answer, which he read aloud from the text as proof (line 6). He did this using an audible voice and without his usual shoulder shrugs to substitute for words he couldn't retrieve quickly. He was also fully engaged in the reading and discussion of the text. He still needed and asked for language help in the classroom, but he was becoming more confident.

Results of the end-of-the-year speech and language evaluation showed positive changes in Vincent's language constructions, and are listed in Figure 8.2. Changes in test scores for language competencies remained at a slightly below average level in the receptive and comprehension areas, but were slowly sliding upward toward age-appropriate levels. Vincent's improved use of word-retrieval strategies was reflected in the standardized test scores, supporting observations in the classroom of his interactions with peers and his teacher. Following months of testing for the presence of a learning disability by the Special Education Department, Vincent was not identified as qualifying for a formal program. His low receptive scores indicated a possible underlying learning disorder that was not clear at this time. The support for successful language and literacy remained with the speech and language pathologist for the next year. Vincent still experienced word-retrieval difficulties, but his secondary problems, such as forced voicing during frustrating episodes, decreased as he interacted more in the classroom and on the school's outdoor fields.

Summary. During this phase of the study, Vincent experienced a new ease in handling language during reading activities and in giving information. In most instances, he used words rather than gestures and shrugs as he interacted verbally in classroom discourse. For example, on one occasion after Vincent had answered a question directed to him by his teacher, a peer commented to me, "He always used to never know, like this" (imitating Vincent's frequent shoulder shrugs).

Not all Vincent's language experiences were smooth. He still sometimes used empty words and substitutions when Ms. Olsen introduced new academic units or when he encountered new vocabulary and content material. However, he had learned to look for clues, ask for help when he really needed it, and trust his own language abilities.

FIGURE 8.2   Speech and Language Assessment Protocol

Student's Name ____Vincent____   Date _____May_____

Student's Homeroom ____Ms. Olsen____   Age/Grade __9 years, 0 months, 2nd__

STUDENT INTERVIEW

Vincent still prefers to work alone in the classroom, with help only from peers. He agrees that "working together in the classroom" with the speech and language teacher and classroom teacher has helped him to "ask better questions." He also states that he appreciates not having to leave the classroom for help all the time.

SPEECH	Test Results:
Informal Deep Testing of speech sounds in words:	76% mastery of /r/ (final position).

LANGUAGE—Comprehensive	Test Results:
Clinical Evaluation of Language Functions— Revised	
Receptive Language:	Standard Score: 78
Expressive Score:	Standard Score: 86

LANGUAGE—Vocabulary	Test Results:
Peabody Picture Vocabulary Test, Form M	Standard Score: 81
Expressive One-Word Picture Vocabulary Test	Standard Score: 90

LANGUAGE—Pragmatics/Problem-Solving	Test Results:
Test of Problem Solving	Standard Score: 52 (mean score of 50)

LANGUAGE—Processing/Word retrieval	Test Results:
Test of Wordfinding in Discourse	
Language Productivity	Standard Score: 89
Wordfinding Behaviors	Standard Score: 91

FLUENCY

No noticeable difficulties.

VOICE

Informal counting tally revealed fewer episodes of forced voicing during classroom discourse.

AUDITORY PERCEPTION—Discrimination/Processing

No medical history of difficulties this school year.

FAMILY/PARENT NOTES

Parents were disappointed that after district testing for a learning disability, Vincent was found not to qualify for special-education services beyond that of speech and language.

TEACHER'S NOTES

Vincent has maintained his placement in the lower reading and math groups. He uses language more appropriately in classroom discourse, but still has some word-retrieval difficulties.

COMMENTS/RECOMMENDATIONS:

Continue classroom-based language and literacy intervention services during next school year.

The teacher's verbal and written accounts of changes in Vincent's language use at the end of the school year supported my own observations that he had progressed in each area of the targeted goals. The modest, but important, gains in academic achievement that accompanied Vincent's increased participation in verbal interaction persuaded his parents to delay further formal testing for other learning disabilities. Vincent would need continued language support in the classroom during the following school year, but he was taking charge of his own participation in classroom discourse.

9 Henry: A Fourth Grader

Student Profile

Henry was the third and oldest child in this study. His language problems first gained his teachers' attention in second grade, when his classroom teacher referred him because of his disfluent pattern of speaking. As I observed him briefly in his classroom, my first impressions were that his breathing was irregular, his language constructions not cohesive, and his phrase reformulations frequent. His parents had also noticed these problems in their home as Henry related school events in a disjointed manner or as he told jokes with awkward rhythm and timing.

Follow-up formal testing of semantic, syntactic, and pragmatic language development revealed age-appropriate competence in language construction. Henry's disfluent language pattern qualified him for special services, which began in November 1990. The foci for remediation included improved breathing rhythm during talking, development of key initiation phrases, and organization of narrative elements. Henry's academic achievement was not a problem at this time. In the resource-room program with two other boys, Henry's fluency and language organization improved. His problems began to take the form of word-retrieval difficulties rather than as dysfluency (stuttering). However, vocabulary enrichment and categorization activities did not help him communicate better in the classroom. His teacher expressed concern about the discrepancy in what she felt he knew and what he shared in classroom discourse.

Henry's medical history was unremarkable. Despite occasional allergic reactions throughout the school year, he took no medication for any health conditions. Henry's younger sister and parents did not exhibit any similar language problems. Figure 9.1 shows the results of Henry's initial speech and language evaluation.

Classroom and Discourse Routines

Henry was a husky, animated fourth grader who actively participated in all classroom activities. He was fairly attentive to teachers and peers, followed directions well, and displayed an average to above-average level of academic achievement in formal and informal evaluations. Much of Henry's use of language in the classroom

FIGURE 9.1   Speech and Language Assessment Protocol

Student's Name _____ Henry _____ Date _____ September _____
Student's Homeroom _____ Ms. Dove _____ Age/Grade __ 9 years, 7 months, 4th __

STUDENT INTERVIEW
Henry noted that he "sometimes forgets words" but that he "really knows them."

SPEECH
No problems observed in classroom discourse. History of misarticulation of th/s (initial position in words) in primary grades.

LANGUAGE—Comprehensive	Test Results:
Clinical Evaluation of Language Functions (Semel & Wiig, 1980)	
*Screening Test	Above Grade/Age Criterion
*Subtest 8: Producing Names on Confrontation	Above Grade/Age Criterion

LANGUAGE—Vocabulary	Test Results:
The Word Test–Revised	Standard Score: 114
Peabody Picture Vocabulary Test–Revised	Standard Score: 113

LANGUAGE—Pragmatics/Problem-Solving
No problems observed.

LANGUAGE—Processing/Word Retrieval	Test Results:
Test of Wordfinding in Discourse (German, 1991)	
Language Productivity	Standard Score: 112
Wordfinding Behaviors	Standard Score: 96

VOICE
Lowered voice in classroom.

AUDITORY PERCEPTION—Discrimination/Processing
No problems noted by nurse, classroom teacher, or SLP.

FAMILY/PARENT NOTES
Parents notice Henry's problems with relating stories in their home. They agree to continue special-education language services, this year in a classroom-based program.

TEACHER'S NOTES
Classroom teacher noted that Henry's difficulties with language expression and self-conscious behavior were negatively affecting his achievement levels.

COMMENTS/RECOMMENDATIONS
Initiate classroom-based language and literacy intervention to support language constructions in discourse.

was interactive; that is, he tried to initiate conversations with peers and asked plenty of questions. Nevertheless, his disfluent language style, especially in classroom discourse, struck teachers and peers as disorganized and appeared to affect his social interactions and self-esteem.

The physical aspects of Henry's classroom changed constantly. His teacher, Ms. Dove, rearranged the desks, including her own, approximately every four weeks as she decided on the configuration that would best meet goals for upcoming curricular units and specific peer interactions. During the first weeks of the school year, the classroom was divided into three sections: an area for all the desks and chairs in the front of the room, arranged in groups of four facing one another; a small-group reading area made up of four long tables pushed together in the back of the room and surrounded by chairs and book shelves; and a smaller, multipurpose area with a table on the other side of the bookshelves, also in the back of the room, used for students' independent quiet work. This arrangement separated groups for reading instruction and quiet seatwork, while allowing the teacher verbal access to any group. Several months later, the room consisted of two main areas: an instructional area with each desk separate from the others and facing forward, and a large table for the small-group teacher-led reading instruction that centered on the back of the room. With the book shelves pushed away from the middle of the room, this latter arrangement created a less crowded, but less collaborative, environment. The children's projects always lined the outer wall of the classroom and partially blocked the door. Content-related informational posters decorated several bulletin boards.

A teacher-aide was available to help individual children and groups with reading problems in the morning and to help the teacher complete clerical tasks in the afternoon. The aide also provided extra help to the four children with learning disabilities in Henry's classroom.

Dynamic Assessment Phase of the Program

Henry was scheduled for sixty minutes of language remediation and support each week, which I divided into two visits to his classroom. I concentrated my time on the two settings in which Henry experienced the most difficulty: small-group basal reading lessons and whole-class content-area discussions. In both settings, teacher-led IRE dominated classroom discourse, leaving few opportunities for student responses longer than one- or two-word phrases. As noted in classroom field notes, Henry seemed more anxious in the daily reading group than in the whole-class discussions, probably because he knew he had to read at least once during his turn and would have to answer comprehension questions. He appeared more comfortable in whole-class discussions because the teacher usually invited only volunteers to answer. In these large discussions, he would join in with an answer when he felt he was prepared, although his language constructions often proved just as awkward and confusing to the teacher and peers as his reading-group contributions did. In these settings, I helped Henry to develop new language strategies that he could use in classroom discourse.

I also helped Henry with language use during selected small-group peer activities in the afternoons. These events focused on project development, such as building an object or writing a paper that was related to a larger unit theme. In working with Henry in this setting, I sought to foster improved language interaction with peers, a goal that was identified in Phase One of the study.

In addition to the classroom-based support I gave Henry, he and I still met for meetings in the halls and occasionally in the resource room. During these sessions, we discussed his problems with word retrieval, compared different situations' level of difficulty for him, and developed strategies for increasing his communication competence in the classroom. Occasionally, I reviewed tape recordings taken from the classroom and used them to give Henry feedback about his language use.

For Henry, as for the other boys in this study, Phase Two began in December of the school year, just before the winter holiday.

Setting Goals

Numerous teachers and the psychologist often described Henry as an underachiever. Several of his previous teachers commented in report-card entries that they viewed his potential academic abilities as higher than he demonstrated in class. His explanations seemed less organized than they expected from him, based on solutions he occasionally offered in class. In Ms. Dove's fourth-grade class, his problems became more obvious.

Ms. Dove asked more questions of Henry than previous teachers had. She expected longer explanations and evidence of more complex reasoning skills, consistent with the increased demands of a fourth-grade class. She used group work and peer interaction to foster the children's own creative ideas. Henry needed help to competently communicate in this classroom.

Based on observations of classroom discourse routines and discussions with Henry, and on suggestions from his classroom teacher, I identified the following language goals:

- develop word-retrieval strategies for more appropriate participation in classroom discourse and more focused explanations;
- eliminate several behaviors that Henry had instituted to mask his language difficulties;
- foster peer interaction to encourage Henry to share his "voice" in classroom decisions.

Henry needed encouragement to accept these goals—he was older than the other two boys in the study and had learned to rely on his own compensatory strategies.

Strategies for Word Retrieval

Henry's frequent word-retrieval problems seemed to make his listeners uncomfortable, judging from the teacher's comments and observations of peers' responses. His word and phrase reformulations elongated and convoluted his responses. His disfluent rhythm and exaggerated gestures diverted attention from his intended message. Henry also changed the pitch of his voice and made animated noises as he qualified his original statements. His body language—unfocused eye contact, subvocalization with shrugs, and continual physical movement—hinted at his own discomfort and defensiveness as he spoke.

Example 9.1 depicts Henry's language difficulties and the confusion they created for the teacher. In this example, the teacher-led reading instruction followed an IRE format, as did most instruction in this classroom. Henry was grouped with nine "average" readers, all of whom were taking turns reading aloud their answers to a comprehension worksheet. A short, teacher-led group discussion of the content material followed.

EXAMPLE 9.1   (September)

1	T:	OK. Good. So, they used the white paint to cover up parts of the burnt house. That's fine. Hands held high . . . Yes, Sue.
2	S:	This is like why the men called it the White House.
3	T:	Right, or called the building the White House. Very good. And that's why you got the name, White House . . . Ed . . . "Designing" [indicating he should read on his worksheet from the word "Designing."]
4	E:	[reads aloud]
5	T:	Excellent. Continue please, Jack.
6	J:	[reads aloud] ELLICOTT'S ASSISTANT WAS . . . LAHVANT.
7	T:	No. Does anybody know who his assistant was? It was in the book. Benjamin . . .
8	S1:	Banaker.
9	T:	Banaker. Very good, Mark. Benjamin Banaker. We'll talk about that later . . .
10	H:	I . . . I . . . kinda understand that . . .
11	T:	You what?
12	H:	I . . . I was . . . That was funny because I was . . . cause I um. . . . I um . . . I was just reading it in um . . . just the last two weeks ago. And I [a few unintelligible words] . . . and it said something about Mr. Banaker.
13	T:	[nodding] Benjamin Banaker? How interesting. Can you tell us anything interesting about him?
14	H:	I think it said something . . . something about . . . about . . . I don't remember . . .
15	T:	That he was an African-American?
16	H:	Yeah. It was about him . . . I don't know . . . saw his name in the newspaper or something . . .
17	T:	How interesting.

18	H:	I . . . I was surprised . . . I didn't read the article. I was just thinking.
19	T:	[Teacher begins to read from her notes, bringing the discussion back to an introduction of key figures.]

An analysis of Henry's discourse revealed difficulties in several areas. He made an awkward attempt to enter the discussion, unappointed by the teacher, with a declarative statement (line 10). He also attempted to initiate a discussion of pertinent new information but lacked details to share (line 12). As this line typified, he generally used "run-on" and often convoluted constructions that distracted his listeners and kept them from understanding his comments (line 12). Henry's syntactic knowledge in this example was appropriate, but his language lacked cohesion. Specifically, he used mostly incomplete phrases punctuated by frequent word reformulations (lines 12, 14, and 16). Moreover, his overuse of the referential pronouns "that" and "it" (lines 12 and 14) caused confusion because they referred to a newspaper article that he didn't mention until several conversational turns later. Also, Henry paused frequently as he spoke, losing the attention of his teacher and extending his turn much longer than the usual allotment. He often lowered his voice so much when he anticipated having difficulty retrieving words (line 12) that others couldn't hear him. After several difficult discourse turns, Henry tried to withdraw from further discussion (line 14). His teacher attempted to continue the conversation, but Henry had little information to add (lines 16 and 18). Intervention would need to focus on more appropriate ways that he could enter classroom discourse and present more organized information.

Although Henry wanted to please his teachers and parents, his language control was slowly slipping, as indicated by changes in his graded assignments from A's to C's on informal classroom assessment. He appeared noticeably self-conscious during extended discourse, using excuses to end conversations early. Clearly, he needed better ways to competently communicate in classroom exchanges. Because he was a fourth grader, I offered him the opportunity to share more of the responsibility for improving his use of language. He initially felt overwhelmed by and defensive about his communication problems, and not as interested in my help as his teacher and I would have preferred. He often "forgot" to come to meetings and to use new strategies in the classroom, offering less-than-substantial excuses and dallying. His resistance would soften, however, early in Phase One. At that point, we began to explore strategies that he considered useful and easy to remember, and he gained some control over his language in classroom discourse.

I gave Henry a simplified but through explanation of word-retrieval difficulties and related expressive language disorders to help him focus on his language problems and understand the reasons behind the strategies I was proposing. Until this school year, my approach to language remediation for Henry had rested predominantly on his vocabulary and categorical organization of knowledge. But he now needed different strategies to use this knowledge in everyday classroom exchanges. I decided to develop these strategies on two levels:

- heightening Henry's awareness of his word-retrieval habits and of cues that he, his classroom teacher, and I could use to facilitate his verbal expression. (These techniques drew from Richard and Hanner's work (1987) on language processing for word-retrieval facilitation.)
- addressing appropriate language strategies for use in the classroom.

Example 9.2 depicts the use of several of these strategies—taking additional time, repeating what had just been said at the beginning of a construction, asking or responding to related questions, providing additional information about the subject, and repeating or reading a word. I had explained and demonstrated each of these to Henry in the resource room, while referring to an audiotaped replay of a small-group reading lesson taken in Henry's class. I wanted him to learn to use these strategies during real classroom talk.

EXAMPLE 9.2   (September)

1	F:	You had trouble getting started [on your answer]. Use phrases. Answer in phrases. You have to try it and tell me if it's better [than using single words].
2	H:	You mean [writes horizontal lines on the blackboard to represent words] it's going along like this, and then this and this [drawing the representation of cloze exercises in a paragraph].
3	F:	Those are "fill-in" sentences. That's how you're trying to answer. And that's where you're having trouble. You could have said, "Being American means apple pie." [I refer to the tape-recorded playback.]
4	H:	Sometimes I do that.
5	F:	Yes, you do and it works well when you do.
6	H:	Yeah. Because I said, "being patriotic."
7	F:	It's easier to "fill-in" when the answer is predictable. Problems occur when the answers aren't predictable.
8	H:	But she [his teacher] calls on me sometimes when I'm not raising my hand.
9	F:	I know, and that's when . . .
10	H:	I'm thinking and she goes, "Henry?"
11	F:	These are five things you can do. I explained these strategies to your teacher, but I haven't told you yet. Here they are [beginning a written list]. One, give yourself additional time to think and answer.
12	H:	OK, the teacher calls on me . . . [gestures as in "What do I do next?"]
13	F:	Is she trying to get you to participate or just calling on you for the answer?
14	H:	I participate in class.
15	F:	What do you do when the teacher calls on you and you're not ready?
16	H:	Stall a little, ramble on . . .
17	F:	Well, then you get lost. Wait and think, and then use a longer phrase.
18	H:	[relaxes and pauses, then . . .] An American is a great person. An American is . . . pretty fair. Being American is . . . giving rights.
19	F:	Strategy Number Two: Repeat the question or comment again to yourself to rethink it, or ask the teacher to repeat the question. You can do this to yourself. [I model.] "What is being an American? Being an American is . . ."

20	H:	. . . Saturday night!
21	F:	I guess that's a joke. When you're with a lot of people, you can go faster. Remember, you can always ask the teacher to repeat the question.
22	H:	Everyone will laugh then.
23	F:	[shake my head "no"] Strategy Number Three: Ask yourself something else about what you wanted to say: "When did it happen?" "Where did it happen?" Or rephrase the question. Or, Strategy Number Four: Picture the word or think of other characteristics about the word or idea.
24	H:	Some . . . something . . . s . . . something . . . some . . . usually I . . . um . . . when I think of America, all of a sudden this big American flag just slaps into my mind with Superman.
25	F:	Oh, then say that: "When I think of an American, I picture an American flag."
26	H:	I always think of him standing in front of an American flag one day [hums patriotic music].
27	F:	So you give yourself information by thinking it in your head or thinking of something else about it. [modeling out loud] "Well, let's see, it looks like . . ." or "I remember doing this at the time" or "It means the same as . . ."
28	H:	I got . . . I got my picture with Superman on the trip.
29	F:	What trip?
30	H:	On my California trip.
31	F:	Real Superman?
32	H:	He was in his ice cave . . . except it was just the Wax Museum.
33	F:	Oh . . . OK. And last comes Strategy Number Five: Look at the answer if you can in the book or repeat it after the teacher. That's the hardest one, just saying the word.
34	H:	That's hard. [changing the topic] Actually, I got my picture in the paper with a lot of guys.
35	F:	[I nod to acknowledge his remark but continue with strategies.] I want you to look over these. We'll go over them another time again.
36	H:	OK.

In this example, Henry tried to use or relate to the new facilitation cues in some meaningful way following many of the strategy explanations. He used the additional time cue by practicing pausing rather than freezing or rushing to retrieve an appropriate word (line 18). He remarked that question repetition would bring negative peer attention (line 22), but added to my modeled sentence for lighthearted practice. To cue using additional information, Henry explained how he could associate the flag in the form of imagery of being an American (line 24). He continued to associate images as he connected Superman to his recent trip to California (line 28). I acknowledged this digression but tried not to encourage it beyond four turns.

Question prompts offered another way for Henry to provide additional information. I modeled a rephrased version of the original question (line 25) for his future reference. Using naming cues, or simple repetition of the word in imitation or after reading the word, proved the most difficult approach, according to Henry (line 34). Although he did seem to attend to the new strategies, he clearly felt uncomfortable talking at length about them, as evidenced by his digressions or topic changes (for example, his returning to the subject of Superman and his trip to California). However, the purpose of this discussion was to expose him to these approaches. By rereading the list at a later, more private time, he could internalize the information. His comments and actions during the meeting described in Example 9.2, along with other similar times, indicated that he still felt very self-conscious about discussing his language.

Taped discussions revealed that, in general, Henry had fewer word-retrieval difficulties in small-group, pull-aside discussions than he did in whole-class discussions. These activities thus let him rehearse for real classroom conversations, boosted his motivation, and helped him to use strategies with my support before trying them in the classroom. For example, in one resource-room meeting, Henry and three peers practiced making presentations to one another that they would later give in front of the class. His slower pace during this rehearsal facilitated his word retrieval and contributed to the fluent nature of his eventual presentation.

Elimination of Related Behaviors

Henry had developed several secondary language and behavioral problems related to his primary ones. For example, to complete his responses quickly, he spoke very quietly during classroom discourse and often slurred or rushed his speech. Usually, his listeners then needed him to clarify his comments. Moreover, to avoid running into language difficulties in the first place, he limited his vocabulary to general words (for example, "thing"). He also used exaggerated arm movements, facial gestures, and vocal variations as he talked, probably to draw attention away from his language.

In addition, Henry made poor eye contact with others or feigned misunderstanding of the subject ("I don't think I know that"), to divert attention away from himself. To compensate for his lack of control over the fluency of his language, he purposefully digressed, or completely changed the topic of conversation, during his extended explanations. Though Ms. Dove emphsized the importance of a clear, persuasive presentation during delivery of reports in class, Henry found it difficult to achieve those qualities. When asked to explain his point of view, to present a report to the class, or to describe an incident in a story, he often added an attention-getting joke or "clowned around" with exaggerated sounds or gestures. In most instances, these interruptions were inappropriate. I thus decided to help Henry stay "on topic" and to take turns entering conversations. Small-group discussions and demonstrations practiced in the resource room with a few classroom peers set the stage for whole-class presentations in the classroom.

Many children with expressive language disorders demonstrate the above behaviors (Richard & Hanner, 1987). Henry's problems distracted his listeners, and drew taunts from peers and reprimands from teachers. During two meetings with him, we discussed eight new strategies that I believed could help him. This first meeting occurred during Phase One. Helping Henry to use these strategies in the classroom was difficult, because he lacked the patience to analyze his language. Judging from his exaggerated facial expressions and occasional comments, he still felt that the teacher completely controlled the use of language in the classroom. I explained to him that he could have control and still work within the teacher's routines.

Example 9.3 provides an excerpt of a meeting that Henry and I had in the hall just outside the classroom. The conversation was an extension of the previous classroom discourse, but in a more isolated environment.

EXAMPLE 9.3   (January)

1	F:	[speaking slowly] Today I thought we could continue the conversations you were having [in the classroom] about the big news on TV . . .
2	H:	[talking quickly] . . . the inauguration.
3	F:	[slowly] Yes. Did you watch it?
4	H:	[quickly] Yeah. Do you want to see baby calluses [referring to cuts on his hands]?
5	F:	What did you . . .
6	H:	Those are really cuts.
7	F:	What did you think about it? First, remember, we've been talking about articulating more slowly, explaining more carefully . . .
8	H:	I'm not very happy with Clinton.
9	F:	. . . and using smaller phrases and sentences to explain details.
10	H:	I'm not really happy with Bill Clinton and that.
11	F:	Really, why not?
12	H:	Well, I'm not happy with the things that make fun of them. Because already they've been saying things.
13	F:	You're not happy with him or with the people that make fun of him?
14	H:	The people that make fun of him.
///		[He recounts several songs and stories that he has heard about Bill Clinton, using a disfluent language pattern full of reformulations and word repetitions.]
15	F:	Let's stop a minute. Before we go any further, let's review the strategies I already told you to remember as you talk. Things I've given you to remember are [I read from a list I had placed in his workbook folder while H looks away from me in a nervous, self-conscious manner] to articulate your sounds more clearly, remember to use eye contact to stay focused, use phrases and shorter sentences, and use the real words. That's one, two, three, four things to remember.
16	H:	I taped Superman last night.
17	F:	. . . and here's number five: "Keep your hands and feet as still as possible." That's because you are easily distracted by all your movements in your chair. When you're "playing around" with a book and talking, you can't really keep your mind on what you're saying. It's hard to stay on the topic. Even now, you're on your knees and you're moving back and forth.
18	H:	[straightens out his posture]

19	F:	The whole idea is to have nothing else to think about except what you're talking about. Clinton used his hands a little today on TV, but only when he really had something that he wanted to . . .
20	H:	. . . get out.
21	F:	Yes, to emphasize.
22	H:	The inauguration is over, now they party.
23	F:	There are still important meetings also. But there is a party.

In this example, Henry identified the topic (line 2) that was presented in his classroom, yet he quickly tried to change it to the calluses on his hands (lines 4 and 6). Henry used this strategy frequently in conversation. He obviously had more control over his vocabulary if he could control the topic of conversation.

As I tried to return to the original topic, I also began to review a new way of conversing (lines 7 and 9). However, Henry clearly did not want to discuss the recommended strategies, nor did he try to practice them. He used rushed language even after I reminded him to slow down (line 7) and to shorten his sentences (line 9). He continued to talk about Bill Clinton in general terms. I followed his lead (lines 11 and 13), modeling preferred, subtle behaviors such as keeping my hands in my lap and using careful, slower phrasing while moving forward with my ideas. Henry's attempt to sit up straighter in his chair (line 17) and then to complete my comments (line 18) indicated that he was listening to my suggestions. Earlier in the discussion I had asked him to clarify the unclear referents or general terms he used ("they" and "things" in line 12). He "picked up" my cues from the previous sentence and expressed himself more clearly (line 14).

Fostering Peer Interaction

With more observation and feedback on Henry's efforts in whole-group class discussion, I began to notice that he also found discourse in small groups awkward. For example, he did not often initiate ideas or suggest changes in a group-developed project. Moreover, he attempted to enter conversations usually by joking or making self-deprecating comments—"You probably wouldn't want to know this . . ." or "We could . . . nah, that's dumb." Yet Henry had good suggestions and smart ideas for implementing them, as evidenced by the information he shared with me privately. He needed to learn that he could share his ideas and to do so more aggressively.

Example 9.4 provides details from a discussion following a classroom activity. All the children had been divided into groups of three or four participants with the task of developing and organizing a colony of settlers. This activity served as part of a larger unit focusing on the experiences of the first American colonists. In Henry's small group, he and his two co-planners sat together on the floor creating unrealistic situations, joking about the characters and materials, disregarding the teacher's continued reminders to brainstorm and write information on paper, and creating noise that distracted the other children.

EXAMPLE 9.4   (November)

1	F:	[signaling to Henry as the activity time ends and the children disperse] I want to talk to you alone for a few minutes. We can go to the end of the hall [just outside the door, but not too conspicuous to passers-by].
2	H:	Science is going to start.
3	F:	I know. We can talk about what we did, what you did in there.
4	H:	I'm just going to leave the colony to them.
5	F:	Why?
6	H:	'Cause.
7	F:	You don't have to leave the colony up to them, or the decisions. You don't seem to understand that you have great ideas.
8	H:	Yeah, but the majority will always be over me.
9	F:	Why do you say that? Why would the majority be over you? Grab some chairs. It's important that you put your input, your information, into every conversation.
10	H:	Yeah . . .
11	F:	You have good ideas.
12	H:	Yeah, but the whole majority will always be over me.
13	F:	Why is that?
14	H:	Because it does. I don't like football, and they like football. So . . .
15	F:	But that has nothing to do with the colony.
16	H:	Yes it does, because they're going to name it after football stars.
17	F:	Then you have to compromise.
18	H:	Oh, have to compromise? Well . . .
19	F:	For example . . .
20	H:	We'd vote. We were going to vote, but then I just saw that they were going to win because it was two against one, so I just . . .
21	F:	The whole conversation wasn't about football. In the first place, you [boys] didn't make a map. If you followed the teacher's directions, the goals that she sets, then you can set goals for yourself. For example, all you had to know when you divided up, the first thing you had to do . . . remember, we talked about being organized . . . is write down what you had to do. Before you move around, before you stand up. Write down what you had to do. Then you will remember more of the words and it will be easier. But when things are out in the open, in the abstract, it's hard for you to figure out what you need to do and say. It's hard for you to use language easily. The whole idea is to use language easily, to be able to just say what you want. But there are things you have to be in control of. We talked about these.
22	H:	[moves around in his chair] Well, uh, this seat . . .
23	F:	Are you uncomfortable in the seat? What did I say about listening?
24	H:	Well, I . . . [mumbles to himself]
25	F:	Then you say, "Mrs. Ross, this seat is uncomfortable. May I please switch or have another one?" And in the classroom, you need to get what you need. You have to ask for paper or whatever you need to do the job.
26	H:	The majority always rules over me and they were going to get the paper.
27	F:	You have to have a voice. You want to have control of your language and what you do. Go to the teacher. Take your time and ask for the paper. I am sure she

		will give you paper or tell you where to get some. You need paper to organize what you're thinking. If, then, some of the boys start to "kid around," then someone's got to say . . . what?
28	H:	[shrugs]
29	F:	"Let's get down to business." What were your goals again? That the teacher gave you?
30	H:	Get a name, new or old [meaning modern or similar to the original colonists], draw a map.
31	F:	Those are your goals. When the teacher tells you what to do, those become your goals. Write them down as soon as you hear them and follow them. You have to take charge. When I was watching, you were letting the others do the talking; you were dropping things on the floor; you weren't paying attention. The most important things are to pay attention and participate. You have to do most of this yourself. I can't follow you around.
32	H:	OK.

Henry's comments that ". . . the majority always rules over me" (lines 8, 12, 20, and 26) implied that he had ideas to contribute but not the power to express them clearly or to convince others of their value. Henry's slow starts and phrase reformulations made it difficult for him to assert himself. In our conversation, I tried to support his ideas and the importance of his language input and personal "voice" in discourse. We did not directly deal with language forms but rather with the need to remain focused on the topic and the importance of following through with the assignment. These suggestions were intended to lend structure to the language Henry would use, facilitating his word retrieval and communication competence.

Summary

The examples above and evaluative information showed that Henry's word-retrieval problems took the form of word and phrase reformulations and insertions of closely related words. He often exhibited "starters," or unfinished syllable initiations. These suggested that he intended to construct a response, but they were distracting to his listeners. His vocal quality was either very soft or very animated, both styles drawing attention away from the words he used. At times, he would continue talking in spite of his language struggles, determined to be included. At other times, he would withdraw ("Never mind") when his listener asked for further clarification. Henry was not as successful in his attempts to participate as he would have liked. Henry had tried throughout his four years of grade school to develop his own language strategies for participation in classroom discourse. As he entered the fourth grade, his teacher sensed his struggles. Henry's constructions appeared disorganized and unprepared. When he knew that his message was unclear, he tried to simplify it but still needed to clarify details. He digressed from the topic when he wanted to share a personal experience because he was more fluent with what he perceived as the less formal organization required in personal narratives. He was beginning to draw negative attention and remarks from friends and peers.

Intervention Phase of the Language Support Program

At first, Henry had been defensive about receiving help in the classroom, explaining to me that "I can do it alone. I think I know it now." He had been used to an isolated resource approach to practicing vocabulary through categorization activities and games. He had received negative remarks from teachers in the past concerning his apparent lack of focus when he answered in class, although his written work and essay responses were always well organized and complete. Now, after three months in the fourth grade, he felt overwhelmed in the classroom and did not think he could remember new cues. Yet Henry was willing to listen to my suggestions in a few pull-aside meetings.

Owing to a more positive attitude and the social interactions of his fourth grade classmates, Henry now had an interest in working to improve his language strategies and skills. He understood the cues as they would occur in the classroom, responding to them when I tried to help him or when the teacher sensed his language struggles. All language support would now be provided in the classroom, where his discourse participation could be meaningful and motivating.

Changes in Language Support

Henry's informal comments to me suggested that he considered himself a fairly social fourth grader ("I want to talk in class. I like to have friends."). Although he worked independently and quietly at his desk, he enjoyed exchanging jokes at lunchtime, entering peer recess activities, and working in organized small groups. His behavioral responses indicated that he was especially sensitive to his peers' often negative reactions to his language problems in classroom activities and he stated his worry that a language support program in the classroom might draw additional attention toward his language difficulties. However, when we began he was comfortable with my presence in the room near him, with my quiet comments between activity routines, and with our individual conferences within the room, but he was not comfortable with any clueing or cueing I offered during classroom language exchanges. During Phase One of the study, he did not volunteer to answer the teacher's questions when I was present.

As a compromise, we agreed that I would visit him in his classroom on Mondays and Thursdays, sitting next to or near his chair but "not all the time." I used mostly nonverbal cues, such as gesturing or facial movements, with follow-up discussions just after each visit. I carefully selected those days in which I would remain next to him and use more obvious support strategies, such as rephrased questions, modeling, and word cueing. Most of my language support occurred before verbal exchanges with the teacher as reminders and after the exchange as feedback, in anticipation of his assuming responsibility for self-monitoring during the rest of the year.

Our initial individual conferences, or discussions, concerned the specifics of working together in the classroom. I assured Henry that my intention was not to increase the pressure he felt when he talked in class by drawing attention to his remarks, but, instead, to decrease his difficulties by developing strategies and providing support. Example 9.5 is an excerpt from one of these discussions, which in this case took the form of a classroom aside following a geography recitation.

EXAMPLE 9.5   (January)

1	F:	Before we finish today, I want to ask you about school. How is school going? Any problems?
2	H:	It's OK.
3	F:	It's going well?
4	H:	Yeah.
5	F:	Good. You've been so quiet these days, but you've been answering exactly right [in class]. You haven't had any trouble with the words, getting the words. You haven't used as many of your old habits, where you would say, "Well, mm . . . well . . . I'm not sure." You just raised your hand, gave the right answer . . . it was perfect. And you gave the right meaning for the word. For example, if the teacher said, "What does a dog do?" you'd say [in the past], "Well . . . I've seen a dog and I have a story about a dog" instead of saying, "A dog barks." Sometimes, before, your answers would not be on target. They didn't always answer the question. But now that's changed. And I think you weren't wiggling around so much. That was excellent. What were the other things you were trying to do?
6	H:	[shrugs]
7	F:	Staying focused, you've done that. Not wiggling, that's better. Oh, give a good answer right away and then add details. You did that when I was watching. I'm going to do that a few more times. I'll come in your classroom and watch to see how it's all going. Then, if you have problems we need to work on, we can discuss them when we're alone.
8	H:	OK. I'm taking medicine that makes me "hyper" as a side effect [to explain wiggling] . . . for allergies.
9	F:	Just for allergies?
10	H:	[nods "yes!"]
11	F:	Thanks for telling me. I'll call your mom tomorrow about it.

In this example, I provided feedback concerning Henry's language use in the classroom (line 5) and indirectly reminded and remotivated him to keep using new language strategies (line 7). Henry still needed help breaking his old language habits. He needed an explanation of the metalinguistic process that he should use to incorporate the new strategies into his everyday language exchanges. His comment that he didn't know what he was doing (line 6) was probably not far from the truth, owing to his self-conscious attitude.

Henry knew that his language problems were interfering with his social acceptance in the classroom ("Sometimes they make fun of me") and his academic performance ("She [the teacher] doesn't wait for me to answer—I know it [the answer]"). But he also knew that his usual defensive attitude toward teachers and adults was no longer effective and admitted that he needed help ("I can really get mixed up"). During occasional small-group resource-room meetings, he invited two of his classroom friends to join us. These friends had similar expressive problems. The resource-room sessions gave them a chance to discuss common struggles and practice new language strategies before "risking" these in the classroom environment. The three boys were also able to "vent" their complaints about teachers' and peers' language habits, for which we discussed appropriate responses. Finally, they learned about each others' language problems, an experience that gave them emotional and language support during school activities.

Henry's teacher, Ms. Dove, expressed an interest in helping Henry. She did not change her expectations for him, hoping to anticipate and adapt to his language problems early in the school year before his negative behaviors became habitual. She felt confident that she would be able to use several of the language-facilitation strategies I had explained to her to help Henry participate in verbal exchanges more appropriately and fluently. This was a difficult undertaking in the beginning of the school year but became easier with time. Example 9.6, from a classroom recitation combining science and social-studies material, shows the teacher's involvement.

EXAMPLE 9.6   (March)

1	T:	Air that moves over the Earth is called . . . Henry? [H has not raised his hand.]
2	H:	[He gestures, moving his hands. He can't find the word; T has asked too fast, and he's unprepared. Gives no verbal response.]
3	T:	[to the class] Everyone together.
4	H:	[with the class] Wind.
///		
5	T:	What were my main ideas today? [points at H, using another question prompt] What was I trying to tell about?
6	H:	[barely audible] Transportation.
7	T:	[another question prompt] What about transportation?
8	H:	What they used.
9	T:	Yes, what they used to travel.

Although Ms. Dove didn't give Henry enough time to respond at first (lines 1 and 2) she subsequently used the naming technique to ask the class to respond (line 3) to the question she had originally posed only to Henry (line 1). She also used question prompts to expand his answer about transportation (line 7), and then provided an expansion of her own as a further model (line 9). She repeated this technique often in future weeks.

Through modeling, I reintroduced word-retrieval strategies in individual asides and discussions, but it was difficult to incorporate these in the classroom without the teacher's help. In Example 9.7, Ms. Dove supported Henry's language again, this time by allowing him the additional time he needed to express himself and by accepting his answer for its content if not for its form. In this small-group reading discussion, the teacher had stopped the reading aloud in order to expand on the concept of "advertising," which was central to the story's meaning. She complemented the discourse with occasional writing on the blackboard, providing lists of key words in the text.

EXAMPLE 9.7   (March)

1	T:	How is choosing a job like choosing clothes?
2	S1:	You have to fit in it.
3	T:	Yes, it has to be right for your needs.
4	H:	Wha . . . If . . . You . . . [slowly] When you pick out clothes, you pick out want you want, and sometimes they're expensive and sometimes they're not. [gestures with his head] OK . . . now if . . . OK . . . let's . . . Well, if clothes fit you but they may be too expensive to get, and a job may be a lot of money.
6	T:	OK. Good analogy.
///		[Other children offer examples.]
7	T:	What can you do to advertise? [looking at Henry, whose hand is raised] What do you need to include when you advertise?
8	H:	We . . . well . . . um . . . maybe . . . like . . . um . . . Put your number up?
9	T:	Yes. Include your phone number in the information you provide.

In our individual conferences, I had encouraged Henry to risk experiencing some difficulty with word retrieval in an effort to share his ideas and knowledge. He tried to do this in the above example (line 8). Successful experiences prompted him to continue trying to complete an answer in a more competent form. Henry's teacher allowed him to answer in another form, if he chose to. In the second part of the lesson, Ms. Dove helped Henry cue himself by rephrasing her question (line 7) and then confirming and rephrasing his answer (line 9). Continued use of the new language techniques was slowly helping Henry to share his knowledge of content information with the class.

Changes in Use of Language Strategies

Henry's most fragile period, reflected in his language, work habits, and self-esteem, came when we first tried to change his language constructions in the classroom in

December. Although he knew that he had problems with his word and phrase refor- mulations, he worried about letting go of the strategies he had developed over time. Henry found it difficult to discuss his language problems, attributing them to causes not within his direct control; for example, a reaction to his allergy medication (see Example 9.5). Hyperactive reactions and other behaviors may have stemmed from the medication, but these constituted only minor parts of his language difficulties in the classroom.

Henry benefited greatly from rehearsals of upcoming presentations and verbal summaries of classroom content material. Neither his classroom nor his home, he explained, lent themselves to practice or out-loud review. For Henry, then, indi- vidual meetings in the classroom or nearby hall offered the only opportunities for him to ease into the language requirements of the classroom. It was here that he first gained confidence to use his language strategies and received positive feedback. During January through March, the exact wording of his language was not as impor- tant as his attempts to achieve a fluency of speech with which he felt comfortable.

Example 9.8 comes from a peripheral meeting in the hall between Henry and me. We verbally reviewed the material presented in a classroom lecture during that day. Our goal was to help Henry focus on the main ideas and to elaborate when necessary. This approach helped Henry to simplify his remarks.

EXAMPLE 9.8   (April)

1	F:	Tell me about the American Revolution. You could tell about whatever aspect you choose, but begin with a summary topic and then keep giving more details.
2	H:	Well, it was called the shot heard 'round the world. And it was uh . . . it was when the uh . . . it was in Lexington. When the British were walking in they had a lot of . . . a lot of . . . uh . . . people and the colonists were in their way. So they told them . . . they told them to get out of the way. They fired and . . . uh . . . the British started firing at the colonists and the colonists started firing at them. So uh . . . that's how it all started.
3	F:	What were they angry about? Why were they shooting at each other?
4	H:	Because they were . . . because King George was uh taxing them for every- thing. For tea and all.
5	F:	You know, you're not wiggling, you're calmer than usual, and you're ap- proaching this in a very organized way. This is a big improvement over the way you would explain everything that you discussed. Have you been doing this in class, too?
6	H:	Yeah.
7	F:	Do you think it's getting a little easier?
8	H:	[smiling and nodding] Mmm hmmm.
9	F:	Have you been trying to stay calm, focused, and give a topic summary?
10	H:	[smiling broadly] Umm hmmm.
11	F:	You have? OK. Why don't you talk about another topic?

The goals mentioned in this interaction—shifting less in his seat, approaching language more calmly, and organizing ideas more carefully (line 5)—were briefly reviewed in this meeting and others. That way, they would be clear enough for Henry to attempt in his regular classroom when I referred to them. I hoped that remembering these strategies would help Henry begin replacing the more inappropriate compensations he was using, such as changing the topic and "clowning around" with acceptable language.

In spite of his protests, Henry benefited from our discussions, as Example 9.9 shows. In this conversation, Henry and I were sitting just outside the classroom door in the hallway. We discussed the class period before our meeting, when the teacher had introduced a portion of a book she had been reading aloud to the class for the past few days. As she began to ask questions to review the events that had occurred in the story from the previous day, Henry started shuffling busily in his chair, possibly to avoid being called on. In the peripheral meeting, captured in Example 9.9, I again urged him to use several new strategies that we had discussed during the previous week.

EXAMPLE 9.9   (April)

1	F	Do you know the author's name?
2	H:	[pauses] No, I don't. She keeps . . . She [teacher] told us a million times . . . I keep forgetting it.
3	F:	That's all right. At least you stopped [to think] when you said that. Do you remember our rules [goals] offhand? If you can tell me what the rules are, those that you're trying . . .
4	H:	OK.
5	F:	. . . then I'll know that you're trying at least one or two at a time, and I'll know what's going on when I observe or listen or help you in class.
6	H:	OK.
7	F:	OK. So what are they?
8	H:	You shouldn't go, y'know, be saying, "Going like that."
9	F:	Right. You should use real words instead of "that" or "going like that," or showing what you're doing, you should just say . . .
10	H:	Use the real words.
11	F:	Use the real words. OK. That's one rule. Great. What's another one? I think we had eight.
12	H:	Another rule would be "Keep still while talking."
13	F:	Keep still, perfect. What are you doing now?
14	H:	Keeping still.
15	F:	More than usual, yes. That's all I can ask.
16	H:	Um . . ."Put your answers in phrases."
17	F:	Yes. Do you know what you did a minute ago? You said, "Another rule is . . ." That was a good way to say it. And that helped you move through it. You're using phrases.
18	H:	[smiling to himself] Gee!

19	F:	Unbelievable!

19 F: Unbelievable!

20 H: I'm not even noticing that I'm using phrases!

21 F: And you're doing a good job.

22 H: Wow. That's weird.

23 F: OK. It's working! Keep going.

24 H: OK. I don't know if I can remember all of them.

25 F: That's all right.

26 H: 'Cause there are eight, but . . .

27 F: That's OK. I just want you to get to know and use some of them.

28 H: Those are the three I've been working on a lot. As you can see, I'm doing better.

29 F: [looking right in his face] That's a hint.

30 H: Eye contact.

31 F: Yes. Watching the person. You've been good about that today, too. You seem a little calmer today.

32 H: That's because I'm having a good day. I can't think of other rules.

33 F: Think of what you do that gets you into trouble.

34 H: I don't think about what I'm saying it?

35 F: Organizing your thoughts, that would be good. I was thinking of your use of run-on sentences.

36 H: I don't do that so much now.

37 F: You've been working on it, have you?

38 H: I don't do it.

39 F: Great.

40 H: Also, when I'm playing with my toys, that go around and move, I don't say, "They're going like that." I tell what they're doing. Even when I'm alone and playing, talking, I don't say it.

41 F: You use the real words. Great. That's up to six [rules].

42 H: Let's see. "Find a comfortable position."

43 F: That's like stay still in your seat. That's good.

44 H: I've been thinking of what I've been doing in school and how I'm improving. Maybe I can think of more.

45 F: If you can remember and use these, you're doing fine. Use these to concentrate when you talk and when you write.

46 H: I was writing the other day and I heard a sound. I thought the world was coming to an end. That's another one, "Stay on subject."

47 F: Stay on the topic.

48 H: Sorry about that.

49 F: It's OK. When you're talking, I don't want you to be thinking about these things every minute. I want these to make your talking easier. Then there's less to worry about. Think about what you want to say and then say it as simply, and as completely, and as quickly, or concisely, as you can . . .

50 H: One number, I think it's three? [pointing to the list I had made during our previous meeting when we developed the strategies together] really helped me a lot . . .

51 F: Putting your answers in phrases. That helped you a lot. Great.

52 H: Yeah. That really helped. So did number one . . .

53	F:	Using real words
54	H:	I haven't been using "it's, "that's," and all. Actually, I think number one and number . . . five . . .
55	F:	Don't use run-on sentences.
56	H:	Yeah. I haven't been doing that. And I use real words.
57	F:	Good. You just said, "This one, number five," not just, "This one."
58	H:	Good, I'm changing my speech. You know what else is helping me? The play [the class will be putting on a play for the school]. Saying all those lines without a lot of "it's," "that's," and run-on sentences.
59	F:	Then you have a good model.
60	H:	Yeah.

In this example, the focus of our meeting shifted from the classroom discourse to Henry's review of important language goals he had remembered to use. These included less use of ambiguous, vague referential terms, such as pronouns without antecedents (lines 8 and 10), increased attention when talking (line 12), construction of language in a larger context (line 20), eye contact with the listener (line 30), and maintaining of his topic focus in discourse (line 46). In addition, Henry provided examples of his own self-monitoring in school and at home. As he discussed these goals and his awareness of them in language interactions, he realized how well he was doing (line 58). He had an extra motivation to carefully self-monitor because he had an important role in the upcoming school play.

During classroom routines, my physical presence and emotional support served as reminders for Henry to experiment with various language strategies and cueing systems that we had discussed and practiced. Ms. Dove knew of all the children's individual differences and needed only a few hints to draw Henry into conversations and encourage his answers. During the second week of the school year, I had explained the five general cueing techniques that have proved useful for facilitating the language of children with word-retrieval and language-processing difficulties. Initially Ms. Dove and I used these to support Henry's language in discourse. Eventually Henry used them to self-monitor his language in the classroom.

Example 9.10 shows the use of word-retrieval strategies in the classroom. This excerpt comes from a small-group reading lesson during which the children read aloud and discussed parts of the text together. The class was reading "Day of the Earthling" from their basal reader. The story was about an earthling on Mars who "hungers" to learn about his homeland and possibly to return to it.

EXAMPLE 9.10   (February)

1	S1:	[reading aloud] PATRIOT ONE . . .
2	T:	What is Patriot One?
3	H:	[raises hand anxiously] The spaceship.
4	T:	The spaceship, good.

///		[Students take turns reading aloud for ten minutes.]
5	S2:	[reading] ALEX CARVER AND JOSSEY JOHNSON WERE . . .
6	T:	Who are Alex and Jossey? Who are they, Henry?
7	H:	They're spacemen.
8	T:	Spacemen, yes. Or they're astronauts, right?
9	H:	Right.
///		
10	S3:	I don't understand what's going on.
11	T:	Someone explain to Carol what's going on. Henry.
12	H:	There's something in his helmet.
13	S3:	Why is he ignoring it?
14	T:	OK. Henry, who are they talking about?
15	H:	They're talking about the spacemen. Y'see he wants . . . um . . . he wants them . . . um. . . to um to land safely . . .
16	S3:	Doesn't he want to figure out about them or what?
17	H:	Well, he just wants to figure out about them and he doesn't want his own kind to die.
18	T:	Right. Exactly.
19	H:	Everything in this story sounds kind of real, y'know?
20	T:	Yes, it does.

In this exchange, Ms. Dove used question repetition when asking about the two space travelers (line 6). Then she "corrected" the word "astronauts" for Henry's "spacemen" (line 8) but not without giving Henry the chance to agree that "astronauts" would be an acceptable word to him (line 9). She knew that he enjoyed this science-fiction story, and helped strengthen his language contributions. Henry also found cues to help himself by expanding on other children's language; for instance, he extended Student 3's question to explain the story line to her (line 17). Henry's short responses were very accurate, clear, and organized (lines 7, 9, 12). And although he experienced difficulties as he rushed to explain about the spacemen (line 15), he continued with his comments slowly, instead of constantly using reformulations. His language contributions in this discussion showed marked improvement over those of the past, and he felt more relaxed and invested in the discussion.

Changes in Discourse Participation

Reluctant to enter classroom discourse in December, Henry made careful, controlled attempts to participate. He had many ideas and experiences that he said he wanted to share, but he had withheld in the past. He would share these if he could do so without "messing up."

Example 9.11 depicts a typical early classroom activity and his participation in it. Before the teacher called on Henry to respond, the class was quietly sharing their answers to worksheet questions that extended the reading skills mentioned in the text. Henry sat at his desk, shuffling papers and looking away from the teacher's glances. He had probably assumed or hoped that she would not call on him until he had located his worksheet or was looking up at her. However, this strategy didn't work for him that day.

EXAMPLE 9.11 (December)

1	T:	What airport is nearest to Culver City?
2	S1:	Santa Monica?
3	T:	Exactly. Santa Monica Transport Airport. Number seven, Henry.
4	H:	I didn't get this done.
5	T:	Why not?
6	H:	I didn't have any time to do this in school.
7	T:	What about last week when you were supposed to do it?
8	H:	I don't know.
9	T:	Number seven, Henry. You can still answer the question. What is the name of the freeway numbered? Picture the freeway numbered one hundred ten, find it . . .
10	H:	[just picks a line, hardly looking to find the correct highway; is nervous because he probably thought the teacher would skip him] San Diego Freeway?
11	T:	Actually, go up a little bit more. You're going south.
12	F:	[to H] Let's go north. You touch it.
13	H:	[follows with his finger; voice relaxes] Harbor Freeway.
14	T:	Right. Harbor Freeway.

In this exchange, Henry had entered the discourse with noticeable nervousness and initially failed to answer the teacher's question. He had not completed the worksheet required for this discussion. However, the assignment involved locating cities on a simple map. He was quite familiar with this skill, because he traveled often with his family. Presumably to end his turn as quickly as possible, he chose to answer the teacher's question with the first highway name he saw on the map (line 10). When he found the correct answer (line 13) with the help of additional information cues (lines 9, 11, 12), he relaxed and attended for the rest of the activity. He eventually answered correctly, without the word insertions or phrase reformulations that usually characterized his speech. Although his first answer was fluent and appropriate, his avoidance behavior, which was secondary to his word-retrieval difficulties, indirectly interfered with his ability to give a more competent, correct answer.

In the above example, Henry seemed to "throw away" all we had talked about just to end his turn. Later, during the second phase of the program, he attempted to stay more focused before being appointed by the teacher, to enter more calmly after being selected, and to answer in phrases using as many cues or clues as he could find in his book or the conversation.

Henry's teacher's concern for his self-esteem, motivation, and success in the classroom was a constant factor throughout the school year. When he began to falter in all of these areas, she continued to "pull him" in to classroom conversations and encourage him to complete his work. Example 9.12, from a small-group reading lesson, shows this support. The teacher was discussing the main character's personality traits as the character attempted to overcome a dilemma.

EXAMPLE 9.12   (April)

1	T:	[asks the children what motivates their efforts] Henry, what about yourself?
2	H:	I'm not sure.
3	T:	Oh, Henry. How about being motivated for your folks? I see you as a person who's really motivated by just wanting to show your family how really terrific you are. OK. Will you think about it and let me know?
4	H:	[nods "yes"]
///		[Other children share in the discussion with the teacher. She returns to Henry, hoping that he will try to participate.]
5	T:	Henry?
6	H:	[no eye contact; shrugs shoulders] I don't know.
7	T:	Henry, what motivates you? What do you think really makes you want to do something?
8	H:	I don't know.
9	T:	There are so many things. For example, now getting in your homework every single day, right? That's a source of motivation.
10	H:	No.
11	T:	No? What then? Help me out.
12	H:	I do that at home.
13	T:	Right, you do. But what motivates you to do it? To do well, right?
14	H:	[getting a little angry] No. I don't want to do it, really.
15	T:	OK. Will you please think about it?
16	H:	Yeah. (He pushes his papers around and watches other children out of the corner of his eye.)
///		[Teacher continues to call on a few other children, who bring the mood of the class back up to a lighter discussion. The topic of conversation changes to one about sports and competition.]
17	S2:	[In chess] you have to get the king so you can move anywhere.
18	T:	Yes, exactly. Very good. Henry?
19	H:	It's always . . . it's also another object that you have to . . . umm . . . in order to get the king, you have to kill all the other things.
20	T:	Exactly.
21	H:	Then you can move back and forth.
22	T:	Yes.
23	H:	You can get them from the back but they're really the toughest people [to get].
24	T:	Right. Jack?
///		[Henry relaxes after successfully entering the discussion and continuing to talk.]
25	T:	Who knows about sacrifice? Mary, what does it mean to sacrifice?
26	M:	[inaudible]

27	T:	All right. To sacrifice means to give up something that's important to you. What about . . .
28	H:	[loudly to himself, in my direction] Oh, oh, in baseball, too.
29	F:	Tell what you know.
30	T:	[seeing the movement and hearing his comment] Explain it.
31	H:	If somebody's on first, you put the batter out and somebody's on first . . . you put the bat out and then the pitcher throws you out and then the other guy gets to second.
32	T:	[speaking slowly and carefully] So you're making a sacrifice for somebody else. You're letting your team go ahead even though you decided that you personally are not going to get to run around the bases. Right?
33	H:	[nods "yes"]
34	T:	So you're really making a very big sacrifice?
35	H:	Yes!
///		[T continues on to another vocabulary word and another child. Henry is very relaxed now; he has been participating successfully after the difficult exchange earlier in the reading lesson.]
36	T:	OK. Let's go ahead and read. Why don't you continue, Henry?
37	H:	[reads one paragraph with inflection, in a slower-than-usual, but fluent, style]
38	T:	[in a very friendly voice] Continue reading, Henry.
39	H:	[reads another two sentences of dialogue, to end at a new paragraph]
40	T:	[assigns another student]
41	H	[now follows the reading of other children]

In this example, Henry at first avoided fully entering the discussion after the teacher called on him (lines 6 and 8). He did not want to participate in the conversation because he was still reluctant to talk at length. Also, the topic seemed to anger him (line 14). Despite his anger, his thoughts were very clear and his language constructions fluent. When he later relaxed and chose to enter the interaction (line 19), his comments were slightly less clearly organized and his language constructions were slightly less fluent. However, he did participate. Henry successfully shared his knowledge of chess and baseball with respect to the term "sacrifice," with only a small amount of encouragement necessary from my cueing (line 29). He was now using classroom discourse to share his knowledge and expertise.

Ms. Dove continued to draw Henry into the discourse (lines 9, 11, and 13). Henry's nervousness eased, but it would take more time for his confidence to grow. He still seemed to have more to share than what he said, but he was no longer holding it back. He also began to show signs of enjoying classroom discourse, continuing his comments for several turns (lines 19, 21, 23). After his unsuccessful contributions about what motivated his efforts, he "regrouped" and tried again to expand his ideas about chess moves (line 21). Last, his teacher was not afraid to confront him nor to return to him later, as she had promised. Still, he had other problems that he had to deal with separately, such as tension with his parents concerning school work.

Sensitive to Henry's problems at home, including parental pressures for high grades and school participation, Ms. Dove intervened when possible. The collaboration among the teacher, Henry, and me continued throughout the school year. Henry was still learning how to adapt his language to the classroom discourse, and his teacher was learning how to adapt to his language. Henry would need this kind of teacher collaboration in the future in order to keep improving his language participation in the classroom.

By the spring, Henry monitored his own language more frequently; he was entering the "handover" stage of the language-remediation program. He had improved the quantity and quality of his language participation in classroom discourse toward the end of the school year. He had more control over his fluency, more patience in expressing his thoughts, more confidence during difficult exchanges, and more use of appropriate methods of entering and maintaining conversations. He still had word-retrieval difficulties, but he and those around him had a better perspective on the problem and know how to deal with it.

As the last example revealed, Henry was beginning to change his language and his attitude toward language participation in the classroom during teacher-directed discourse. He understood the rhythm and rules of the classroom routines and that he could "fit" his language into those routines. He recalled six of eight helpful strategies to facilitate word retrieval. For example, he used specific words in line 8, offered his responses in the form of phrases in line 16, and maintained eye contact with the listener in line 30. Later, he admitted to practicing these strategies in the classroom. After observing his participation in the classroom a day later, I added two more goals to his last list: First describe or tell the most important details; then pause to think more often.

Figure 9.2 shows results of the end-of-the-year speech and language evaluation, mildly supportive of Henry's progress in language and literacy constructions. Tests for language competencies were not repeated in May if they indicated an age-appropriate level of performance. Classroom observations by the speech and language pathologist and by the classroom teacher had already revealed the high potential for achievement in literacy activities, supported by standardized test results. The changes that were important to recheck were those involving expressive language constructions. The scores for word-retrieval strategies indicated improved levels of performance. Along with Henry's increased communicative competence, his fluency level was more appropriate, and his voice was louder. The test results supported Henry's own admission that he felt more confident when he interacted in the classroom. The teacher's notes further supported these balanced evaluation results. Henry was enrolled in the speech and language program for another year to continue his progress and prepare him for enrollment in middle school.

Summary. Henry worked hard this school year trying to assume responsibility for modifying and monitoring his language during classroom discourse. He knew he would need to work on his language skills and classroom attitude in the next school

FIGURE 9.2 Speech and Language Assessment Protocol

Student's Name _____Henry_____	Date _____May_____
Student's Homeroom _____Ms. Dove_____	Age/Grade ___10 years, 3 months, 4th___

STUDENT INTERVIEW
Henry states that he is more comfortable "telling stories and giving answers" in the classroom. He feels that he has a few more friends than before because he can "talk easier" now. He admits that he still has some difficulties constructing his responses, but that "it's OK now."

SPEECH
No noticeable problems.

LANGUAGE—Comprehensive
No need to retest.

LANGUAGE—Vocabulary
No need to retest.

LANGUAGE—Pragmatics/Problem-Solving	Test Results:
Test of Problem Solving	Standard Score: 59 (mean score of 50)

LANGUAGE—Processing/Word Retrieval	Test Results:
Test of Wordfinding in Discourse (German, 1991)	
Language Productivity	Standard Score: 111
Wordfinding Behaviors	Standard Score: 98

FLUENCY
Informal evaluation during classroom discourse and individual conferencing interactions. Breathing patterns are within normal limits. Fluency is slightly disrupted by word-retrieval difficulties.

VOICE
Voice is audible in classroom discourse.

AUDITORY PERCEPTION—Discrimination/Processing
No problems with auditory perception.

FAMILY/PARENT NOTES
Parents are comfortable with changes in Henry's language constructions and achievement levels. They requested an end to direct intervention services now that Henry will be in his last year at this elementary school.

TEACHER'S NOTES
Ms. Dove notices an improvement in Henry's language fluency and in his achievement level, secondary to increased language participation in literacy activities and with peers during socialization (lunch, physical education) periods, as reflected in final report card.

COMMENTS/RECOMMENDATIONS:
Continue language support through monthly consultation meetings with classroom teacher.

year, as well. During his first four years in elementary school, he had developed alternative language and behavioral strategies, such as exaggerated gesturing and digressive monologues, that were not useful to him in the classroom. His teachers and parents, who had remarked to me about his obvious language difficulties and his decreased self-confidence in the classroom throughout previous school years, were now seeing subtle changes in Henry's language use. His progress was slow but forward moving, a significantly different result from previous years' remediation efforts. Henry's teacher's comments described his positive efforts and growing participation, although he always seemed capable of sharing more information. He may not have reached what his parents and teacher felt was his true potential, but he was no longer criticized for problematic language and behavior.

Specifically, Henry became more vocal, more involved, and more fluent as his competence and focus grew. His confidence in his ability to participate increased, as well, allowing him to discover his language capabilities and to overcome some of his anger and frustration with his difficulties. He also interacted more with other students in more appropriate ways. Some of them began understanding him more, and even respected him for his knowledge.

However, Henry was not always comfortable or successful with classroom discourse yet. Individual peripheral meetings helped him remember how important strategy use was in his language routines. At the end of the school year, Henry was just beginning to work on using language-facilitation strategies in classroom discourse. He had needed time to give up his own less competent participation tactics and to replace them with new, more effective ones. He knew that he would benefit from language support in the classroom in the next school year. But, he finished the school year stating that he was pleased with his present improved communication skills.

SECTION FOUR

Reflections

10 A Retrospective Look at the Intervention Programs

Change in the structure of any school-based program requires reorganization of the policies and social systems that support it. As new approaches toward instruction are introduced and modeled, new perspectives evolve among administrators, teachers, students, and support personnel concerning the nature of classroom interactions and learning experiences. The case studies of Mickey, Vincent, and Henry serve as examples of proposed approaches to supporting students who struggle with language and literacy constructions in the classroom. The changes that occurred throughout the year-long study represent the kinds of modifications in thought and procedure that often accompany school reform. Indeed, the process of change is inseparable from the reactions and responses of the participants. In this study, as the initial changes in the site of instruction were introduced, the teachers' input and students' progress influenced future changes in implementation of remedial and compensatory language and literacy strategies. Looking back on the year-long program, there were three core elements of change that occurred: noticeable improvement in students' communicative competence in the classroom; development of a collaborative, constructivist spirit among teachers, students, and the language specialist; and new policy and procedures in the school and district toward special-needs education.

Development in Communicative Competence

Each focal child's language and role changed in the classroom as he began to participate more often and more competently in classroom discourse than he had in the past year. Previously, the boys had learned a strategy in the resource room, practiced it there, and, unfortunately, left it there. Now, each child came to understand that he would be expected to slowly and confidently assume responsibility for and control over the strategies that he chose to use in classroom conversations. The hardest parts of their new task were to trust my suggestions and to risk experiencing more frustration as they practiced new language strategies for the first time. At first they knew to follow my lead. Sooner than expected, they wanted to take the lead themselves.

Later, they needed to apply these lessons in everyday classroom language situations in which I was not present.

All three children experienced improvement in their classroom language competence for the first time in several years of school. Their roles in the classroom changed from reluctant respondents to more active participants. Mickey, who needed prodding to enter discourse in the first few months of the school year, managed to assert himself (occasionally) in classroom discourse with competent comments, expand his language constructions using phrases, and anticipate language opportunities by attending carefully to discourse. Vincent, who overused ambiguous pronouns and growled, learned to self-monitor his word retrieval using visual cues and attempted longer phrases. Henry's periodic successes encouraged him to assertively enter classroom discourse with appropriate, if not always fluent, language constructions. All the teachers noted these changes; in several cases, peer relationships changed as well. Each of the boys seemed happier, or more confident, now that he finally "fit in" better.

Their growing communicative competence helped them specifically tackle the classroom language routines set by teachers and, less directly, students. In each of the three classrooms studied, strict IRE patterns of interaction dominated learning activities, allowing limited opportunities for students to control conversation or organize activities. Therefore, the language strategies that the three focal boys were beginning to master would be most useful in the next school years, when teachers would adhere to these same routines. These strategies would also prove valuable in other kinds of language routines that occur in the classroom, such as students' collaborating on mutual projects or peer-review activities, and teachers' participation in student interaction. Accordingly, the intervention program helped the children self-monitor their use of language strategies and apply them flexibly. I often struggled with balancing lessons on changing the students' language constructions and personal perspectives in discourse. I tried to move from direct instruction to indirect support as necessary. I hoped that these children would generalize the strategies they learned when new language routines presented themselves in the classroom.

Collaboration with Teachers

The teachers, like the students, were unaccustomed to having another educator in the classroom and to the additional conferencing that occurred between the students and myself as they were teaching. Although the movement of teacher-aides around the classroom as they worked with an individual student caused some distraction, the aides received direct instructions from the teachers. The teachers were uncertain about what I was teaching the children and felt that they had little control over my comments as they taught, a situation that challenged their role as overseer in the classroom. We resolved this problem through informal collaborative discussions. The teachers remained the primary decision-makers in their classrooms, but we often alternated in implementing new language strategies for the focal children.

One of the teachers' main roles in this research study was to learn more about the children's problems through classroom observation and occasional in-service meetings, and to make informed changes in the way they questioned and accepted the children's responses. This was difficult for them to do with classrooms of almost twenty-five students. The teachers had three main challenges: They needed additional information about the children's specific language problems; they needed to see modeling of effective teaching strategies in the classroom; and they wanted extra planning time to organize strategies and adaptations. Because all three teachers wanted to do the best job possible, they experienced extra stress. These feelings are reflected in teachers' evaluations of their own performances and efficacy (Ringlaben & Price, 1981; Ross & Wax, 1993).

My role in the classroom was to make the children's and teachers' jobs in this study look easy—while instructing new language strategies and conducting occasional in-class individual conferences. The teachers' cooperation was an integral part of the successes the children experienced. By introducing goals for competent language and then modeling examples of applicable cues, I made the lessons appear more manageable for teachers and students alike. I also provided simple but meaningful explanations of the boys' language problems and described possible solutions. The teachers' cooperation in this research study was voluntary, so they had to feel comfortable in their roles. And because the theories supporting situated learning were clear and applicable, the teachers easily accepted my role as leader in bringing these strategies into the classroom.

One of the many important components of a successful integrated language program is communication with the classroom teacher to ensure generalization of new strategies into a child's everyday classroom language routines. Children often leave the language resource room with "improved strategies" and "successful experiences" in that isolated context, only to suffer failure and regression in the school hallways or classrooms. For a language remediation program to work, all the child's teachers must use the cues and clues developed by the language or learning specialist.

All three classroom teachers in this study modified their interactions in discourse and their expectations for the three focal students with some degree of success. This success, in turn, led to more competent contributions to classroom discourse by these children. The examples provided in this book show these changes. I frequently explained the evolving theories of language use and learning strategies to the teachers. These conversations gave them additional knowledge to draw on as they created their own adaptations of language routines for the boys.

Throughout this study, all the teachers practiced the IRE format of verbal interaction in their classroom language routines. I worked within that structure to develop competent communication strategies for the three boys. Teachers made some modifications within the IRE format—for instance, giving more time for answers, acknowledging "out-of-turn" contributions, and giving more cues—to accommodate the children's needs. Nevertheless, they most frequently posed "pseudo-questions," that is, less authentic questions, in search of the "correct" answer. The impact of the teachers' use of restricted language routines on Mickey's, Vincent's, and Henry's language participation was originally very limiting, marginalizing them within the classroom discourse. My presence in the classroom during the year provided the necessary opportunities for me to model more appropriate and expanded forms of question routines (i.e., open-ended, interactive, higher level in nature) that helped to scaffold the boys' responses. Still, it was important for Mickey, Vincent, and Henry to learn how to "make room" for their responses in classrooms in which teachers use traditional language routines.

One of the keys to developing a language and literacy program to fit the particular needs of struggling students is through frequent consultation among team members. The traditional view of consultation services follows the expert service model (Caplan, 1970). That is, one individual with expertise in an existing area of knowledge assists another in dealing with a specific problem as it occurs and for generalization to future instances. In this model, the consultant is not typically involved in the implementation of the recommended course of action; rather, he or she primarily provides diagnostic and prescriptive advice (Brown, Wyne, Blackburn, & Powell, 1979). This model has important limitations owing to a general lack in continuity of the services and an inequality in the roles of participants. It also weakens the credibility of "in-house" staff members and leaves accountability for meetings and follow-up services unclear. Thus, this model is not optimal for school-based professional consultants. It clearly did not prove highly successful in prior trials at the school chosen for this study.

A more effective model for the educational setting includes ongoing collaboration among the professionals (Brown, Wyne, Blackburn, & Powell, 1979; Coufal, 1990; Pryzwansky, 1985). In this model, the suggestions for interventions by the consultee originate from team discussions and mutual decisions. Tharp and Wetzell (1969) refer to this team of client, consultant, and consultee as the "triadic relationship" typical of effective consultative models. In cases of school-based problems, the team consists of the teacher, the specialist, and the child.

This second model is client centered (Carkhuff, 1969; Rogers, 1951). Team members mutually develop goals based on shared participation, resources, and accountability, and built on trust, parity, and interdependence (Friend & Cook, 1990). In a research study of consultative methodology, Coufal (1990) refers to this process of negotiation as collaborative consultation to emphasize both the manner and process of interaction. Her studies provide evidence of the advantages of this process. I introduced and attempted collaborative consultation informally in each boy's classroom during this study.

Models of the consultation process vary. There are usually at least four progressive stages: identification of a problem, formulation of alternative approaches, intervention, and conclusion of services. The nature of these stages—that is, the specific details and solutions—depend on the context in which the model applies and the involvement of participants. The length of time devoted to each stage also varies.

In the cases of the three children in this study, the goals for collaborative consultation were offshoots of those listed in each child's educational program, and focused on mitigating word-retrieval difficulties. Classroom teachers and I met informally at the request of either of us and at scheduled times. This approach is consistent with Coufal's (1993) observations that collaborative consultation does not occur in a single setting or within traditional time constraints of an assigned "clinical hour." Instead, she notes, it features a holistic approach to ongoing discussions of assessment and treatment options. Conversations in this study included comparisons of the boys' performance in the areas of school work and their use of specific strategies for improvement. The teachers and I also discussed situations that intensified stress for each child and relevant social or emotional issues.

Changes in the School

This research study inspired valuable—and surprising—change in many aspects of the school beyond the language of the focal children. Specifically, the school transitioned toward new forms of classroom organization and assessment methods, and the district began implementation of a new inclusive policy for educating children with special needs and individual differences. Each of these changes in turn influenced the research study, as will be explained below. Together, these changes created a complex and often stressful atmosphere in the classrooms.

The changes in assessment and classroom organization occurred slowly, following educational input from teachers' discussions, in-service presentations, my own suggestions, and experiential successes. The building principal was only beginning to acknowledge and provide for collaborative work among teachers and special staff members in terms of time allotments, but individual teachers experimented with new applications of language and literacy teaching developments.

For example, classrooms that at the beginning of the school year had one central teaching area consisting of individual rows of desks facing one blackboard evolved into rooms with pairs of desks facing the board and then four-desk groupings or tables around the room. The teachers made reference materials such as informational books and primary source materials more readily available in educational interest areas called "centers." These changes both created and reflected changes in classroom teaching and learning styles; for example, encouraging peer conferencing and support, and introducing student-directed learning. Despite the emphasis on IRE format, teachers and students began developing questions and answers together. In the past, the children with expressive language problems would have provided structured, often contrived, answers. Now they negotiated those answers with help from me or another student. As the adult introducing these supportive language strategies, I could easily provide such assistance and attract little notice as I sat and moved with the children in their smaller groups. By modeling the strategies in different contexts,

I helped transfer the responsibility for support to the classroom teachers, the students' peers, and the students themselves.

Changes in assessment methods also reflected the adaptations I had requested of the three teachers. In the past, language and learning specialists had used standardized assessment instruments to evaluate students' progress in reading, writing, and language development and determine group or track placements. This imposed unfair restrictions on the judgments about the focal children's true language and literacy skills. Questions derived from contrived textual material lacked the contextual cues the children needed to retrieve words quickly and appropriately. The use of less formal assessment strategies, such as portfolio development, classroom observation, and choices for completion of a task gave all three children the opportunity to demonstrate their actual abilities.

Finally, the school district decided to include all children in regular classes, following an investigation into the potential impact of this change. Children with moderate-to-severe cognitive or physical impairments, limited English proficiency, and learning disabilities were assigned special teacher aides to assist them in adapting to the classroom routines. This sent a message to classroom teachers that they would now be responsible, at least in part, for integrating these children into everyday classroom activities and for adapting the curriculum accordingly. This was a large responsibility for these selected teachers, but it set the stage for collaboration in the classrooms I was studying.

Not surprisingly, this new policy proved a mixed blessing. It worked to my advantage in that adaptations for the children I was studying seemed rather simple compared to those for children with multiple and more severe handicaps. However, the students I had chosen to help did not have any teacher aides assigned to them as did the new inclusionary students. Thus, I was the helper, but I was limited in the time I had available. I needed to consult and collaborate with the teachers to support their new responsibilities, but their busy schedules often made this difficult. The teachers' emotions swung from anxiety about accomplishing the added tasks to relief as the new language strategies began to get results. I had anticipated only positive reactions to the support services I would provide.

New Insight into Students' Difficulties

During the school year following this study, the children received similar support services in the school. However, the teacher preparation and collaboration proved less fluid. It is difficult to replicate relationships. Still, the boys had gained a good dose of self-sufficiency and self-esteem, both of which supported the efforts of teachers and a language specialist in the continued program. As the following year progressed, new information became available about each boy's language and literacy difficulties, and this encouraged further fine-tuning of their intervention programs.

Mickey's continued problems with socialization prompted special educators to again pursue a medical diagnosis. Subsequent observation and expanded access to information through Internet browsing revealed that Mickey's language and learning characteristics conformed to Asperger Syndrome. A previously little known subcategory of pervasive developmental disorder (*DSM-IV*, 1994), Asperger Syndrome is a "shadow syndrome" of autism. That is, like autism, it is a social communicative disorder. It shares many of the ritualistic behavior and obsessive/compulsive psychological tendencies of autism but has several dissimilar symptoms as well. More recently, Asperger Syndrome has been included in the larger category of Autistic Spectrum Disorders (Wetherby & Prizant, 2000). The behavioral characteristics of Asperger Syndrome include narrowed, egocentric interests, obsessive habits, awkward socialization strategies, mild sensory-motor deficits, and an average to above average range of intelligence (Atwood, 1997; Frith, 1991; Twachtman-Cullen, 1996; Wetherby & Prizant, 2000; Williams, 1995). Students with Asperger Syndrome are articulate and responsive, and can read, write, and reason, albeit in rather concrete forms. Problems arise in the area of abstract thinking, humor, and taking of alternative perspectives. Critical thinking is limited to concrete, predictable comments. Still, Mickey benefitted from the changes in language routines that this study engendered. The positive changes in his language and literacy strategies support the argument that children with language disorders can function in the classroom with appropriate support from specialists and teachers.

Vincent was reevaluated during the following school year by the special-education department, and was found to have specific learning disabilities in language and reading. He received resource services outside the classroom. He struggled with academic achievement during this year but maintained friendships and used strategies for participating in language and literacy activities. Vincent voiced his dissatisfaction with the "pull-out" program, but still cooperated with it. His gains in self-esteem, social participation, and language development continued.

Henry did not receive any resource services after the year of the study but was retained on the special-education roster through consultative services. He continued his schooling without any incidents or problems. He took a proactive approach to problem-solving when he experienced language or literacy difficulties, seeking help through questioning or individual conferences with the teachers. Henry's language and literacy development had been age appropriate, but his strategies for applying these had caused him the initial difficulties. With a new view of communicative competence—that boosting and improving his participation was more beneficial than the actual language he used—Henry completed his elementary-school years armed with language and literacy strategies that would help him succeed in middle school.

11 Future Considerations

The information provided in these chapters extends beyond the confines of this particular study. It provides important information concerning the procedures, the problems, and the promise of integrating special-education programs involving children with language difficulties into regular-education classroom activities and discourse. It provides a glimpse into three separate but similar attempts to remediate children's language difficulties in a shared domain, while recognizing the significant responsibilities and contributions of each participant—the special-education teacher, the regular-education teacher, and the student. This inside view can help alert all school personnel, including regular- and special-education staff members and senior administrators, to the need for flexible programming and meaningful communication within our schools today. Although the case-study methodology used for this research affords a detailed look at only a small sample of children with expressive language difficulties, it supports new perspectives on education of children with special needs.

For example, the sites of assessment and remediation need to match the context in which the language problems crop up, so that the student can directly apply solutions. Classroom-based language assessment and instruction must constitute a major part of remediation programs for children with language disorders and similar special needs, especially in classrooms where teachers assume more collaborative roles in organizing daily activities and providing educational services. The decision-making process that occurs as speech and language pathologists identify children as having language difficulties and develop remediation programs ranks as another crucial area of consideration. Within this setting, educators can address language problems other than expressive constructions and word retrieval primarily in the classroom.

Another consideration for classroom-based language and literacy support programs would involve intervention in classrooms with diverse student populations and discourse routines that vary from the traditional IRE pattern. A larger range of interactional discourse would provide more opportunities to address different forms of language constructions for competent models and remediation programs. Teachers need to make modifications within and beyond the IRE format, giving more time for answers, acknowledging "out-of-turn" contributions, and giving more cues to accommodate the children's needs. Collaboration and communication among all participants can provide the key to making these changes.

Boosting collaborative consultation between special-education specialists and regular-education teachers can strengthen the expertise of all educators. Specifically, it can close the gaps between regular-education teachers' knowledge of language accommodation and special-education teachers' knowledge of curricular content. As a result, all the children in the classroom benefit. At a time when children with physical handicaps, cognitive impairments, and limited English proficiency are finally being included with their peers in regular classrooms, educators must make individual adaptations to accommodate children's special needs.

This last point has generated debate since the passage of legislation supporting inclusionary education. For example, the Education for All Handicapped Children Act (PL 94-142) mandates that students be placed in the least restrictive educational environment. (See Marozas & May, 1988, for a more complete review of that important step.) It also opens classrooms to children with language difficulties who would have been excluded in the past. Once a child has qualified for special-education services, the teacher specifies a set of language goals for integration into the regular-education program, as set by the child's Individual Education Program (IEP). Besides the language specialist, the classroom teachers and aides often become part-time implementers of these goals.

Thus, the prime responsibility for implementation of special language strategies is shifting from the special educator alone to a shared collaboration of teacher, child, and language specialist. Helping the classroom teacher understand a child's problem and offering suggestions for enhancing the child's language empowers both teacher and child. How well these consultative programs function hinges on participants' attitudes and the program model.

More specifically, the language negotiation process in the classroom requires metalinguistic awareness on the parts of teachers and students during verbal exchanges. Students with language difficulties benefit from encouragement and reinforcement in their struggles and successes. The teachers need modeling and support to individualize conversational styles; for example, varying language and literacy discourse routines by including more critical inquiry, encouraging connections with text through increased question uptake and digressions, and shaping and scaffolding responses through student-student interaction. Consideration of these factors further define the collaborative process. Many teachers resent the extra effort they must expend to accommodate special students because they have not received sufficient information to understand the nature of the problems or to feel in control of the situations in which difficulties disrupt discourse (Ross & Wax, 1993). Teacher cooperation through consultative collaboration forms an important component in a successful language-support program.

Teachers also need to approach classroom organization and management in new ways. Children's working in groups, sharing and comparing new information, strengthens the learning of each member. Students actively sharing in their education, selecting and critiquing texts and topics, allows for meaningful learning (Pappas, Keifer, & Levstik,, 1999; Wells & Chang-Wells, 1992). The children in this study had less difficulty with language that they initiated and that interested them than they did with material selected for them or questions that struck them as contrived. This is true of all children's language and literacy skills; information that children can connect to their own experiences and needs has the most value to them.

Possibly, curriculum directors should change the vocabulary used to explain the orientation of educational programs before language and learning specialists implement the programs. The term "special" as it is used in the schools has taken on an all-inclusive definition; that is, any student who is not "average" is special. "Special" has thus come to mean "different," with a negative connotation. Yet changes in the characteristics and needs of schoolchildren have unfolded rapidly in the past few years and promise to challenge teachers and administrators of the future even more. There are fewer and fewer "average" children in classes today. Rather than separating and segregating children with special needs and backgrounds, classroom teachers, with collaborative and consultative support from language and learning specialists, can educate all children together so as to acknowledge and support their unique strengths and difficulties. All students are special individuals with differences to share.

REFERENCES

Allington, R. (1980). Teacher interruption behavior during primary-grade reading. *Journal of Educational Psychology, 72,* 371–377.

American Psychological Association. (1994). *Diagnostic and statistical manual of mental disorders* (4th ed.). Washington, DC: Author.

American-Speech-Language-Hearing Association. (1996, Spring). Inclusive practices for children and youths with communication disorders: A position statement and technical report. *ASHA, 38* (Suppl. 6, pp. 35–44).

Atwood, T. (1998). *Asperger's Syndrome: A guide for parents and professionals.* Philadelphia, PA: Jessica Kingsley Publishers.

Au, K. H., & Jordon, C. (1981). Teaching reading to Hawaiian children: Finding a culturally appropriate solution. In H. T. Trueba, G. P. Guthrie, & K. H. Au (Eds.), *Culture and the bilingual classroom: Studies in classroom ethnography* (pp. 139–152). Rowley, MA: Newbury House.

Baker, J., & Zigmond, N. (1990). Are regular education classes equipped to accommodate students with learning disabilities? *Exceptional Children, 58,* 515–527.

Bakhtin, M. M. (1981). *The dialogic imagination: Four essays by M. M. Bakhtin.* Austin, TX: University of Texas Press.

Bakhtin, M. M. (1986). *Speech genres and other late essays.* Austin, TX: University of Texas Press.

Ball, E. W. (1997). Phonological awareness: Implications for whole language and emergent literacy programs. *Topics in Language Disorders, 17*(3), 14–16.

Barnes, D. (1976). *From communication to curriculum.* Harmondsworth, UK: Penguin.

Barton, M., Maruszewski, D., & Urrea, D. (1969). Variations of stimulus context and its effect on word finding ability in aphasics. *Cortex, 5,* 351–364.

Bauwens, J., & Hourcade, J. J. (1997). Cooperative teaching: Pictures of possibilities. *Intervention in School and Clinic, 33*(2), 81–85.

Bean, R. M., Zigmond, N., & Eichelberger, R. T. (1990, April). Effects of an in-class model on instruction received by remedial students from their classroom reading teachers. Paper presented at the annual meeting of the American Educational Research Association, Boston, MA.

Beck, A. R., & Dennis, M. (1997). Speech-Language Pathologists' and Teachers' Perceptions of Classroom-Based Interventions. *Language, Speech and Hearing Services in the Schools, 28*(2), 146–153.

Benson, D. F., & Geschwind, N. (1969). The alexias. In P. J. Vinken & G. W. Bruyn (Eds.), *Disorders of speech, perception, and symbolic behavior. Vol. 4: Handbook of Clinical Neurology* (pp. 112–140). Amsterdam: North-Holland.

Bernstein, B. (1990). The structuring of pedagogic discourse: Class codes and control (Vol. IV). London: Routledge and Kegan Paul.

Blachman, B. A. (1994). Early literacy acquisition. In G. P. Wallach & K. G. Butler (Eds.), *Language learning disabilities in school-age children and adolescents: Some principles and applications* (pp. 253–274). New York: McMillan College Publishing Company.

Blalock, G. (1997). Strategies for school consultation and collaboration. In E. A. Polloway & J. R. Patton (Eds.), *Strategies for teaching learners with special needs* (520–552). Upper Saddle River, NJ: Prentice Hall, Inc.

Bland, L. E., & Prelock, P. A. (1995). Effects of collaboration on language performance. *Journal of Children's Communication Development, 17,* 31–37.

Bloom, L. A., Perlmutter, J., & Burrell, L. (1999). The General Educator: Applying Constructivism to Inclusive Classrooms. *Intervention in School & Clinic, 34*(3), 132–136.

Bloome, D. (1982). *School culture and the future of literacy.* National Institute of Education.

Bloome, D., & Theodorou, E. (1988). Analyzing teacher-student and student-student discourse. In J. Green, J. Harker, & C. Wallet (Eds.), *Multiple perspective analyses of classroom discourse* (pp. 217–248). Norwood, NJ: Ablex Publishing Corp.

Blosser, J. L., & Kratcowski, A. (1997). PAC's: A framework for determining appropriate service delivery options. *Language, Speech, and Hearing Services in Schools, 28,* 99–107.

Blumenfeld, P. C. (1992). Classroom learning and motivation: Clarifying and expanding goal theory. *Journal of Educational Psychology, 84*(3), 272–281.

Bowers, L., Jorgenson, C., Huisingh, R., Barrett, M., Orman, J., & LoGiudice, C. (1994). *Test of problem-solving–revised.* East Moline, IL: LinguiSystems, Inc.

Boyle, J. R., & Danforth, S. (1997). *Cases in special education* (pp. 126–179). Boston, MA: McGraw-Hill.

Brown, D., Wyne, M. D., Blackburn, J. E., & Powell, W. C. (1979). *Consultation: Strategy for improving education.* Boston: Allyn and Bacon.

Bruner, J. S. (1983). *Child's talk.* London: Oxford University Press.

Calkins, L., Montgomery, K., & Santman, D. (1998). *A teacher's guide to standardized reading tests: Knowledge is power.* Portsmouth, NH: Heinemann.

Campione, J. C. (1989). Assisted assessment: A taxonomy of approaches and an outline of strengths and weaknesses. *Journal of Learning Disabilities, 22*(3), 151–165.

Caplan, G. (1970). *The theory and practice of mental health consultation.* New York: Basic Books.

Carkhuff, R. R. (1969). *Helping and human relations* (Vols. I & II). New York: Holt, Rinehart, & Winston.

Catts, H. W., & Kamhi, A. G. (1999). *Language and reading disabilities.* Boston: Allyn & Bacon.

Cazden, C. B. (1988). *Classroom discourse.* Portsmouth, NH: Heinemann.

Cazden, C. B. (1998). *Two meanings of "discourse."* Paper presented at the 20th Annual Meeting of the American Association for Applied Linguistics (Seattle, WA, March, 1998).

Chalfant, J., Pysh, M., & Moultrie, R. (1979). Teacher assistance teams: A model for within building problem solving. *Learning Disabilities Quarterly, 2,* 85–86.

Chall, J. S. (1996). *Learning to read: The great debate* (3rd ed.). Orlando, FL: Harcourt Brace.

Chomsky, N. (1975). *Reflections on language.* NY: Random House.

Christie, F. (1985). Curriculum genres: Towards a description of the construction of knowledge in schools. A paper given at the working conference on interaction of spoken and written language in education settings, held at the University of New England, Armidale, November 11–15, 1985.

Christie, F. (1987). The morning news genre: Using a functional grammar to illuminate educational issues. *Australian Review of Applied Linguistics, 10*(2), 182–198.

Christie, F. (1995). Pedagogic discourse in the primary school. *Linguistics and Education, 7,* 221–242.

Cirrin, F. M., & Penner, S. G. (1995). Classroom-based and consultive speech delivery models for language intervention. In M. E. Fey, J. Windsor, & S. F. Warren (Eds.) *Language intervention: Preschool through the elementary years* (pp. 333–362). Baltimore, MD: P. H. Brooks Publishers.

Coates, R. D., (1989). The regular education initiative and opinions of regular classroom teachers. *Journal of Learning Disabilities, 22,* 532–536.

Cook, L., & Friend, M. (1996). Co-Teaching: Guidelines for creating effective practices. In E. L. Meyen, G. A. Vergason, & R. J. Whelan (Eds.), *Strategies for teaching exceptional children in inclusive settings* (pp. 155–182). Denver, CO: Love Publishing Company.

Coufal, K. L. (1990). *Collaborative consultation: An alternative to traditional treatment for children with communicative disorders.* (Doctoral dissertation, University of Nebraska-Lincoln, 1989). Dissertation Abstracts International, 51/02, 694A.

Coufal, K. L. (1993). Collaborative consultation for speech-language pathologists. *Topics in Language Disorders, 14*(1), 1–14.

Damico, J. S., & Damico, S. K. (1993). Language and social skills from a diversity perspective:

Considerations for the speech-language pathologist. *Language, Speech, and Hearing Services in the Schools, 24*(4), 236–243.

De Hirsch, K. (1960). Stuttering and cluttering: Developmental aspects of dysrhythmic speech. *The Journal of Special Education, 3,* 143–153.

Dewey, J. (1990). *The school and society; and, The child and the curriculum: A centennial edition.* Chicago, IL : University of Chicago Press.

Dohan, M., & Schultz, H. (1998). The speech-language pathologist's changing role: Collaboration within the classroom. *Journal of Children's Communicative Development, 20*(1), 9–18.

Dollaghan, C., & Campbell, T. (1992). A procedure for classifying disruptions in spontaneous language samples. *Topics in Language Disorders, 12*(2), 56–67.

Donahue, M. L. (1994). Differences in classroom discourse styles of students with learning disabilities. In D. N. Ripich & N. A. Creaghead (Eds.), *School discourse problems*, 2nd edition (pp. 97–124). San Diego, CA: Singular Publishing Co., Inc.

Duchan, J. F., Hewitt, L. E., & Sonnenmeier, R. M., (Eds.). (1994). *Pragmatics: From theory to practice.* Englewood Cliffs, NJ: Prentice-Hall.

Dunn, L. M., & Dunn, L. M. (1997). *Peabody Picture Vocabulary Test-Revised.* Circle Pines, MN: American Guidance Service.

Edelsky, C., Altwerger, B., & Flores, B. (1991). *Whole language: What's the difference?* Portsmouth, NH: Heinemann.

Edwards, D., & Mercer, N. (1987). *Common knowledge: The development of understanding in the classroom.* New York: Routledge.

Eisenhart, M. A., & Cutts-Dougherty, K. (1991). Social and cultural constraints on students' access to school knowledge. In E. H. Hiebert (Ed.), *Literacy for a diverse society* (pp. 28–43). New York: Teachers College Press.

Eisner, E. (1985). *The educational imagination.* New York: Macmillan.

Elksnin, L. K. (1988). Case method of instruction. *Teacher Education and Special Education, 21*(2), 95–108.

Elksnin, L. K. (1997). Collaborative speech and language services for students with learning disabilities. *Journal of Learning Disabilities, 30,* 414–426.

Elksnin, L. K., & Capilouto, G. J. (1994). Speech-language pathologists' perceptions of integrated service delivery in school settings. *Language, Speech, and Hearing Services in Schools, 25,* 258–267.

Erikson, F. (1977). Some approaches to inquiry in school community ethnography. *Anthopology and Education Quarterly, 22*(2), 177–183.

Evans, D., Townsend, B. L., Duchnowski, A., & Hocutt, A. (1996). Addressing the challenges of inclusion of children with disabilities. *Teacher Education and Special Education, 19*(2), 180–191.

Falk-Ross, F. C. (1995). *Addressing language difficulties in the classroom: A communicative competence perspective.* Unpublished doctoral dissertation, University of Illinois at Chicago.

Falk-Ross, F. C. (November, 1996). *Classroom-based language remediation programs: Roles, routines, and reflections.* Paper presented at the Annual Convention for the Illinois Speech-Hearing-Language Association, Chicago, Illinois.

Falk-Ross, F. C. (1997). Developing metacommunicative awareness in children with language difficulties: Challenging the typical pull-out system. *Language Arts, 74*(3), 206–216.

Falvey, M. A. (1995). *Inclusive and heterogeneous schooling: Assessment, curriculum, and instruction.* Baltimore, MD: Paul H. Brookes Publishing Company.

Farber, J. G., & Klein, E. R. (1999). Classroom-based assessment of a collaborative intervention program with kindergarten and first-grade students. *Language, Speech, and Hearing Services in Schools, 30,* 83–91.

Feagans, L., & Short, E. J. (1984). Developmental differences in the comprehension and production of narratives by reading-disabled and normally achieving children. *Child Development, 55,* 1727–1736.

Feagans, L., & Short, E. J. (1986). Referential communication and reading performance in learning-disabled children over a 3-year period. *Developmental Psychology, 22*(2), 177–183.

Feuerstein, R. (1980). *Instrumental enrichment: An intervention program for cognitive modifiability.* Baltimore, MD: University Park Press.

Fey, M. E., Windsor, J., & Warren, S. F. (1995). *Language intervention: Preschool through the elementary years.* Baltimore, MD: Paul H. Brookes Publishing Co.

Firth, J. R. (1950). Personality and language in society. *Sociological Review, 14,* 37–52.

Flanders, N. A. (1970). *Analyzing teacher behavior.* Reading, MA: Addison-Wesley.

Freire, P. (1970). *Pedagogy of the oppressed.* New York: Continuum Publishing Company.

Friend, M., & Bursuck, W. D. (2002). *Including students with special needs: A practical guide for classroom teachers* (3rd ed.). Needham Heights, MA: Allyn & Bacon.

Friend, M., & Cook, L. (1992). *Interactions: Collaboration skills for school professionals.* White Plains, NY: Longman.

Friend, M., & Cook, L. (1990). Collaboration as a predictor of success in school reform. *Journal of Educational and Psychological Consultation, 1,* 69–86.

Frith, U. (1991). *Autism and asperger syndrome.* Cambridge, UK: Cambridge University Press.

Garcia, G. E. (1992). Ethnography and classroom communication: Taking an "emic" perspective. *Topics in Language Disorders, 12*(3), 54–66.

Gardner, M. (1981). *Expressive one-word picture vocabulary test.* Novato, CA: Academic Therapy Publications.

Gardner, W. I. (1982). Why do we persist? *Education and Treatment of Children, 5,* 369–378.

Gee, J. P. (1999). *An introduction to discourse analysis: Theory and method.* New York: Routledge.

Geertz, C. (1987). *The interpretation of cultures.* New York: Basic Books.

German, D. J. (1979). Word-finding skills in children with learning disabilities. *Journal of Learning Disabilities, 12*(3), 43–48.

German, D. J. (1984). Diagnosis of word-finding disorders in children with learning disabilities. *Journal of Learning Disorders, 17*(6), 353–359.

German, D. J. (1986). *National College of Education Test of Word-Finding (TWF).* Allen, TX: DLM Teaching Resources.

German, D. J. (1987). Spontaneous language samples of children with word-finding problems. *Language, Speech, and Hearing Services in Schools, 18*(3), 217–230.

German, D. J. (1991). *National College of Education Test of Word-Finding in Discourse (TWF-D).* Allen, TX: DLM Teaching Resources.

German, D. J. (1992). Word-finding intervention for children and adolescents. *Topics in Language Disorders, 13*(1), 33–50.

German, D. J., & Simon, E. (1991). Analysis of children's word-finding skills in discourse. *Journal of Speech and Hearing Research, 34*(2), 309–316.

Glaser, B., & Strauss, A. (1967). *The discovery of grounded theory.* Chicago: Aldine.

Glyden, D. R. (1994). Stuttering Severity Instrument. Austin, TX: PRO-ED, Inc.

Goldman, R., & Fristoe, M. (1986). *The Goldman-Fristoe Test of Articulation-Revised.* Circle Pines, MN: American Guidance Service.

Goodman, K. S. (1986). *What's whole in whole language?* Portsmouth, NH: Heinemann.

Green, J. L. (1983). Exploring classroom discourse: Linguistic perspectives on teaching-learning processes. *Educational Psychologist, 18*(3), 180–199.

Green, J., & Harker, J. (1988). *Multiple perspective analyses of classroom discourse.* Norwood, NJ: Ablex Publishing Corp.

Green, M. (1985). Talk and doubletalk: The development of metacommunication knowledge about oral language. *Research in the Teaching of English, 19,* 9–24.

Gumperz, J. J. (1983). *Language and social identity.* New York: Cambridge University Press.

Gutierrez, K. D. (1995a). Script, counterscript, and underlife in the classroom: James Brown versus Brown v. Board of Education. *Harvard Educational Review, 65*(3), 445–471.

Gutierrez, K. D. (1995b). Unpackaging academic discourse. *Discourse Processes, 19*(1), 21–37.

Gutierrez, K. D. (1997). A cultural-historical view of learning and learning disabilities: Participating in a community of learners. *Learning Disabilities Research and Practice, 12*(2), 123–131.

Halliday, M. A. K. (1978). *Language as social semiotic.* Baltimore, MD: University Park Press.

Halliday, M. A. K. (1993). Toward a language-based theory of learning. *Linguistics and Education, 5,* 53–116.

Halliday, M. A. K., & Hasan, R. (1976). *Cohesion in English.* New York: Longman.

Halliday, M. A. K., & Hasan, R. (1985). *Language, context, and text: Aspects of language in a social-semiotic perspective.* Walton Street, Oxford: Oxford University Press.

Hamel, J., Dufour, S., & Fortin, D. (1993). *Case study methods.* Newbury Park, CA: Sage Publications, Inc.

Hammersley, M. (1990). *Reading ethnographic research: A critical guide.* New York: Longman.

Hines, R. A. (1994). The best of both worlds? Collaborative teaching for effective inclusion. *Schools in the Middle, 3*(4), 3–6.

Hoffman, P. R. (1997). Phonological intervention with storybook reading. *Topics in Language Disorders, 17*(2), 69–88.

Holquist, M. (1990). *Dialogism: Bakhtin and his world.* New York: Routledge.

Hubbard, R. S., & Power, B. M. (1993). *The art of teacher inquiry: A handbook for teacher-researchers.* Portsmouth, NH: Heinemann.

Huisingh, R., Barrett, M., Bowers, L., LoGiudice, C., & Orman, J. (1990). *The Word Test–Revised.* East Moline, IL: LinguiSystems, Inc.

Hymes, D. (1985). *Foundations in sociolinguistics: An ethnographic approach.* Philadelphia, PA: University of Pennsylvania Press.

Idol, L., Nevin, A., & Paolucci-Whitcomb, P. (1999). *Models of curriculum-based assessment: A blueprint for learning* (3rd ed.). Austin, TX: PRO-ED, Inc.

Johnson, D., & Myklebust, H. (1967). *Learning disabilities: Educational principles and practices.* New York: Grune & Stratton.

Kaplan, E., Goodglass, H., & Weintraub, S. (1976). *Boston Naming Test* (Experimental Ed.). Boston: VA Hospital.

Kearney, C. A., Durand, V. M. (1992). How prepared are our teachers for mainstreamed classroom settings? A survey of postsecondary schools of education in New York State. *Exceptional Children, 59*(1), 6–11.

Klein, H. B., & Moses, N. (1999). *Intervention planning for children with communication disorders: A guide for clinical practitioners and professional practice.* Boston: Allyn & Bacon.

Kutash, K., & Duchnowski, A. J. (1997). Creating comprehensive and collaborative systems. *Journal of Emotional and Behavioral Disorders, 5*(2), 66–75.

Larson, V. L., & McKinley, N. L. (1989). If kids need speech and language help, are your schools prepared to give it? *The American School Board Journal, 176,* 30–33.

Larson, V. L., McKinley, N. L., & Boley, D. (1993). Service delivery models for adolescents with language disorders. *Language, Speech, and Hearing Services in Schools, 24,* 36–42.

Lemke, J. (1985). *Using language in the classroom.* Geelong, VIC (Australia): Deakin University Press. [Republished 1989, Oxford University Press.]

Lerner, J. (1996). *Children with learning disabilities: Theories, diagnosis, and teaching strategies.* Boston, MA: Houghton Mifflin Company.

Lesar, S., Benner, S. M., Habel, J., & Coleman, L. (1997). Preparing general education teachers for inclusive settings: A constructivist teacher education program. *Teacher Education and Special Education, 20*(3), 204–220.

Lewis, R. B., & Doorlag, D. H. (1999). *Teaching special students in general education classrooms.* Upper Saddle River, NJ: Prentice-Hall.

Liles, B. Z. (1982). *Procedure for the analysis of cohesion in spoken narratives.* Hartford, CT: University of Connecticut.

Liles, B. Z. (1985). Cohesion in the narratives of normal and language-disordered children. *Journal of Speech and Hearing Research, 28,* 123–133.

Lincoln, Y. S., & Guba, E. G. (1985). *Naturalistic inquiry.* Newbury Park, CA: Sage.

Linder, T. W. (1993). *Transdisciplinary play-based assessment: A functional approach to working with young children,* rev. ed. Baltimore, MD: Paul H. Brookes.

Lindsfor, J. W. (1987). *Children's language and learning.* Englewood Cliffs, NJ: Prentice-Hall.

Lipsky, D. K., & Gartner, A. (1997). Inclusion, school restructuring, and the remaking of American society. *Harvard Educational Review, 66*(4), 762–796.

Marvin, C. A. (1987). Consultation services: Changing roles for SLP's. *Journal of Children's Communication Disorders, 11*(1), 1–15.

McCauley, R. J., & Swisher, L. (1984). Use and misuse of norm-referenced tests in clinical assessment: A hypothetical case. *American Speech-Language-Hearing Association.*

McCollom, P. (1991). Cross-cultural perspectives on classroom discourse and literacy. In E. H. Hiebert (Ed.), *Literacy for a diverse society: Perspectives, practices, and policies* (pp. 108–121). New York: Teachers College Press.

McCormick, L., Loeb, D. F., & Schiefelbusch, R. L. (1997). *Supporting children with communication difficulties in inclusive settings: School-based language intervention.* Boston: Allyn & Bacon.

McGregor, K. K., & Leonard, L. B. (1989). Facilitating word-finding skills of language-impaired children. *Journal of Speech and Hearing Disorders, 54*(2), 141–147.

McGregor, K. K., & Windsor, J. (1996). Effects of priming on naming accuracy. *Journal of Speech and Hearing Research, 39*(5), 1048–1058.

McIntosh, R., Vaughn, S., Schumm, J. S., Haager, D., & Lee, O. (1994). Observations of students with learning disabilities in general education classrooms. *Exceptional Children, 60,* 249–261.

Madden, N., & Slavin, R. E. (1983). Mainstreaming students with mild handicaps: Academic and social outcomes. *Review of Educational Research, 53,* 519–569.

Malinowski, B. (1923). The problem of meaning in primitive languages. Supplement 1 in C. K. Ogden & I. A. Richards (Eds.), *The meaning of meaning.* London: Keagan Paul.

Marozas, D. S., & May, D. C. (1988). *Issues and practices in special education.* New York: Longman.

Martin, J. R., Christie, F., & Rothery, J. (1987). Social processes in education: A reply to Sawyer and Watson. In Ian Reid (Ed.), *The place of genre in learning: Current debates* (pp. 58–82). Typereader Publications, Number 1, Center for Studies in Literary Education. Geelong, Australia: Deakin University Press.

Menyuk, P., & Chesnick, M. (1997). Metalinguistic skills, oral language knowledge, and reading. *Topics in Language Disorders, 17*(3), 75–87.

Mercer, C. D., & Mercer, A. (1998). *Teaching students with learning problems.* Upper Saddle River, NJ: Prentice-Hall.

Merritt, D. D., & Culatta, B. (1996). *Collaborative language intervention in the classroom.* San Diego, CA: Singular Publishing Group.

Meyen, E. L., Vergason, G. A., & Whelan, R. J. (1996). *Strategies for teaching exceptional children in inclusive settings.* Denver, CO: Love Publishing Company.

Minke, K. M., Bear, G. G., Deemer, S. A., & Griffen, S. M. (1996). Teachers' experiences with inclusive classrooms: Implications for special education reform. *Journal of Special Education, 30*(2), 152–186.

Minuchin, P. (1985). Families and individual development: Provocations from the field of family therapy. *Child Development, 56*(2), 289–302.

Moody, S. W., Vaughn, S., Hughes, S. T., & Fischer, M. (2000). Reading instruction in the resource room: Set up for failure. *Exceptional Children, 66*(3), 305–316.

Morine-Dershimer, G. (1988). Comparing systems: How do we know? In J. L. Green & J. O. Harker (Eds.), *Multiple perspective analyses of classroom discourse* (pp. 195–214). Norwood, NJ: Ablex.

Nelson, N. W. (1993). *Childhood language disorders in context: Infancy through adolescence.* New York: Macmillan.

Nelson, N. W., & Sturm, J. M. (1997). Formal classroom lesson: New perspectives on a familiar discourse event. *Language, Speech, and Hearing Services in Schools, 28*(3), 255–273.

Nippold, M. A. (1992). The nature of normal and disordered word finding in children and adolescents. *Topics in Language Disorders, 13*(1), 1–14.

Norris, J. A. (1997). Functional language intervention in the classroom: Avoiding the tutoring trap. *Topics in Language Disorders, 17*(2), 49–68.

Nystrand, M., Gamoran, A., Kachur, R., & Prendergast, C. (1997). *Opening dialogue: Understanding the dynamics of language and learning in the English classroom.* New York: Teacher's College Press.

Olswang, L., & Bain, B. A. (1991). When to Recommend Intervention. *Language, Speech & Hearing Services in the Schools, 22*(4), 255–263.

Owens, R. E. (1995). *Language disorders: A functional approach to assessment and intervention,* 2nd ed. Boston: Allyn & Bacon.

Oyler, C. (1996). *Making room for students: Sharing authority in room 104.* New York: Teachers College Press.

Palinscar, A. S., & Brown, A. L. (1983). *Reciprocal teaching of comprehension-monitoring activities.* Champaign, IL and Cambridge, MA: Bolt Beranek and Newman, Inc.

Palinscar, A. S., & Brown, A. L. (1986). Interactive teaching to promote independent learning from text. *The Reading Teacher, 39,* 771–777.

Pappas, C. C. (1991). Young children's strategies in learning the "book language" of information books. *Discourse Processes, 14,* 203–225.

Pappas, C. C. (1997). Reading instruction in an integrated language perspective: Collaborative interaction in classroom curriculum genres. In S. Stahl & D. A. Hayes (Eds.), *Instructional models in reading* (pp. 283–311). Hillsdale, NJ: Erlbaum.

Pappas, C. C., Keifer, B. Z., & Levstik, L. S. (1999). *An integrated language perspective in the elementary classroom: An action approach.* White Plains, NY: Longman.

Pennington, M. C. (1998). *Classroom discourse frames.* Paper presented at the 20th Annual Meeting of the American Association for Applied Linguistics (Seattle, WA, March, 1998).

Phillips, W. L., Alfred, K., Brulle, A., & Shank, K. (1990). *REI: The will and skill of regular educators.* Eastern Illinois University (ERIC Document Reproduction Service No. ED 320 323).

Prelock, P. A., & Lupella, R. O. (1989). Views of children's word-finding difficulties: Disciplinary inferences. In Dana Kovarsky (Ed.), *Language interaction in clinical and educational settings.* ASHA Monographs, No. 30.

Prelock, P. A., Miller, B. E., & Reed, N. L. (1993). *Working with the classroom curriculum: A guide for analysis and use in speech therapy.* Tucson, AZ: Communication Skill Builders.

Pryzwansky, W. (1985). The preservice training and supervision of consultants: Reactions and extensions. *Counseling Psychologist, 13*(3), 410–413.

Rainforth, B., York, J., & MacDonald, C. (1992). *Collaborative teams for students with severe disabilities.* Baltimore, MD: Paul H. Brookes.

Ramirez, A. (1988). Analyzing speech acts. In J. L. Green & J. O. Harker (Eds.), *Multiple perspective analyses of classroom discourse* (pp. 135–163). Norwood, NJ: Ablex.

Rankin, J. L., & Aksamit, D. L. (1994). Perceptions of elementary, junior high, and high school student assistant team coordinators, team members, and teachers. *Journal of Educational and Psychological Consultation, 5,* 229–256.

Reinhiller, N. (1996). Coteaching: New variation on a not-so-new practice. *Teacher Education and Special Education, 19*(1), 34–48.

Reynolds, M. C., Wang, M. C., & Walberg, H. J. (1987). The necessary restructuring of special and regular education. *Exceptional Children, 53,* 391–398.

Reynolds, W. M., & Wepman, J. M. (1987). *The Wepman Test of Auditory Discrimination* (2nd ed.). Los Angeles, CA: Western Psychological Services.

Richard, G. J., & Hanner, M. A. (1987). *Language Processing Remediation.* IL: LinguiSystems, Inc.

Ringlaben, R. P., & Price, J. R. (1981). Regular classroom teachers' perceptions of mainstreaming effects. *Exceptional Children, 47,* 302–304.

Ripich, D. N., & Creaghead, N. A. (1994). *School discourse problems* (2nd ed.). San Diego, CA: Singular Publishing Company.

Rogers, C. (1951). *Client-centered therapy.* Boston, MA: Houghton Mifflin.

Rogoff, B. (1990). *Apprenticeship in thinking.* New York: Oxford University Press.

Roman, L. G., & Apple, M. W. (1990). Is naturalism a move away from positivism? Materialist and feminist approaches to subjectivity in ethnographic research. In E. W. Eisner & A. Peshkin (Eds.), *Qualitative inquiry in education* (pp. 38–73). New York: Teachers College Press.

Routman, R. (1991). *Invitations: Changing as teachers and learners K–12.* Portsmouth, NH: Heinemann.

Ross, F. C. (1992). Word retrieval difficulties in the classroom: A case study of Susan. Unpublished manuscript.

Ross, F. C., & Wax, I. (1993). *Inclusionary programs for children with language and/or learning disabilities: Issues in teacher readiness.* Paper presented at the 43rd Annual Meeting of the National Reading Conference, Charleston, SC.

Schubert, W. H. (1986). Curriculum research controversy: A special case of a general problem. *Journal of Curriculum and Supervision, 1*(2), 132–147.

Secord, E. (Ed.). (1990). *Best practices in school speech-language pathology: Collaborative programs in the schools: Concepts, models, and procedures.* San Antonio, TX: Psychological Corporation.

Semel, E. M., Wiig, E. H., & Secord, W. (1995). *CELF: Clinical evaluation of language functions.* Columbus, OH: Charles E. Merrill.

Shuy, R. (1988). Identifying dimensions of classroom language. In J. L. Green, & J. O. Harker (Eds.), *Multiple perspective analyses of classroom discourse* (pp. 115–134). Norwood, NJ: Ablex.

Silliman, E. R., Ford, C. S., Beasman, J., & Evans, D. (1999). An inclusion model for children with language learning disabilities: Building classroom partnerships. *Topics in Language Disorders, 19*(3), 1–8.

Silliman, E. R., & Wilkinson, L. C. (1991). *Communicating for learning: Classroom observation and collaboration.* Gaitherburg, MD: Aspen Publishers, Inc.

Simon, C. S. (1979). *Communicative competence: A functional-pragmatic approach to language therapy.* Tucson, AZ: Communication Skill Builders, Inc.

Simpson, R. L., & Myles, B. S. (1996). The general education collaboration model: A model for successful mainstreaming. In E. L. Meyen, G. A. Vergason, & R. J. Whelan (Eds.), *Strategies for teaching exceptional children in inclusive settings* (pp. 435–450). Denver, CO: Love Publishing Company.

Slavin, R. E. (1995). *Cooperative learning: Theory, research, and practice.* Boston: Allyn & Bacon.

Snow, C. E. (1994). What is so hard about learning to read? In J. F. Duchan, L. E. Hewitt, & R. M. Sonnenmeier (Eds.), *Pragmatics: From theory to practice* (pp. 164–184). Englewood Cliffs, NJ: Prentice Hall.

Stainback, W., & Stainback, S. (1984). A rationale for the merger of special and regular education. *Exceptional Children, 51,* 102–111.

Stake, R. E. (1998). Case studies. In N. K. Denzin & Y. S. Lincoln (Eds.), *Strategies of qualitative inquiry* (pp. 86–109). Thousand Oaks, London: Sage Publications, Inc.

Strauss, A., & Corbin, J. (1990). *Basics of qualitative research: Grounded theory procedures and techniques.* Newbury Park, CA: Sage.

Teale, W. H., & Sulzby, E. (1986). *Emergent literacy: Writing and reading.* Norwood, NJ: Ablex.

Tenenberg, M. (1988). Diagramming question cycle sequences. In J. H. Green, & J. O. Harker (Eds.), *Multiple perspective analyses of classroom discourse* (pp. 165–193). Norwood, NJ: Ablex.

Tharp, R. G., & Gallimore, R. (1988). *Rousing minds to life: Teaching, learning, and schooling in social context.* Cambridge, UK: Cambridge University Press.

Tharp, R. G., & Wetzell, R. J. (1969). *Behavior modification in the natural environment.* New York: Academic Press.

Thousand, J., Diaz-Greenberg, R., Nevin, A., Cardelle-Elawar, M., Beckett, C., & Reese, R. (1999). Perspectives on a Freirean dialectic to promote inclusive education. *Remedial and Special Education, 20*(6), 323–327.

Thousand, J. S.,Villa, R. A., & Nevin, A. I. (1994). *Creativity and collaborative learning: A practical guide to empowering students and teachers.* Baltimore, MD: Paul H. Brookes Publishing Co.

Tierney, R. J. (1998, February). Literacy assessment reform, shifting beliefs, principled possiblilties, and emerging practices. *The Reading Teacher, 51*(5), 374–390.

Troia, G. A., Roth, F. P., & Yenikomshian, G. H. (1996). Word frequency and age effects in normally developing children's phonological processing. *Journal of Speech and Hearing Research, 39*(5), 1099–1108.

Twachtman-Cullen, D. (1996). Blinded by their strengths: The topsy-turvy world of Asperger's Syndrome. *The Advocate.* Autism Society of America Newsletter.

Udvari-Solner, A. (1997). A process for adopting curriculum in inclusive classrooms. In R. A. Villa & J. S. Thousand (Eds.), *Creating an inclusive school.* Alexandria, VA: Association for Supervision and Curriculum Development.

U.S. Department of Education. (2000). *Digest of education statistics 1999.* National Center for Education Statistics 2000-031. Washington, DC: Government Printing Office.

Vaughn, S., Bos, C. S., & Schumm, J. S. (1997). *Teaching mainstreamed, diverse, and at-risk students in the general education classroom.* Boston, MA: Allyn & Bacon.

Vaughn, S., Schumm, J. S., & Kouzekanani, K. (1993). What do students with learning disabilities think when their general education teachers make adaptations? *Journal of Learning Disabilities, 21*(2), 82–89.

Vaughn, S. H., Terejo, M., Klingner, J. K., & Schumm, J. S. (1998). A collaborative effort to enhance reading and writing instrcution in inclusive classrooms. *Learning Disabilities Quarterly, 21*(1), 157–174.

Vygotsky, L. S. (1978). *Mind in society: The development of higher psychological processes.* In M. Cole, V. John-Steiner, S. Scribner, & E. Souberman (Eds.). Cambridge, MA: Harvard University Press.

Wallach, G. P., & Butler, K. G. (1994). *Language learning disabilities in school-age children and adolescents: Some principles and applications.* New York: Merrill.

Walther-Thomas, C., Kovinek, L., & McLaughlin, V. L. (1999). Collaboration to support students' success. *Focus on Exceptional Children, 32*(3), 1–18.

Walther-Thomas, C. (1996). Planning for effective co-teaching: The key to successful inclusion. *Remedial and Special Education, 17*(4), 255–264.

Wang, M. C., Haertel, G. D., & Walberg, H. J. (1998). Models of Reform: A Comparative Guide. *Educational Leadership, 55*(7), 66–71.

Wang, M. C., Peverly, S., & Randolf, R. (1984). Comparison of a full-time mainstreaming program and a resource room approach. *Exceptional Children, 51,* 33–40.

Wang, M. C., Reynolds, M. C., & Walberg, H. J. (1986). Rethinking special education. *Educational Leadership, 44,* 1, 26–31.

Wells, G. (1994). *Changing schools from within: Creating communities of inquiry.* Toronto, Canada: Ontario Institute for Studies in Education Press. (Distributed by Heinemann Press.)

Wells, G. (1998). Some questions about direct instruction—why? to whom? how? and when? *Language Arts, 76*(1), 27–35.

Wells, G. (1999). *Dialogic inquiry: Towards a sociocultural practice and theory of education.* Cambridge, UK: Cambridge University Press.

Wells, G., & Chang-Wells, G. L. (1992). *Constructing knowledge together.* Portsmouth, NH: Heinemann.

Wertsch, J. V. (Ed.). (1985). *Culture, communication, and cognition: Vygotskian perspectives.* Cambridge, UK: Cambridge University Press.

Wetherby, A., & Prizant, B. (2000). *Communication and language intervention series: Vol 9. Autism spectrum disorders: a transactional developmental perspective* (pp. 11–30). Baltimore, MD: Brookes Publishing.

Wiig, E. H., & Semel, E. M. (1984). *Language assessment and intervention for the learning disabled.* Columbus, OH: Charles E. Merrill.

Wilcox, M. J., Louri, T. A., & Caswell, S. B. (1991). Early language intervention: A comparison of classroom and individual treatment. *American Journal of Speech-Language Pathology, 1,* 49–52.

Will, M. C. (1986). Educating children with learning problems: A shared responsibility. *Exceptional Children, 52,* 411–415.

Williams, K. (1995). Understanding the child with Asperger syndrome: Guidelines for teachers. *Focus on Autistic Behavior, 10*(2), 9–16.

Wolcott, H. F. (1992). Posturing in qualitative research. In M. D. LeCompte, W. L. Millroy, & J. Preissle (Eds.), *The handbook of qualitative research* (pp. 30–52). New York: Academic Press.

Wolf, M. (1991). Naming speed and reading: The contribution of the cognitive neurosciences. *Reading Research Quarterly, 23,* 159–177.

Wolman, C. (1991). Sensitivity to causal cohesion in stories by children with mild mental retardation, children with learning disabilities, and children without disabilities. *Journal of Special Education, 25*(2), 135–154.

Woodruff, G., & McGonigel, M. J. (1988). *Early intervention team approaches: The transdisciplinary model.* Council for Exceptional Children. Reston, VA: ERIC Clearinghouse on Handicapped and Gifted Children, (ERIC Document Reproduction Service No. ED 302 971).

Young, R. (1992). *Critical theory and classroom talk.* Philadelphia, PA: Multilingual Matters Ltd.

Ysseldyke, J. E., Algozzine, B., Shinn, M. R., & McGue, M. (1982). Similarities and differences between low achievers and students classified as learning disabled. *Journal of Special Education, 16,* 73–85.

Key to Transcriptions

Turn:	Numbered portions of language designating each speaker's contribution to discourse.
F:	Fran Falk-Ross's turn
M:	Mickey's turn
V:	Vincent's turn
H:	Henry's turn
S1, S2	Consecutive students' conversational turns
"Initial"	Refers to speakers: teacher (T), class (Ss), or student (child's initial)
///	Break in reported discourse
Information in italics	Contextual information/field notes
[ ]	Interpreted, explanatory information
CAPS	Actual reading from a book
Underscore	Emphasis
. . .	Short pause in speaker's utterance

INDEX